Freedom of the Press

Freedom of the Press

A Reference Guide to the United States Constitution

Lyrissa Barnett Lidsky
and R. George Wright

REFERENCE GUIDES TO THE
UNITED STATES CONSTITUTION, NUMBER 10
Jack Stark, *Series Editor*

PRAEGER

Westport, Connecticut
London

Library of Congress Cataloging-in-Publication Data

Lidsky, Lyrissa Barnett, 1968–
  Freedom of the press : a reference guide to the United States Constitution / Lyrissa Barnett
Lidsky and R. George Wright.
      p. cm.—(Reference guides to the United States Constitution, ISSN 1539-8986 ; no. 10)
    Includes bibliographical references and index.
    ISBN 0-313-31597-3 (alk. paper)
    1. Freedom of the press—United States. I. Wright, R. George. II. Title. III. Series.
KF4774.L53 2004
342.7308'53—dc22   2004009836

British Library Cataloguing in Publication Data is available.

Library of Congress Catalog Card Number: 2004009836
ISBN: 0-313-31597-3
ISSN: 1539-8986

First published in 2004

Praeger Publishers, 88 Post Road West, Westport, CT 06881
An imprint of Greenwood Publishing Group, Inc.
www.praeger.com

Printed in the United States of America

The paper used in this book complies with the
Permanent Paper Standard issued by the National
Information Standards Organization (Z39.48-1984).

10 9 8 7 6 5 4 3 2 1

To David A. Anderson,
My professor, mentor, and friend
Who continues to teach me about freedom of the press.

—L.B.L.

For Mary, once more.

—R.G.W.

Contents

Series Foreword

JACK STARK

One can conceive of the United States Constitution in many ways. For example, noting the reverence in which it has been held, one can think of it as equivalent to a sacred text. Unfortunately, most of its devotees have had less knowledge and even less understanding of the document than they have had reverence for it. Sometimes it is treated as primarily a political document and on that basis has been subjected to analysis, such as Charles Beard's *An Economic Interpretation of the Constitution of the United States*. One can plausibly argue that the Constitution seems most astounding when it is seen in the light of the intellectual effort that has been associated with it. Three brief but highly intense bursts of intellectual energy produced, and established as organic law, most of the Constitution as it now exists. Two of these efforts, sustained over a long period of time, have enabled us better to understand that document.

The first burst of energy occurred at the Constitutional Convention. Although some of the delegates' business, such as the struggle between populous and non-populous states about their representation in Congress, was political, much of it was about fundamental issues of political theory. A few of the delegates had or later achieved international eminence for their intellects. Among them were Benjamin Franklin, Alexander Hamilton, and James Madison. Others, although less well known, had first-rate minds. That group includes George Mason and George Wythe. Many of the delegates contributed intelligently. Although the Convention's records are less than satisfactory, they indicate clearly enough that the delegates worked mightily to constitute not merely a polity but a rational polity—one that would rise to the standards envisioned by the delegates' intellectual ancestors. Their product, though brief, is amazing. William Gladstone called it "the most wonderful work ever struck off."

Despite the delegates' eminence and the Constitution's excellence as seen from our place in history, its ratification was far from certain. That state of affairs necessitated the second burst of intellectual energy associated with that document: the debate over ratification. Soon after the Convention adjourned, articles and speeches—some supporting the Constitution and some attacking it—began to proliferate. A national debate commenced, not only about the document itself but also about the nature of the polity that ought to exist in this country. Both sides included many writers and speakers who were verbally adroit and steeped in the relevant political and philosophical literature. The result was an accumulation of material that is remarkable for both its quantity and its quality. At its apex is the *Federalist Papers,* a production of Alexander Hamilton, James Madison, and John Jay that deserves a place among the great books of Western culture.

Another burst, not as impressive as the first two but highly respectable, occurred when the Bill of Rights was proposed. Some delegates to the Constitutional Convention had vigorously asserted that such guarantees should be included in the original document. George Mason, the principal drafter of the Virginia Declaration of Rights, so held, and he walked out of the Convention when he failed to achieve his purpose. Even those who had argued that the rights in question were implicit recognized the value of adding protection of them to the Constitution. The debate was thus focused on the rights that were to be explicitly granted, not on whether any rights *ought* to be explicitly granted. Again many writers and speakers entered the fray, and again the debate was solidly grounded in theory and was conducted on a high intellectual level.

Thus, within a few years a statement of organic law and a vital coda to it had been produced. However, the meaning and effect of many of that document's provisions were far from certain; the debates on ratification of the Constitution and the Bill of Rights had demonstrated that. In addition, the document existed in a vacuum, because statutes and actions had not been assessed by its standards. The attempt to resolve these problems began after Chief Justice John Marshall, in Marbury v. Madison, asserted the right of the U.S. Supreme Court to interpret and apply the Constitution. Judicial interpretation and application of the Constitution, beginning with the first constitutional case and persisting until the most recent, is one of the sustained exertions of intellectual energy associated with the Constitution. The framers would be surprised by some of the results of those activities. References in the document to "due process," which seems to refer only to procedures, have been held also to have a substantive dimension. A right to privacy has been found lurking among the penumbras of various parts of the text. A requirement that states grant the same "privileges and immunities" to citizens of other states that they granted to their own citizens, which seemed to guarantee important rights, was held not to be particularly important. The corpus of judicial interpretations of the Constitution is now as voluminous as that document is terse.

As the judicial interpretations multiplied, another layer—interpretations of interpretations—appeared, and also multiplied. This layer, the other sustained intellectual effort associated with the Constitution, consists of articles, most of them published in law reviews, and books on the Constitution. This material varies in quality and significance. Some of these works of scholarship result from meticulous examination and incisive thought. Others repeat earlier work, or apply a fine-tooth comb to matters that are too minute even for such a comb. Somewhere in that welter of tertiary material is the answer to almost every question that one could ask about constitutional law. The problem is finding the answer that one wants. The difficulty of locating useful guidance is exacerbated by the bifurcation of most constitutional scholarship into two kinds. In "Two Styles of Social Science Research," C. Wright Mills delineates macroscopic and molecular research. The former deals with huge issues, the latter with tiny issues. Virtually all of the scholarship on the Constitution is of one of those two types. Little of it is macroscopic, but that category does include some first-rate syntheses such as Jack Rakove's *Original Meanings*. Most constitutional scholarship is molecular and, again, some fine work is included in that category.

In his essay, Mills bemoans the inability of social scientists to combine the two kinds of research that he describes to create a third category that will be more generally useful. This series of books is an attempt to do for constitutional law the intellectual work that Mills proposed for social science. The author of each book has dealt carefully and at reasonable length with a topic that lies in the middle range of generality. Upon completion, this series will consist of thirty-seven books, each on a constitutional law topic. Some of the books, such as the book on freedom of the press, explicate one portion of the Constitution's text. Others, such as the volume on federalism, treat a topic that has several anchors in the Constitution. The books on constitutional history and constitutional interpretation range over the entire document, but each does so from one perspective. Except for a very few of the books, for which the special circumstances dictate minor changes in format, each book includes the same components: a brief history of the topic, a lengthy and sophisticated analysis of the current state of the law on that topic, a bibliographical essay that organizes and evaluates scholarly material in order to facilitate further research, a table of cases and an index. The books are intellectually rigorous—in fact, authorities have written them—but, due to their clarity and to brief definitions of terms that are unfamiliar to laypersons, each is comprehensible and useful to a wide audience, one that ranges from other experts on the book's subject to intelligent non-lawyers.

In short, this series provides an extremely valuable service to the legal community and to others who are interested in constitutional law, as every citizen should be. Each book is a map of part of the U.S. Constitution. Together they map all of that document's territory that is worth mapping. When this series is complete, each book will be a third kind of scholarly work that combines the macroscopic and the molecular. Together they will explicate all of the important constitutional topics. Anyone who wants assistance in understanding either a topic in constitutional law or the Constitution as a whole can easily find it in these books.

Acknowledgments

The authors wish to thank David Anderson and Bill Page for their helpful comments on the initial draft of the book. This book also has benefited tremendously from the research and editing skills of Angela Brayer, Tomasz Bartosz, Sherica Bryan, Michael Pike, Natalie Tanner, Sara Rich, Robin Tubesing, Theresa Gheen, and David Arizmendi. Thanks, too, to Marilyn Henderson for tirelessly inputting changes and keeping track of the various drafts of the book. The assistance of Judy McAlister and Faith Long Knotts was likewise invaluable.

The Text and History of the First Amendment

AN INTRODUCTION

The language of the First Amendment to the United States Constitution seems simple enough: "Congress shall make no law . . . abridging the freedom of speech, or of the press . . ." Yet the First Amendment's protections are both broader and narrower than this seemingly simple text suggests. The modern First Amendment is the product of a complex layer of interpretations imposed on the text by courts, particularly the United States Supreme Court, which bears the ultimate responsibility of interpreting the Constitution in our federal system.

The language of the First Amendment seems to guarantee absolute protection for freedom of the press. Indeed, Justice Hugo L. Black famously announced that when the First Amendment "says 'no law,' . . . that is what I believe it means."[1] In practice, however, the Supreme Court has never construed the First Amendment as literally preventing the federal or state governments from passing *any* laws affecting the press' ability to gather or publish information. For example, the Court has interpreted the First Amendment to allow government regulation of speech that falls into narrowly defined categories of "low-value" speech, like obscenity or "fighting words." In some instances, the Court has even permitted government regulation of speech within a fully protected category, like political speech. Indeed, no single principle or philosophy governs all First Amendment cases: Sometimes the words "no law" mean "no law," but very often they do not.

If "no law" does not really mean "no law" in the First Amendment, then neither is "Congress" the only branch of government forbidden from passing laws abridging press freedom. All branches of the federal government are covered by the First Amendment, and since 1925, the First Amendment's prohibitions have applied to state and local governments as well by virtue of the Fourteenth Amendment. In that year, the Supreme Court held that freedom of the press is a fundamental liberty protected from deprivation by a state without due process of law. (Gitlow v. New York, 1925) Thus, the Fourteenth Amendment forbids state governments from passing laws that the First Amendment forbids the federal government from passing.

The First Amendment is broader than its language suggests in another respect as well. At the time the First Amendment was written, "freedom of the press" referred to mass publications produced by a printing press. However, the First Amendment today extends not only to newspapers and magazines but also to other types of mass media, including television, radio, cable, and the Internet.

It should be clear at this point that the language of the First Amendment is merely a starting point for analysis. A true understanding of press freedom in the United States is only gained by studying the complex body of law interpreting the First Amendment. The authors have undertaken just such a study, and we present it to you in this volume.

A HISTORY OF THE PRESS CLAUSE

By studying the intent of the Framers of the Constitution, scholars are able to clarify the sometimes murky language of constitutional provisions. In the case of the First Amendment, however, the Framers left little direct evidence indicating what they meant by the term "freedom of the press."

The American colonists inherited from English common law a narrow conception of freedom of the press. English law had long repressed speech and publications critical of religious or political authorities.[2] Sir William Blackstone, author of the most influential treatise on English common law, wrote in 1769 that the punishment of "blasphemous, immoral, treasonable, schismatical, seditious, or scandalous libels" did not infringe "the liberty of the press, properly understood."[3] According to Blackstone, the "liberty of the press" under English common law consisted merely "in laying no previous restraints upon publications, and not in freedom from censure for criminal matter when published."[4] In other words, liberty of the press merely meant that a publication could not be censored prior to publication. Publishers could, however, be punished *after* publication.

The most common form of "previous" or prior restraint in England was the licensing system. Every publication had to receive a license from government censors or risk severe punishment. The English government instituted the licensing system to suppress publications critical of the government, after the printing press made the widespread dissemination of such publications possible around 1500. England officially abolished licensing of the press in 1695.[5] Even so, the English government continued to punish works *after* publication as "seditious libels," subjecting the authors to both civil and criminal penalties. The government also used taxation to put English newspapers out of business.

The colonial government in America subjected colonial printers to many of the same repressive measures that were used at home in England.[6] Licensing continued in the American colonies for at least 25 years after it was abolished in England, and several colonial printers were prosecuted for seditious libel. Indeed, as historian Leonard Levy has documented, colonial legislatures were particularly zealous in punishing those who criticized them. Yet there is also evidence that a more expansive notion of press freedom was taking hold in the colonies. Colonial printers felt free to engage in heated discussions of matters of public interest, and as one historian has written, "no governmental institution, political faction, or individual was free from attacks such as few newspapers today would dare to print."[7] The 1735 trial of John Peter Zenger illustrated American hostility to the use of the common law of seditious libel as a means of suppressing press freedom. Zenger, a newspaper printer, was jailed and charged with seditious libel for publishing criticisms of New York governor William Cosby. When a grand jury refused to indict Zenger, the colony's attorney general brought seditious libel charges under his own authority. Under the common law, Zenger was not allowed to defend himself by saying that the criticisms of Cosby were accurate, for the law considered a true statement more dangerous than a false one. This was so because a true statement was more likely to incite violence or diminish respect for government. The common law also gave the judge, who was a loyal appointee of Governor Cosby, the role of deciding if Zenger's criticisms were illegal. The only role for the jury was to decide whether Zenger published the criticisms.

Zenger's lawyers skillfully appealed to popular sentiment to win a victory for freedom of the press. Zenger's lawyers convinced the jury that the real issue in the case was Zenger's freedom to print the truth and that the jury should therefore decide that Zenger's words were not libelous. Disregarding the judge's instructions on the law, the jury acquitted Zenger of publishing seditious libel. Reports of the *Zenger* trial were published widely, and the jury's decision was heralded as a victory for both freedom of the press and for the jury as a protector of press freedom from government tyranny. The *Zenger* trial effectively signaled the end of seditious libel (at least for the next 40 years) as a weapon to silence the press.[8]

Forty years later, the American Revolution forced Americans to consider the proper role of the press in a democracy. During the revolutionary period, Americans began to view press freedom as essential to the functioning of a government that derived its authority from the consent of the governed. Nine of the eleven state constitutions that emerged during this period included guarantees of freedom of the press.[9] A free press was to play a structural role in the new governments. It would act as a check on government abuses of power and allow citizens to scrutinize and, if necessary, recall their elected representatives. Thus, the American revolutionaries considered freedom of the press integral to preserving the "desired relation between the people and their government."[10]

The original federal Constitution, however, did not guarantee freedom of the press. At the time of the adoption of the Constitution, the Federalists, an influential group of supporters of a strong federal government, argued that a bill of rights (and a press clause) would be superfluous. The new federal government, they argued, was a government of limited powers only, and it would therefore lack the power to infringe on individual liberties. However, there was widespread criticism of the absence of a bill of rights, and particularly the absence of protection for freedom of the press. The First Congress responded by drafting the Bill of Rights, which became the first ten amendments to the new Constitution.

What is now the First Amendment was actually third on the list in the original Bill of Rights; it became the First Amendment only because the original First and Second Amendments were not ratified. We know that the First Amendment, initially proposed by James Madison, went through five versions in the legislative process. However, there is no indication that the Framers of the First Amendment engaged in sustained debate on the meaning of freedom of the press. Nevertheless there is evidence that the Senate rejected a motion that would have made press freedom under the Bill of Rights only as broad as press freedom under the common law.[11] The intent of those who drafted and passed the First Amendment, therefore, sheds very little light on the meaning of the press clause.

Just 7 years later, however, the controversy surrounding the Sedition Act of 1798 propelled a national debate over the meaning of press freedom under the First Amendment.[12] The Federalists, who controlled both the Congress and the Presidency, passed the Sedition Act in 1798 to prevent the Jeffersonian Republican Party (including Vice President Thomas Jefferson) from winning the election of 1800. The Act made it a crime to print "false, scandalous, and malicious writings or writings against the government of the United States," the Congress, or the President "with intent to defame."[13] Significantly, the Act did not make it a crime to defame the Vice President, and the Act expired in 1801, *after* the election. Under the Act, Federalists brought 15 indictments against Republican printers, resulting in ten convictions and in three Republican newspapers ceasing to print. The Act therefore demonstrated the potency of criminalizing seditious libel (for the Act was merely a statutory version) as a weapon for silencing critics of the government. Yet the controversy over the Act also established, at least in the court of public opinion, that the First Amendment restricted the power of the federal government to punish seditious libel.

During the Sedition Act controversy, James Madison and Thomas Jefferson articulated expansive and influential conceptions of press freedom. In resolutions adopted by the Kentucky and Virginia legislatures, Madison and Jefferson contended that the federal government had exceeded its express powers in passing the Sedition Act and had violated the First Amendment. Madison, in particular, decried the Sedition Act for "repress[ing] that information and communication among the people, which is indispensable to the just exercise of their electoral rights,"[14] and he forcefully argued that the First Amendment protected the press not only from "previous restraint" but from subsequent punishment as well. The Virginia Resolutions also declared that the federal government's exercise of power in passing the Sedition Act should produce "universal alarm, because it is leveled against the right of freely examining public characters and measures, and [of] free communication among the people thereon, which has ever been justly deemed the only effectual guardian of every other right."[15] Although the Supreme Court never passed on the constitutionality of the Act, the public debate over the Act helped define a distinctively American conception of press freedom, and public hostility to prosecutions under the Sedition Act fueled the victory for the Republican Party in the election of 1800.

THE FIRST AMENDMENT IN THE EARLY TWENTIETH CENTURY

It was not until the twentieth century, however, that the Supreme Court began to develop our modern, libertarian conception of freedom of the press. Although libertarian radicals during the nineteenth century argued "that speech on virtually any subject should be protected from legal regulation by the state," these arguments met with judicial hostility.[16] Indeed, both federal and state judges embraced the notion that suppressing speech with a "bad tendency"—speech like libel, contempt of court, obscenity, and breach of the peace—did not abridge speech or press freedoms. Another reason the First Amendment played a negligible role in speech and press controversies of the nineteenth century was that its prohibitions applied only to the federal government, which lacked the vast powers it possesses today. Even the adoption of the Fourteenth Amendment in 1868, which guaranteed that the states could not deprive a person of "liberty" without due process of law, did not signal immediately that the First Amendment would now apply to the states. In 1907, therefore, the Supreme Court could still maintain that press freedom meant no more than freedom from prior restraints and thus could find punishment of an editor for criticizing a judge entirely constitutional. (Patterson v. Colorado, 1907)

The modern era of First Amendment jurisprudence began with World War I and the prosecution of both radicals and ordinary citizens for what today seem like innocuous criticisms of war policy. The government pursued most of these prosecutions under the Espionage Act of 1917. This Act was essentially a modern form of seditious libel, making it a crime punishable by 20 years' imprisonment to make false statements that would interfere with the war effort, "to attempt to cause insubordination" in the military forces, or to "obstruct the recruiting or enlistment" of soldiers.[17]

Initially the Supreme Court unanimously upheld convictions under the Espionage Act, holding that the First Amendment did not forbid punishment of those who had "abused" their rights of free speech. Schenck v. United States, for example, upheld a felony conviction under the Act for publishing pamphlets critical of the government's war effort. The defendant targeted the pamphlets to men who had been drafted to fight in World War I. Writing for the Court, Justice Oliver Wendell Holmes quickly rejected any First Amendment defense to the defendant's conviction under the Act. According to Holmes, the relevant question in evaluating the constitutionality of the Espionage Act was whether the speaker's words created such "a clear and present danger that they bring about the substantive evils that Congress has a right to prevent." Applying this "clear and present danger" test, Justice Holmes found that the pamphlets did constitute a clear and present danger to the war effort, despite the highly tenuous connection between the defendant's speech and actual interference with the draft.

Schenck was not Justice Holmes' finest hour as a defender of free speech. In time, however, Justice Holmes' recast the clear and present danger test to reflect a libertarian concern for government suppression of radical dissent. In a series of cases involving Espionage Act prosecutions, Holmes, together with Justice Louis Brandeis, began arguing that the Act was being used to punish citizens who criticized their government, something the First Amendment had long forbidden. In a series of dissenting opinions, Holmes and Brandeis contended that speech could only be suppressed when it posed a "clear and present danger" (that is, a real and immediate danger) of harm to society. They argued that many of the prosecutions under the Espionage Act were based on only a speculative connection between the speech at issue and any substantive harms. (See, e.g., Abrams v. United States, 1919 (Holmes, J., dissenting); Gitlow v. New York, 1925 (Holmes, J., dissenting); Whitney v. California, 1927 (Brandeis, J., concurring).)

Justices Holmes' and Brandeis' dissent in Abrams v. United States illustrates their emerging theory of the First Amendment. In *Abrams,* five Russian socialist immigrants were convicted under the Espionage Act for distributing pamphlets, mostly written in Yiddish, advocating a strike in a munitions factory. Justice Holmes wrote that the government may not suppress speech unless it presents an imminent threat of *immediate* harm. The government's mere speculative assertion that the defendants had hindered the war effort would not do. In a now famous passage defending the defendants' First Amendment rights, Holmes wrote:

Persecution for the expression of opinions seems to me perfectly logical. . . . To allow opposition by speech seems to indicate you think the speech impotent, . . . , or that you do not care whole-heartedly for the result, or that you doubt either your power or your premises. But when men have realized that time has upset many fighting faiths, they may come to believe even more than they believe the very foundations of their own conduct that the ultimate good desired is better reached by free trade in ideas—that *the best test of truth is the power of the thought to get itself accepted in the competition of the market,* and that truth is the only ground upon which their wishes safely may be carried out. That at any rate is the theory of our Constitution. (emphasis added)[18]

Although the marketplace of ideas metaphor originated with John Milton and John Stuart Mill, it was Holmes who introduced it into the First Amendment lexicon. The marketplace of ideas metaphor represents a libertarian conception of freedom of expression; for Holmes and Brandeis, and for many thinkers today, the corrective for "evil counsels" is more speech, not government suppression. The marketplace of ideas is a forum for debate and discussion, where citizens can come together free from government interference to discuss a diverse array of ideas and opinions. Ideally, the truth emerges from the clash of opposing viewpoints in the competition of the market. Open discussion in the marketplace of ideas thus produces better individual decisions as well as more "rational social judgment."[19] This, at least, is the theory underlying the marketplace metaphor, and its rhetorical force has made it the dominant underpinning of modern speech and press cases.

Yet it was Justice Brandeis who wrote the most eloquent and impassioned defense of freedom of expression. Brandeis wrote:

Those who won our independence believed that the final end of the State was to make men free to develop their faculties; and that in its government the deliberative forces should prevail over the arbitrary. They valued liberty both as end and as a means. They believed liberty to be the secret of happiness and courage to be the secret of liberty. They believed that freedom to think as you will and to speak as you think are means indispensable to the discovery and spread of political truth; that without free speech and assembly discussion would be futile; that with them, discussion affords ordinarily adequate protection against the dissemination of noxious doctrine; that the greatest menace to freedom is an inert people; that public discussion is a political duty; and that this should be the fundamental principle of American government. (Whitney v. California, 1927 (Brandeis, J., concurring))

Brandeis' opinion has been described as an essay on "civic courage."[20] Brandeis rejected fear as the basis for suppression of speech, arguing that the "remedy" for dangerous speech "is more speech, not enforced silence." In few but memorable words, Brandeis alludes to what are still the dominant justifications for protecting freedom of expression today: It fosters the search for truth, allows the individual to develop his faculties, and is a precondition for democratic self-governance.

It was not until the 1950s that the Supreme Court acknowledged that the Holmes-Brandeis conception of the First Amendment had become the dominant view. Even then, the Court used a variation of the clear and present danger test to uphold the conviction of Communist Party members for conspiring to overthrow the government by force. (Dennis v. United States, 1951 (plurality)) The clear and present danger test thus failed to protect the speech of dissidents in the face of a perceived national emergency.

Even so, the dissents of Holmes and Brandeis today form the theoretical underpinning of many court cases striking down laws suppressing speech and press freedoms. The legacy of their libertarian conception of the First Amendment to freedom of press in the United States is the terrain this book will explore. Thus, the remainder of this book is, in a very real sense, a history of judicial developments in the law governing freedom of the press since Holmes and Brandeis.

THE PRESS CLAUSE TODAY

Although the press clause is separate from the speech clause in the language of the First Amendment, the Supreme Court typically treats them as merely different facets of the more general concept of freedom of expression. Indeed, the Court has often stated that the press is entitled to no greater First Amendment protection than the general public, and most of the First Amendment decisions involving the media are grounded at least as much in the free speech clause of the First Amendment as in the press clause. One implication of this is that many of the First Amendment victories won by members of the mass media have also benefited individual speakers. Another implication is that the press clause today has little *independent* vitality as a constitutional right. The constitutional right of freedom of the press guarantees the media the same free speech rights as individual speakers, but (as it currently stands) little more.

Historically, it is clear that the Framers viewed the press clause as protecting a right distinct from freedom of speech. The Framers saw the press as an important check on the abuse of power by government officials; whereas freedom of speech was "more closely related to the incipient notion of individual autonomy."[21] Justice Potter Stewart was the most famous modern proponent of the theory that the First Amendment provides distinct protection for the "organized press." Justice Stewart argued that "the primary purpose of the constitutional guarantee of a free press was . . . to create a fourth institution outside the government as an additional check on the three official branches." For Stewart, therefore, the press clause was a "structural provision of the Constitution," designed to protect the press as an institution with a special role to play in our system of government. Stewart's belief in the special role of a "strong and independent press" led him to oppose government attempts to "convert the communications media into a neutral 'marketplace of ideas.'"[22] Stewart believed that the press (but not individuals) had a First Amendment privilege not to disclose confidential news sources to a grand jury and that the press (but not individuals) deserved special protections against being held liable for defamation of public officials. According to Stewart, these privileges and others were necessary to enable the press to perform its checking function on government abuses of power. Although Stewart's view has historical support, the Court has been reluctant to ground its First Amendment decisions involving the press on the press clause alone, routinely rejecting the invitation to create special privileges available only to the mass media.

Chief Justice Burger offered an alternative theory of the press clause in First National Bank v. Bellotti. Burger rejected the notion that the institutional press deserved "any freedom from government restraint not enjoyed by all others." Burger viewed the press clause from a functional rather than a structural perspective. He argued that the speech clause protects the liberty to express ideas and beliefs, and the press clause merely protects the liberty to disseminate such ideas and beliefs widely. By implication, therefore, anyone who publishes his ideas to a mass audience should qualify for First Amendment protection, whether or not he is a member of the institutional press.

Although Chief Justice Burger may have been incorrect as a matter of history, he did identify a critical problem with according special constitutional status to the institutional press, namely the problem of defining who "counts" as a member of the institutional press. Any definition of the "press" would hinge on "such variables as content of expression, frequency or fervor of expression, or ownership of the technological means of dissemination." (First National Bank v. Belloti, 1978 (Burger, C.J., concurring)) Perhaps this threshold problem explains the Court's reluctance to extend special constitutional status to the institutional press. That said, because the institutional press has greater incentives and resources to litigate First Amendment issues than other citizens, many of the Supreme Court's most important First Amendment decisions are shaped by its needs and interests. Even without special constitutional status, the status of the institutional press receives a great deal of legal protection. In most jurisdictions, for example, reporters have a privilege, whether based on a statute, common law, or state constitutional law, that protects them against compelled disclosure of confidential sources. Even though the First Amendment does not demand it, the press often receives preferential tax treatment and other kinds of subsidization by law. These form an important part of what we think of as press freedom, even if the First Amendment's press clause does not require them.

TECHNOLOGY AND THE FIRST AMENDMENT: THE BROADCAST PARADIGM

Most of the First Amendment principles discussed in this book apply equally to newspapers, broadcasters, cable television, Internet publishers, and other mass media. Whether a defamatory statement about a public official is broadcast on NBC, aired on CNN, or published in the *Washington Post*, the First Amendment requires the public official to prove actual malice and falsity if she is to have any hope of a monetary recovery. By the same token, the First Amendment equally forbids the government from enjoining television programs, radio broadcasts, or magazine articles. However, there are some instances in which the First Amendment permits regulation of broadcasters that would be forbidden when applied to other media. The usual justification for this differential treatment of broadcasters is the unique nature of the broadcast medium as a scarce public resource. This justification, however, has always had its critics, and it is becoming more and more questionable as the technological differences between broadcast, cable, and other media erode. Moreover, as new technologies of mass communication arise, courts must decide whether the First Amendment should apply differently to different segments of the media.

To appreciate the difference between the First Amendment paradigm applied to broadcasters with the paradigm applied to the print media, consider that federal law *requires* licensing of broadcasters. Until recently, federal law charged the Federal Communications Commission (FCC)—the federal agency that regulates the electronic media—with the task of licensing broadcast stations in accordance with the "public interest, convenience, and necessity."[23] Even now the FCC is charged with basing license renewal decisions in part on the public interest.[24] In other words, the FCC's decision whether to renew a broadcast license is based at least partially on the content that the television or radio station broadcasts. There is no doubt that a similar licensing scheme applied to the print media would be unconstitutional. Although much is unclear about the history of the First Amendment, it is absolutely certain that the founding fathers regarded licensing of printing presses as inimical to press freedom. Yet licensing by government bureaucrats is not only tolerated but encouraged in the broadcast medium. Why?

The answer has to do with the history and physical characteristics of the medium. During the 1920s, hundreds of radio stations began broadcasting with little or no government oversight. As described by the Supreme Court, "the allocation of frequencies was left entirely to the private sector, and the result was chaos." (Red Lion Broad. Co. v. F.C.C., 1969) Competing stations began broadcasting at the same frequencies in the same geographic locations. The signal interference thus created meant that none of the broadcasts could get through to listeners. The resulting chaos made it "apparent that broadcast frequencies constituted a scarce resource whose use could be regulated and rationalized only by the Government." (Red Lion Broad. Co. v. F.C.C., 1969) Congress therefore created the Federal Radio Commission, which later became the Federal Communications Commission, to allocate the portion of the electromagnetic spectrum available for commercial and public broadcasting in a manner "consistent with the public interest, convenience [and] necessity." The FCC performs these duties by issuing licenses to broadcasters, renewing licenses periodically, insuring that broadcasters comply with technical and operations rules, and developing rules to regulate broadcasting. Broadcasters, then, unlike newspaper publishers, are subject to pervasive governmental regulation because there is a need for an administrative body to allocate a limited resource—the electromagnetic spectrum—among competing users.[25]

The argument that an efficient and effective system of broadcasting demands that the government allocate the airwaves is often referred to as the "scarcity rationale." The scarcity rationale is the primary explanation for why the First Amendment tolerates content regulation of broadcasting that it would forbid in other mass media. Compare, for example, Miami Herald v. Tornillo with Red Lion Broadcasting v. F.C.C., two Supreme Court cases with very similar facts but with widely divergent answers to the question of whether government can regulate to foster public access to the mass media. The *Tornillo* case dealt with the constitutionality of a Florida "right of reply" statute. The statute required newspapers that "assailed" the character or record of a political candidate to print the candidate's response. Although the Court recognized that the statute's purpose was to "ensure that a wide variety of views reach the public," it nonetheless found the statute unconstitutional. "A responsible press," as the Court eloquently stated, "is an undoubtedly desirable goal, but press responsibility is not mandated by the Constitution and like many other virtues cannot be legislated." The Court was unequivocal in its condemnation of "government-enforced access" to newspapers, characterizing the statute as a content-based penalty on speech. The "compelled printing of a reply" consumes resources that a paper might prefer to use in a different manner. It also potentially "dampen[s] the vigor" of political reporting to the extent editors forego criticism of political candidates to avoid having to print their replies. Under these circumstances, the Court had no trouble concluding that the First Amendment does not tolerate governmental interference with "editorial control and judgment."

In Red Lion v. FCC, however, the Supreme Court held that the First Amendment *does* tolerate governmental interference with the editorial control and judgment of broadcasters, at least for the purpose of ensuring that the public receives a full range of views on issues of public concern. *Red Lion* involved a challenge to two "right of reply" rules imposed on broadcasters by the FCC: the "political editorial" rule and the "personal attack" rule. These two rules were merely specific applications of the FCC's "fairness doctrine," which requires broadcasters to give fair coverage to important public issues. The "political editorial" rule required a broadcaster who endorsed or opposed a political candidate in an editorial to notify the opposed candidate and give a "reasonable opportunity" to respond. The "personal attack" rule required broadcasters who aired attacks on the character of a person or group during discussion of a public issue to give the person or group attacked an opportunity to respond. The Supreme Court held that these "right of reply" rules did not violate the First Amendment, explicitly rejecting the argument that the rules would dampen the vigor of public debate and encourage undue "self-censorship" among broadcasters. (Red Lion Broad. v. F.C.C., 1969)

The Court justified its decision in *Red Lion* on the technological characteristics of broadcasting, specifically on "the scarcity of broadcast frequencies, the government's role in allocating those frequencies, and the legitimate claims of those unable without governmental assistance to gain access to those frequencies for expression of their views." Under the *Red Lion* scarcity doctrine, the government can impose affirmative programming obligations on broadcasters because they have been given a license to use a limited public resource. When a licensee accepts the privilege of using the public airways, that licensee must also accept the responsibility of acting as a fiduciary or "proxy for the entire community." In its role as fiduciary, the broadcaster is required to safeguard the First Amendment interests of its listening audience by giving "suitable time and attention to matters of great public concern."

The scarcity doctrine that underlies *Red Lion* is a highly questionable basis for according broadcasters diminished First Amendment protection. Newspaper ownership is concentrated in an ever smaller number of hands, and yet this "economic scarcity" did not convince the *Tornillo* Court that government-enforced access was constitutional. Moreover, the "physical scarcity" of the broadcast spectrum stems from the fact that the government has only chosen to dedicate a small portion of all available frequencies to commercial and public broadcasting. From a technological perspective this form of "allocational scarcity" may soon be a thing of the past. As Professor Christopher Yoo has noted, "[t]he impending arrival of a series of new broadcast technologies, including digital transmission, program storage, video-on-demand, spread spectrum, and packet switching, holds the promise of eliminating spectrum as a physical constraint even if broadcasting is viewed in isolation from other media."[26]

Even the FCC itself has concluded that "the dramatic transformation in the telecommunications marketplace provides a basis for the Court to reconsider its application of diminished First Amendment protection to the electronic media." Indeed, the FCC today imposes very few affirmative programming obligations on broadcasters, although it periodically contemplates imposing more.[27]

Despite the clamor against the scarcity doctrine, however, the Supreme Court continues to cling to it even while rejecting invitations to apply it to other media. In Reno v. ACLU, the Supreme Court refused to apply the broadcast paradigm to the Internet specifically because the Internet is not a scarce resource. Instead, the Court accorded Internet publishers the same First Amendment rights as their print counterparts. Likewise, the Court in Turner Broadcasting System, Inc. v. Federal Communications Commission ("Turner I") refused to apply the broadcast paradigm to cable operators because of the "fundamental technological differences between broadcast and cable transmission." Cable technology does not result in "signal interference," eliminating the need for government allocation, although the "physical infrastructure" of cable may depend on government permission to use public rights-of-way. Moreover, cable is not characterized by physical scarcity: "Given the rapid advances in fiber optics and digital compression technology, soon there may be no practical limitation on the number of speakers who may use the cable medium." (Turner Broad. Sys. v. F.C.C., 1994) The Court went to great pains to stress that physical scarcity rather than mere economic scarcity was the reason that its decisions accorded broadcasting diminished First Amendment protection. Indeed, the Court cited *Tornillo* for the principle that market dysfunction or "failure in a speech market, without more, is not sufficient to shield a speech regulation from the First Amendment standards applicable to nonbroadcast media." Although there is some dicta in the case that casts doubt on the Court's commitment to the scarcity doctrine, the overall tenor of the decision suggests that the Court will continue to tolerate limited governmental interference with editorial discretion in the broadcast medium but will vigilantly police such interference with other media.[28]

NOTES

1. Edmond N. Cahn, "Justice Black and the First Amendment 'Absolutes': A Public Interview," 37 *N.Y.U. L. Rev.* (1962) 548.

2. Leonard Levy, *Emergence of a Free Press* (New York, Oxford: Oxford University Press, 1985).

3. Common law is "law created by judges primarily in the process of deciding cases rather then by legislation." Larry L. Chubb, "Economic Analysis in the Courts: Limits and Constraints," 64 *Ind. L.J.* (1989) 769, 771–72.

4. William Blackstone, 4 *Commentaries on the Laws of England* (Oxford: Clarendon Press, 1765–69) 151–52.

5. Licensing in England was closely connected to the royal grant of printing monopoly to a private corporation, the Stationers' Company. *See* Lyman Ray L. Patterson, *Copyright in Historical Perspective* 6 (Nashville: Vanderbilt University Press, 1968). For a classic critique of this system, see John Milton, *Areopagitica* (1644).

6. See generally Levy, *Emergence of a Free Press.*

7. Merrill Jensen, "Book Review," 75 *Harv. L. Rev.* (1961) 456, 457.

8. Harold L. Nelson, "Seditious Libel in Colonial America," 3 *Am. J. Legal History* (1959) 160, 170.

9. Bernard Schwartz, *The Bill of Rights: A Documentary History* (New York: Chelsea House Publishers, 1971) 256.

10. David A. Anderson, "The Origins of the Press Clause," 30 *UCLA L. Rev.* (1983) 455, 489.

11. Anderson, "The Origins of the Press Clause," 480–81.

12. As David Anderson has shown, it would be wrong to assume that the legislators of the Fifth Congress were the same legislators who passed the First Amendment: "Of the ninety-five senators and representatives who served in the First Congress, only eighteen remained when the Sedition Act was enacted in July 1798, and of those only ten voted 'aye.' It was thus not, in any literal sense, 'the Framers' who passed the Sedition Act." Anderson, "The Origins of the Press Clause," 517.

13. The Sedition Act, Ch. 74, 1 Stat. 596 (1798) (expired 1801).

14. James Madison, The Virginia Report of 1799–1800, at 222, in *Freedom of the Press from Zenger to Jefferson* (Leonard Levy, ed., 1966) (Durham, N.C.: Carolina Academic Press, 1996).

15. *Documents of American Constitutional and Legal History*, 160 (Melvin Urofsky, ed., 1989) (bringing forth the Virginia Resolutions) (Philadelphia: Temple University Press, 1989).

16. David M. Rabban, "Free Speech in Its Forgotten Years" (Cambridge, U.K., New York: Cambridge University Press, 1997) 2. Professor Rabban's book is by far the most comprehensive book on free speech controversies and the development of free speech theory during the nineteenth and early twentieth centuries.

17. The full text of this provision, as well as an extended explanation of the legislative history of the Espionage Act, can be found in David Rabban, "Free Speech in Its Forgotten Years," 254, 248–98. Rabban notes that approximately two thousand prosecutions were brought under the Espionage Act. "Free Speech in Its Forgotten Years" 256.

18. See Marc A. Franklin, David A. Anderson, & Fred H. Cate, *Cases and Materials on Mass Media Law* (Mineola, N.Y.: Foundation Press, 2000) 10 (tracing the metaphor to Milton's *Areopagitica* and in the writings of John Stuart Mill). (emphasis added)

19. Thomas I. Emerson, *The System of Freedom of Expression* (New York: Random House, 1970) 6–9.

20. Vincent Blasi, "The First Amendment and the Ideal of Civic Courage: The Brandeis Opinion in Whitney v. California," 29 *Wm. & Mary L. Rev.* (1988) 653, 690–91.

21. Anderson, "The Origin of the Press Clause," 534.

22. Potter Stewart, "Or of the Press," at 636.

23. 47 U.S.C.A sec. 303 (2000).

24. Telecommunications Act of 1996, 47 U.S.C. sec. 309(1) (2000) (revising licensing criteria but still requiring the FCC to base license renewal, in part, on the public interest).

25. As the Supreme Court said in National Broadcasting Co. v. United States (1943): "[T]he radio spectrum simply is not large enough to accommodate everybody. There is a fixed natural limitation upon the number of stations that can operate without interfering with one another. Regulation of radio was therefore as vital to its development as traffic control was to the development of the automobile."

26. Christopher S. Yoo, "The Rise and Demise of the Technology-Specific Approach to the First Amendment," 91 *Geo L.J.* (2003) 245, 267.

27. See 91 *Geo. L.J.* (2003) 245, 264. Since 1983, the FCC has been considering deleting both the political editorial rule and the personal attack rule, which were not eliminated by the 1987 repeal of the Fairness Doctrine. The D.C. Circuit Court of Appeals finally issued a writ of mandamus requiring the FCC to repeal them in 2000. (Radio-television News Directors Ass'n v. FCC, 2000)

28. But see Time Warner Co. v. Federal Communications Comm'n, in which the D.C. Circuit Court of Appeals applied the "same relaxed standard of scrutiny that the court has applied to the traditional broadcast media" to the direct broadcast satellite. The court noted that "the United States has only a finite number of satellite positions available for DBS use."

The Supreme Court recently upheld a provision of the Bipartisan Campaign Reform Act of 2002 that requires broadcasters to maintain records of "politically related broadcasting requests." The Court, citing *Red Lion*, justified its decision based in part on the FCC's "'broad' mandate to assure broadcasters operate in public interest." (McConnell v. Federal Election Comm'n, 2003)

2

First Amendment Theory and Method

THEORETICAL JUSTIFICATIONS FOR PROTECTING PRESS FREEDOM

Freedom of speech and freedom of the press are often referred to collectively as "freedom of expression." This term recognizes that speech and press freedoms are interrelated. The freedom to speak protects communication of one's ideas and beliefs, and the freedom of the press protects the dissemination of one's ideas and beliefs to a wide audience via print, broadcast, cable, or the Internet.[1] Thus, many of the same justifications for protecting freedom of speech also apply to freedom of the press. Yet the press as a social institution also plays a unique role in informing the public, shaping public opinion, and checking abuses of government power. This unique role is suggested by the term "the Fourth Estate": The press acts as a fourth, unofficial check on the three official branches of government.[2] While this concept may influence First Amendment decisions involving the press, courts are reluctant to rely on it as the *sole* basis for a decision.

Because freedom of speech and freedom of the press are interrelated, the theoretical justifications for protecting them are largely the same. These justifications include both consequentialist and deontological theories: In other words, theorists have argued for protecting freedom of expression both because it leads to good consequences for society and because it is a good in and of itself.

The Marketplace of Ideas and the Search for Truth

John Milton and John Stuart Mill both famously argued that the free exchange of ideas fosters the search for truth. The "marketplace of ideas" metaphor, which was introduced to First Amendment jurisprudence by Justice Oliver Wendell Holmes, is perhaps the dominant theoretical justification for protecting freedom of expression. Yet this theory is open to serious challenge. As a practical matter, many viewpoints never enter the marketplace of ideas. Many citizens lack the money or education required to become serious participants in the marketplace of ideas. Other citizens are barred from meaningful participation because class, race, or gender biases impair their ability to make themselves heard. Moreover, many have argued that the concentration of mass media ownership allows a relatively small number of giant corporations to dominate the marketplace of ideas. Driven by profit, a handful of corporations sets the parameters of public debate based on what they think will be profitable rather than on what an informed public should know. Although the Internet has given more citizens access to a medium of mass communications, it has not guaranteed them the opportunity to be heard. Indeed, even in cyberspace the most powerful speakers tend to be the same media corporations that dominate "real space." Thus, for many citizens, the marketplace of ideas metaphor is little more than a hollow aspiration.

Another potential problem with the marketplace of ideas as the dominant metaphor in First Amendment law is its assumption that truth will ultimately prevail. The persistence of popular delusions, like the widespread belief in UFOs, casts doubt on the potential for rational discourse. And if we do not have faith in citizens' abilities to weed out false information, why should society allow blatant and sometimes harmful lies, like those disseminated by Holocaust deniers, to pollute the marketplace of ideas? Finally, the "search for truth" rationale presupposes that truth is out there, waiting to be discovered; it does not concede that truth may be merely subjective, relative, historically and socially contingent. Although these criticisms of the marketplace of ideas have force, the alternative—ceding power to a government authority to decide what citizens ought to hear—is a dangerous remedy that few First Amendment scholars are willing to embrace.

Individual Fulfillment and Self-Realization

Freedom of expression fosters not only the individual's search for truth but also his or her quest for self-realization and self-determination. If an individual is to achieve his or her potential as a human being, he or she must have access to a wide range of ideas and experiences. Freedom of expression in the arts, sciences, literature, and music all contribute to the range of possibilities the individual may explore. Yet the individual must also be free to develop and express his or her potential in ways he or she has chosen. In other words, freedom of expression fosters self-determination, and government suppression is therefore an affront to individual dignity.

The "individual self-realization" rationale is a powerful justification for speech and press freedoms, for it rests on the premise that the individual should have access to the widest possible range of ideas and information. Still, some have questioned whether all paths to self-realization are equally valid. Both the individual and society might benefit if information about becoming a hit man or a terrorist were suppressed. Moreover, the self-realization argument has limits. There are many activities that are not protected by the First Amendment that an individual may consider crucial to his or her self-realization. The First Amendment, for example, does not guarantee the right to open a restaurant or to marry a person of the same sex or to enter a bigamous marriage, even though the individual may consider these crucial to his or her self-fulfillment. Moreover, if an individual is to realize his or her potential as a human being, he or she may require access to subsidized education, housing, and health care, yet the First Amendment does not give him or her a right to these things. Is it fair, then, to question whether freedom of expression is the front of all other freedoms?

Democratic Self-Governance and Social Stability

A fundamental premise of democratic society is that government authority derives from the consent of the governed. An informed citizenry is essential to a self-governing society, and a free press is essential to an informed citizenry. The press gathers and disseminates information about public affairs, laying the foundation for discussion, debate, and citizen participation in public decision-making. Closely linked to this idea is the argument that freedom of expression promotes social stability. Citizens who can make themselves heard through the political process need not make themselves heard through force of arms. Thus, orderly change can take place without undue disruption of the social fabric if freedom of expression is allowed to flourish.

The most influential proponent of the idea that press freedom is essential to "democratic self-governance" was Alexander Meiklejohn, who argued that the First Amendment protects only those forms of expression "by which we 'govern.'"[3] In other words, the First Amendment protects only *political speech*. This notion has been enshrined in law by a series of Supreme Court decisions holding that speech on matters of public concern lies at the core of the First Amendment. Yet the "democratic self-governance" rationale for protecting freedom of expression fails as a general theory of the First Amendment. As Professor Zechariah Chaffee pointed out soon after Meiklejohn presented his thesis in 1948, many types of expression that are not related directly to politics nonetheless deserve protection in a free society.[4] Neither Van Gogh's *Starry Night* nor Walt Whitman's *Crossing Brooklyn Ferry* are overtly political, but few of us would want to live in a society where the government could suppress them. Meiklejohn responded to such criticisms by expanding the definition of "political speech" to include literary, artistic, philosophical, and scientific speech, arguing that they relate to political matters because voters derive from them the "knowledge, intelligence, [and] sensitivity to human values" that allow them to make "sane and objective judgment[s]."[5] Defined broadly, however, it becomes difficult to draw a line excluding any speech from the definition of political speech.

Other theories have been offered to justify speech and press protection. One scholar has argued, for example, that the protection of diverse and even offensive speech creates a tolerant society.[6] Yet courts, unlike scholars, have never felt compelled to adhere to a single justification for protecting freedom of expression. Instead they have treated the justifications discussed above as overlapping, adapting the justification or justifications that are most resonant in individual cases.

METHODS OF ANALYSIS IN FIRST AMENDMENT CASES

Courts have used various analytical tools and legal doctrines to test the constitutionality of laws involving the freedom of expression. However, courts have never felt compelled to adopt a single method for analyzing every press freedom case but have instead applied the theory that they felt best suited for the particular circumstances. These theories include, but are not limited to, absolutism, balancing, and the clear and present danger test.

Absolutism

One of the less frequently employed legal doctrines used to resolve First Amendment cases is absolutism. Absolutism originates in the text of the First Amendment: The First Amendment says Congress can pass "no law" abridging freedom of expression, and any and every law that abridges freedom of expression is unconstitutional. Absolutism, associated most famously with Justice Hugo Black (who served on the Supreme Court from 1937 to 1971), is attractive in its simplicity. Justice Black, for example, interpreted the First Amendment to forbid all regulations except for those that placed only incidental restrictions on the time, place, and manner of an individual's freedom of expression. Absolutism tries to tie the hands of judges so that they will not be swayed by the temptation to restrict speech in response to historical "emergencies" (like the Red Scare of the 1950s or the war on terrorism today). But absolutism forced even Justice Black to unduly narrow the scope of what counts as speech in order to reach what he felt was the "correct" result in a speech case. In Cohen v. California, for example, Justice Black argued that a state could constitutionally punish one of its citizens for a jacket that said "Fuck the Draft." (Black, J., joining in the dissent written by Blackmun, J.); (Adderley v. Florida, 1966). Expressing this type of antiwar sentiment on one's jacket, said Justice Black, was not speech but was instead a type of physical conduct in a courthouse corridor that the state could legitimately regulate. Because Justice Black's absolutism did not allow him to balance the State's interests against the right to freedom of expression, he was forced to resort to this strained argument in order to avoid what to him was an unacceptable constitutional outcome.

Balancing

An obvious alternative to absolutism of this sort is a balancing process that weighs First Amendment freedoms against other important societal interests. Balancing is the dominant method of analyzing First Amendment cases today. A simple example of balancing occurred in the Supreme Court's decision in New York v. Ferber. There, the Court held that a state statute criminalizing the distribution of child pornography was constitutional because "the evil . . . restricted so overwhelmingly outweigh[ed] the expressive interests, if any, at stake." The Court evaluated both the State's interest in protecting children with society's and the individual defendant's interest in the expression (child pornography) and found the balance tipped in favor of regulation.

When balancing interests, the Supreme Court often specifies not simply that the State's interest must outweigh the First Amendment interest at stake but must outweigh it by a specified amount. Because First Amendment freedoms occupy such a central role in our democracy (what is sometimes referred to as a "preferred position"), the Supreme Court has often said that freedom of expression may not be regulated unless a State can show a *compelling* or *important* interest in such regulation. In addition, the State is often required to show that the regulation it has chosen is narrowly tailored to achieve its interest, or that it is the least restrictive means of achieving that interest. This type of balancing test, in which the Court tips the scale heavily in favor of freedom of expression, is known as "strict scrutiny" and is applied in many First Amendment cases.

The Supreme Court has often chosen to balance the competing interests in First Amendment cases on an ad hoc basis. In other words, the Court assigns a weight to the interests based on the specific facts of the case it is deciding. However, the balance struck is so fact-specific to that case that the Court's decision gives little guidance to resolve future cases. Thus the virtue of such ad hoc balancing, its flexibility, is also its vice, its unpredictability.

The second type of balancing commonly employed by the court, categorical balancing, is less subject to the criticism of unpredictability. When the Court employs categorical balancing, it attempts to assign a weight to general categories of speech; the weight assigned transcends the merits of the particular case at hand and is designed to be applied to every case involving that category of speech, regardless of the specific facts. The Court's decision in Chaplinsky v. New Hampshire is the classic illustration of categorical balancing. In *Chaplinsky*, the Court declared "fighting words, inherently injurious words," or "words likely to cause an average addressee to fight" to make so little contribution to the "exposition of ideas" as to be totally unworthy of constitutional protection. Thus, "fighting words" are typically of such low value that the balance must be struck in favor of regulation.

Categorical balancing, however, does not always provide clear resolutions for future cases because it is often not easy to know whether the speech at issue falls into an unprotected category. Can the state forbid the use of racial epithets on the grounds that they are fighting words? What about insults to a person's mother? Obscenity, another category of "low value" speech, has been so notoriously difficult to define that one justice was forced to proclaim, "I know it when I see it." (Jacobellis v. Ohio, 1964) This type of analysis is no more predictable than ad hoc balancing. To further complicate matters, the Supreme Court recently said that the State may not even punish the use of low value speech like fighting words if the State's purpose is to single out particular content or viewpoints for sanction. (R.A.V. v. City of St. Paul, 1992) Categorical balancing does not obviate the need for judges to make difficult value choices in individual cases.

The Clear and Present Danger Test

As discussed in the first chapter, the clear and present danger test originated with Justices Oliver Wendell Holmes and Louis Brandeis, who contended that speech could only be suppressed when it posed a "clear and present danger" (that is, a real and immediate danger) of harm to society. Holmes and Brandeis developed the clear and present danger test in a series of cases involving the prosecution of citizens who criticized U.S. policy during World War I. In most of these cases, the two justices argued that the government had shown only a speculative connection between the speech at issue and any substantive harms to the war effort. A majority of the Court eventually endorsed this view, and the "clear and present danger" test for speech restrictions was the dominant method of analyzing First Amendment cases for a large portion of the twentieth century.

Today, the libertarian conception of the First Amendment developed by Holmes and Brandeis is still ascendant, but the clear and present danger test has only limited importance as a legal doctrine. The clear and present danger test has given way to the "incitement" test of Brandenburg v. Ohio. This test is used primarily for speakers who allegedly "incite" violence by their audience. *Brandenburg* involved a hooded Ku Klux Klan speaker who exhorted his audience, some of whom were armed, to "[s]end the Jews back to Israel" and to "bury the niggers." In striking down Ohio's prosecution of the speaker for advocating criminal activity, the Supreme Court held that the First Amendment does not allow "a State to forbid or proscribe advocacy of the use of force or of law violation except where such advocacy is directed to inciting or producing imminent lawless action and is likely to incite or produce such action." (Brandenburg v. Ohio, 1969) In other words, a State must show that the speaker intended to incite another to imminent violence in a context that made it highly likely such violence would actually occur. Drawing on notions developed by Holmes and Brandeis, *Brandenburg* rests on the premise that most Americans are not susceptible to the impassioned rhetoric of a radical speaker. The continuing relevance of *Brandenburg's* incitement test to the mass media is that courts often apply it in cases in which the media (usually television or movies) are blamed for causing people to harm themselves or others. As we shall see, however, the incitement test, which was developed to prevent a fiery orator from inciting a mob to violence, does not adapt well to such cases.

NOTES

1. This was the view espoused by Chief Justice Burger in First Nat'l Bank v. Bellotti. Justice Burger argued that this was the Framer's understanding of the press clause in the First Amendment. However, Burger was probably incorrect as a historical matter. The Framers appear to have been primarily concerned with the role of the press in checking government abuses of power and thus likely viewed the press clause as protecting the press as an institution. Nonetheless, Burger's argument that the press clause is a functional protection rather than a structural one seems to be ascendant in the case law.

2. Potter Stewart, "Or of the Press," 26 *Hastings L.J.* (1975) 631, 635 ("The primary purpose of the constitutional guarantee of a free press was a similar one: to create a fourth institution outside the government as an additional check on the three official branches. . . . The relevant metaphor, I think, is the metaphor of the Fourth Estate.").

3. Alexander Meiklejohn, "The First Amendment Is An Absolute," 1961 *Sup. Ct. Rev.* 245, 255.

4. For further discussion of Chaffee's views, see Zechariah Chaffee, *Free Speech in the United States* (Cambridge, Mass.: Harvard University Press, 1941).

5. Alexander Meiklejohn, *The First Amendment Is an Absolute*, 1961 Sup. Ct. Rev. 245, 256.

6. Lee C. Bollinger, *The Tolerant Society: Freedom of Speech and Extremist Speech in America* (New York: Oxford University Press; Oxford: Clarendon Press, 1986), 237–38.

3

Prior Restraints

Prior restraints are an especially disfavored form of media regulation. In fact, prior restraints on the publication of ideas and information are presumptively unconstitutional. A prior restraint is a government regulation that restricts speech in advance of or *prior to* publication. Prior restraints usually take the form of licensing systems, gag orders, or gag laws. The distinction between prior restraints and punishments imposed on expression *after* publication is constitutionally important because the First Amendment reserves special opprobrium for prior restraints. Even expression that the government constitutionally could punish after publication ordinarily may not be suppressed by the government prior to publication.

THE HISTORICAL EXPLANATION FOR THE SPECIAL
OPPROBRIUM ATTACHED TO PRIOR RESTRAINTS

The classic prior restraints were the English licensing laws. Henry VIII adopted the first comprehensive licensing scheme in 1538, requiring pre-publication review of religious books by ecclesiastical authorities and review of all other books by his Privy Council.[1] Queen Elizabeth I put even more exacting limitations upon the press with the establishment of the Star Chamber.

The Star Chamber, which had both legislative and judicial authority, proclaimed in 1586 that all printing presses had to be registered with the Stationers Company, and all printed materials had to be submitted to the Company for approval by issuance of a license.[2] In return for its government-granted monopoly on printing, the Company was expected to defend the interests of the Crown. The Company was authorized to search for and destroy any printing presses that were not properly registered. The Star Chamber meted out harsh punishments, including torture, to those who did not adhere to this licensing scheme. Parliament continued this tradition of censorship with the Licensing Act of 1662, which "was allowed to expire in 1694, apparently not so much from opposition to the principle of the statute as from frustration with the absurdities and inequities of its administration."[3] Nevertheless, by the end of the eighteenth century, both in England and America "prior restraints" in the form of licensing schemes had become associated with government tyranny. Indeed, a primary purpose of the Framers in adopting the First Amendment was to prevent governmental licensing of the press.

The special dangers of licensing schemes are well and succinctly described by Professor Thomas Emerson:

A system of prior restraint is in many ways more inhibiting than a system of subsequent punishment: It is likely to bring under government scrutiny a far wider range of expression; it shuts off communication before it takes place; suppression by a stroke of the pen is more likely to be applied than suppression through a criminal process; the procedures do not require attention to the safeguards of the criminal process; the system allows less opportunity for public appraisal and criticism; the dynamics of the system drive toward excesses, as the history of all censorship shows.[4]

From this perspective, licensing schemes deserve special opprobrium not just because of their historical association with tyranny, but also because licensing schemes are a more insidious threat to freedom of expression than subsequent punishment. Licensing schemes block some expression from ever reaching the marketplace of ideas, with little opportunity for the public to scrutinize the decision-making of the censors.

MODERN FORMS OF PRIOR RESTRAINTS

Licensing schemes are relatively rare today, and for good reason. The Supreme Court has condemned attempts by the executive branch to institute licensing in no uncertain terms. One of the few areas in which the Supreme Court has tolerated licensing schemes is in the context of obscenity. Even here, the Court requires that any preliminary injunction entered must be immediately appealable and the procedure employed must "assure a prompt final judicial decision [that the speech is unprotected] to minimize the deterrent effect of an interim and possibly erroneous denial of a license." (Freedman v. Maryland, 1965)

Far more common than licensing are judicial or legislative attempts to censor the press in advance of publication. When the judiciary issues an order to the press to refrain from publishing something, it is known as a "gag order." A gag order may take the form of a temporary restraining order, a preliminary injunction or, more rarely, a permanent injunction against publication.[5] When the legislature passes a statute forbidding the press from publishing on certain topics, the statute is known as a "gag law." Both are treated as prior restraints and bear a heavy presumption against their constitutionality.

Near v. Minnesota ex rel. Olson, the first great Supreme Court case on prior restraints against the press, involved neither a gag order nor a gag law, but a strange combination of both. The Minnesota legislature passed a statute providing for "abatement, as a public nuisance, of a malicious, scandalous and defamatory newspaper, magazine or other periodical." (Near v. Minnesota ex rel. Olson, 1931) Relying on this statute, the Hennepin County Attorney sought a permanent injunction against the Saturday Press. The trial judge entered the injunction against the Saturday Press because it had published articles alleging that "a Jewish gangster was in control of gambling, bootlegging and racketeering in Minneapolis, and that law enforcing officers and agencies were not energetically performing their duties." The United States Supreme Court looked beyond the unusual features of the Minnesota statute and labeled it a prior restraint based on its "operation and effect." Even though the permanent injunction against future publication was, in a sense, a punishment for past publication, the effect of the injunction was to restrain publication in the future. If the Press did wish to resume publication, it would have to comply with the trial judge's order to "operate [its] newspaper in harmony with the public welfare," or else face contempt charges. This, the Court said, "is the essence of censorship." (Near v. Minnesota ex rel. Olson, 1931)

Near is a landmark case not only because of its strong condemnation of prior restraints but also because it looked beyond the form of the Minnesota statute to its operation and effect as a prior restraint. The *Near* decision also makes the distinction between prior restraints and subsequent punishments a critical one for First Amendment purposes, because *Near* expressly stated that the publisher of the Saturday Press could still be "punished," civilly or criminally, for publishing "malicious, scandalous and defamatory" material. Perhaps even more critically, the *Near* decision did not condemn prior restraints in all circumstances; indeed, the Court stated, for example, that prior restraints might properly be used to protect national security, to prevent dissemination of obscenity, or to prevent incitements to violence and overthrow of the government. (Near v. Minnesota ex rel. Olson, 1931)

PRIOR RESTRAINTS AND NATIONAL SECURITY

The Pentagon Papers case, New York Times Co. v. United States, tested the breadth of the national security exception to the First Amendment's prohibition on prior restraints.[6] While the controversy over the Vietnam War was at its height, the *New York Times* obtained and began publishing portions of what came to be known as the "Pentagon Papers," a forty-seven volume classified history of U.S. involvement in the war. The Nixon Administration (via the Justice Department) sued to obtain an injunction against further publication on the grounds that it would jeopardize national security interests. In the interim, the *Washington Post* also began publishing portions of the Pentagon Papers, and the Administration quickly brought a second action against them. Within seventeen days after the *New York Times* began publishing the Pentagon Papers articles, both cases were heard before the Supreme Court. The government argued that further publication would embarrass U.S. allies, compromise intelligence sources and endanger U.S. troops. The Court rejected this claim, holding simply that the government had failed to overcome the "heavy presumption against [the] constitutional validity" of prior restraints. (New York Times Co. v. United States, 1971) The fact that each of the nine Justices then felt compelled to write his own opinion in the case testifies to the significance of the Court's decision. The Pentagon Papers case was, and is, seen as a test of the American commitment to press freedom; the outcome proves that we are willing to pay a very great price for press freedom, even in the face of threats to national security.

THE COLLATERAL BAR AND THE DANGERS OF VIOLATING INJUNCTIONS

Although injunctions are treated as a form of prior restraint, they do not pose the same threats to freedom of expression as licensing schemes. A party seeking injunctive relief must convince a judge, at a hearing in open court, of the propriety and constitutionality of suppressing a specific article, book, or movie. And judges, unlike the bureaucrats who censor speech under licensing systems, "have no vested interest in the suppression of speech," as Professor John Jeffries has noted. Jeffries, in an important article called "Rethinking Prior Restraints," argues that the primary reason for treating injunctions as prior restraints is the procedural impact of the collateral bar rule.[7] Under the collateral bar rule, "the legality of an injunction may not be challenged by disobeying its terms."[8] If an enjoined party chooses to publish in violation of an injunction, that party can be charged with criminal contempt and is "barred" from asserting the unconstitutionality of the injunction as a defense. (See Pittsburgh Press Co. v. Pittsburgh Comm'n on Human Relations, 1973)

The collateral bar rule encourages obedience to judicial authority, but it does so at a cost to freedom of expression. By delaying publication, an injunction may destroy the newsworthiness of the enjoined information. Moreover, injunctions are often ineffective because an injunction against one media outlet does not prevent its competitors from publishing the same information.

Two federal appellate courts and some state courts have avoided the harsh effects of the collateral bar rule by carving out an important exception to it. (See, e.g., State ex rel. Superior Court of Snohomish v. Sperry, 1971; State v. Coe, 1984; Wood v. Goodson, 1972; People v. Gonzalez, 1996) Specifically, these courts have stated that speakers may challenge a "transparently invalid" prior restraint in the form of a court order by violating the order. (Procter & Gamble Co. v. Bankers Trust Co., 1996) Given the heavy presumption against the constitutionality of prior restraints, almost every prior restraint would seem to be transparently invalid. Recognizing the danger that the transparently invalid exception would swallow the collateral bar rule, the Court of Appeals for the First Circuit attempted to limit the exception. The First Circuit required that "a publisher, even when it thinks it is the subject of a transparently unconstitutional order of prior restraint, [must] make a good faith effort to seek emergency relief from the appellate court." (In re Providence Journal Co., 1987) Only if the publisher cannot gain "timely access to the appellate court" or an appellate decision, may the publisher "proceed to publish and challenge the constitutionality of the order in the contempt proceedings." Even with this limitation, the "transparently invalid" exception to the collateral bar rule does much to ameliorate the threat the bar poses to First Amendment values.

PRIOR RESTRAINTS IN INTELLECTUAL PROPERTY CASES

One context in which preliminary injunctions are routinely granted, with little thought given to the First Amendment implications, is in cases involving copyright infringements or trade secret violations. Copyright infringement cases and trade secret cases often involve a defendant's choice of expression. If, for example, an author writes a parody of *Gone with the Wind*, the author is clearly engaged in creative expression; however, the work can still be enjoined as a copyright infringement if it relies too heavily on the original work. If an employee of Microsoft criticizes its new operating system, in the process revealing key elements of its design, the employee is clearly engaged in expression of ideas but can nonetheless be enjoined from revealing trade secrets.

Why these cases have traditionally been treated as immune from the First Amendment restrictions on prior restraints is not immediately clear. Some have argued that intellectual property law protects property rights, and it should therefore trump First Amendment concerns. (See, e.g., Dallas Cowboys Cheerleaders, Inc. v. Scoreboard Posters, Inc., 1979) Others have argued that the government's interest in protecting intellectual property is compelling and that copyright law, for example, encourages speech by protecting creative works. (See, e.g., Harper & Row Publishers, Inc. v. Nation Enterprises, 1985) None of these arguments, however, hold up under analysis. As Professors Mark Lemley and Eugene Volokh have argued, libel law protects a form of reputational "property," and yet prior restraints cannot be used to prevent libelous speech.[9] Moreover, the government's interest in protecting national security could surely be described as compelling in many cases; yet even in cases involving national security, prior restraints are subject to such rigorous restrictions that they will almost never be constitutional.

The fact that copyright law is explicitly authorized by the Constitution gives a strong indication of the importance of promoting the expression of authors, artists, musicians and others. Even so, the use of prior restraints to protect copyrights still runs the risk of suppressing constitutionally protected expression, which is precisely the reason prior restraints are constitutionally barred in other contexts. Moreover, although copyright law creates financial incentives for the expression of ideas, it also can be used to suppress speech, as in the case in which the author J.D. Salinger used copyright law to suppress (permanently) the publication of letters he had written to a friend. (Salinger v. Random House, Inc., 1987) Partly on the basis of these arguments, Lemley, Volokh, and other commentators have decried the anomalous treatment of injunctions in intellectual property cases.[10] Thus far, a few courts are becoming more hostile, on First Amendment grounds, to granting prior restraints in intellectual property cases, but it is too early to say that the tide has turned. (See, e.g., Ford Motor Co. v. Lane, 1999; State ex. rel Sports Mgmt. News, Inc. v. Nachtigal, 1996)

FREE PRESS VS. FAIR TRIAL: PRIOR RESTRAINTS TO PREVENT PREJUDICIAL PUBLICITY

The Supreme Court has held that prejudicial publicity before and during criminal trials can sometimes taint the jury's impartiality so much that the criminal defendant is denied his constitutional right to a fair trial. (Sheppard v. Maxwell, 1966) The criminal defendant's right to a fair trial is particularly at risk in sensational cases that set off a media "feeding frenzy." The classic example is the trial of Bruno Hauptmann for kidnapping the baby of Charles Lindbergh, the famous aviator. A "'carnival' atmosphere" infected the trial, at which Hauptmann was quickly convicted. (Nebraska Press Ass'n v. Stuart, 1976) A more recent example is the 1995 murder trial of O.J. Simpson, a trial which dominated almost every media outlet for months and which turned the names of the judge, prosecutors, defense attorneys, police, and even witnesses into household names. (Of course the Simpson trial, unlike many other high-publicity criminal trials, ultimately resulted in an acquittal of Simpson.)

To protect the integrity of the criminal trial, prosecutors or criminal defendants sometimes seek preliminary injunctions against the press to stem prejudicial publicity. Because the right to a fair trial is itself of constitutional status, these cases present special challenges not exhibited in other prior restraint cases. The Supreme Court dealt with prior restraints in the trial context in Nebraska Press Association v. Stuart. The case involved the brutal murder of six members of a family in Sutherland, Nebraska, a town of about 850 people. The case triggered extensive publicity in local, regional and national media. At the request of the criminal defense attorney and the prosecutor, a judicial order was entered prohibiting the media from publishing information thought to be prejudicial to the criminal defendant's right to a fair trial. This information included: (1) the existence or contents of the criminal defendant's confession, (2) statements made to other people, (3) the contents of a note written by the defendant, (4) some aspects of the medical testimony given at an open preliminary hearing, (5) the identity of the victims of sexual assault by the defendant prior to the murders, and (6) even the nature of the assaults prior to the murders. In addition, the order forbade the press from publishing the specific prohibitions of the restrictive order (presumably for fear that this might indirectly reveal the prejudicial information). The trial judge's restrictive order on the media was upheld, with slight modifications, by the Nebraska Supreme Court. The U.S. Supreme Court unanimously reversed this decision, reiterating the heavy presumption against the constitutionality of prior restraints.

In this sense, *Nebraska Press* was a victory for press freedom. However, the Supreme Court rejected the notion that the prohibition of prior restraints is absolute. It even rejected the notion that prior restraints based on fair trial grounds must meet the very high standards set in Near v. Minnesota and the Pentagon Papers case. Even so, the Court laid down strict requirements that must be satisfied before a trial court can issue a restrictive order against the media on fair trial grounds.

First, the Court said, a court must determine whether the nature and extent of pretrial publicity is likely to impair the criminal defendant's right to a fair trial. (Nebraska Press Ass'n v. Stuart, 1976) Second, a court must make express findings on the record that no alternatives short of a prior restraint on the press would protect the criminal defendant's Sixth Amendment right. Alternatives include changing the venue (or location) of the criminal trial, postponing the trial to allow publicity to subside, "searching questioning of prospective jurors" to weed out those who cannot be impartial, instructing jurors to decide the case only on the basis of evidence presented in open court, and sequestering jurors during trial. The Supreme Court also suggested that trial judges issue orders to restrain lawyers, police officers, and witnesses in the case rather than trying to control the press. Obviously, this requirement is very difficult for a trial court to surmount, because it will be very difficult to show that none of the alternatives will suffice to protect the integrity of the trial.

The third requirement is probably even more difficult to meet. Even if a trial court can show the ineffectiveness of alternatives to a prior restraint, the court must show that a prior restraint would be effective to protect the right to fair trial. This is difficult to show because a trial judge only has the power (jurisdiction) to issue orders that will bind the media in a limited area. But in sensational cases, media coverage is likely to be national in scope, thereby making a restrictive order ineffective. Furthermore, gossip and rumors about sensational cases may be just as prejudicial as news accounts, which also makes restraints on the media futile.

In addition to these three requirements, a court cannot forbid the media from reporting events that occur in open court, which is a significant limitation in light of the First Amendment right of the press and public to attend most criminal trials. (See Richmond Newspapers, Inc. v. Virginia, 1980) And finally, the terms of the prior restraint must be narrow and precise in order to avoid infringing the First Amendment rights of the media any more than necessary to safeguard the criminal defendant's Sixth Amendment rights. (Nebraska Press Ass'n v. Stuart,

1976) The Supreme Court found that the lower court's orders in *Nebraska Press* did not satisfy these exacting requirements, and suggested that it was a typical rather than exceptional case in this regard. In fact, Justice White's concurring opinion suggested that the requirements imposed by the Court were so stringent that he doubted if a prior restraint would ever be permissible. Thus, Nebraska Press Ass'n v. Stuart stands as a great victory for press freedom.

It was not a complete victory, however. Certainly the decision has meant that prior restraints to protect fair trial rights have been exceedingly rare, and the Supreme Court has never upheld a prior restraint against the press. However, the Court's rejection of an absolute prohibition on prior restraints has sometimes led lower courts to impose them in situations where the requisite findings cannot or have not been made. On occasion, trial judges even issue prior restraints that would be held unconstitutional if appealed far enough, but never are. For example, in 1990, Cable News Network (CNN) obtained and began publishing tapes of conversations between Panamanian General Manuel Noriega and his attorneys. At the time of the conversation, Noriega was in jail in Miami on drug trafficking charges. Noriega's attorneys obtained a temporary restraining order against further publication of the tapes, and the district court judge ordered CNN to turn over the tapes to him so that he could determine whether they threatened Noriega's right to a fair trial by disclosing confidential attorney-client communications. CNN refused to turn over the tapes and broadcast one of them in violation of the judge's order. CNN's attempt to obtain emergency relief in the appellate courts was unavailing. The Eleventh Circuit Court of Appeals denied relief, stating that CNN was required to provide the tapes to the trial judge so that he could determine the proper scope, if any, of any restraining order. (United States v. Noriega, 1990) The Supreme Court subsequently denied CNN's application to stay the order and denied certiorari. (Cable News Network, Inc. v. Noriega, 1990) As a result, CNN turned over the tapes to the district judge, who determined that further publication would not jeopardize Noriega's fair trial rights. However, CNN was held in criminal contempt and fined $85,000 for broadcasting one of the tapes in violation of the court's temporary restraining order. CNN was able to avoid paying a more substantial fine only by agreeing to broadcast an apology for violating the order. What the CNN case illustrates is that trial courts can sometimes be persuaded to grant prior restraints to protect fair trial rights, despite the seemingly insurmountable barriers placed against the issuance of such restraints by Near v. Minnesota and Nebraska Press Ass'n v. Stuart.

NOTES

1. Michael I. Meyerson, "The Neglected History of the Prior Restraint Doctrine: Rediscovering the Link Between the First Amendment and the Separation of Powers," 34 *Ind. L. Rev.* (2001) 295, 298.

2. Myerson, "The Neglected History of the Prior Restraint Doctrine: Rediscovering the Link Between the First Amendment and the Separation of Powers," 299.

3. John Calvin Jeffries, Jr., "Rethinking Prior Restraint," 92 *Yale L.J.* (1983) 409, 412.

4. Thomas I. Emerson, *The System of Freedom of Expression* (New York: Random House, 1970) 506.

5. "The term 'prior restraint' is used 'to describe administrative and judicial orders *forbidding* certain communications when issued in advance of the time that such communications are to occur.' Temporary restraining orders and permanent injunctions, *i.e.,* court orders that actually forbid speech activities, are classic examples of prior restraints." (Alexander v. United States, 1993) (emphasis supplied by the Court).

6. For more on the historical background of the case, see generally David Rudenstine, "The Pentagon Papers Case: Recovering Its Meaning Twenty Years Later," 12 *Cardozo L. Rev.* (1991) 1869.

7. Jeffries, Jr., "Rethinking Prior Restraint," 426–27.

8. Jeffries, Jr., "Rethinking Prior Restraint," 431.

9. Mark A. Lemley & Eugene Volokh, "Freedom of Speech and Injunctions in Intellectual Property Cases," 48 *Duke L.J.* (1998) 147, 182–83. Lemley and Volokh summarize and refute all of the potential arguments for immunizing copyright law from "normal First Amendment procedural guarantees." They ultimately conclude that copyright injunctions should be applied with more consideration for First Amendment values and recommend a four-factor test to be applied before granting of a preliminary injunction.

10. See generally Lemley and Volokh, "Freedom of Speech and Injunctions in Intellectual Property Cases," 199–210 (arguing that the copyright law context presents a "comparatively weak" case for allowing preliminary injunctions of otherwise protected speech); Michael W. Shiver, Jr., "Objective Limitations or, How the Vigorous Application of 'Strong Form' Idea/Expression Dichotomy Theory in Copyright Preliminary Injunction Hearings Might Just Save the First Amendment," 9 *UCLA Ent. L. Rev.* (2000) 361, 383–87 (proposing a more reserved judicial approach in copyright infringement cases, where injunctions would be issued only when necessary to prevent use of expressive elements of a copyrighted work).

4

Content-Based Restrictions
on the Media

AN INTRODUCTION

In First Amendment law, courts frequently distinguish between *content-based* and *content-neutral* governmental regulations of expression. This distinction is an important one, since courts almost invariably strike down content-based regulations.[1] The distinction is easy to illustrate and justify, at least superficially. But the content-based/content-neutral distinction can quickly become complex, murky, contested, and subjective in its application, formulation, and rationale.[2]

The Supreme Court has declared that "above all else, the First Amendment means that government has no power to restrict expression because of its message, its ideas, its subject matter, or its content." (Arkansas Writers' Project, Inc. v. Ragland, 1987 (quoting Police Dept. of Chicago v. Mosley, 1972)) This broad declaration shows a special judicial concern about content-based regulations. Let us set aside the categorical nature of this formulation for a moment, and focus on the underlying distinction itself. The idea is roughly that content-based regulations limit communication "because of the message conveyed."[3] In contrast, content-neutral regulations restrict communication "without regard to the message conveyed."[4] A bit more particularly, if still vaguely, some speech regulations are thought to regard the "communicative impact"[5] of the speech, and others are not. The former regulations alone are said to be content-based.

From a constitutional standpoint, content-based regulations seem generally worse than content-neutral regulations. We can, of course, imagine highly restrictive content-neutral regulations.[6] Denying all journalists any professional use of electricity could be a content-neutral restriction. But even as a content-neutral restriction, it would clearly undermine the First Amendment. And we can imagine content-based regulations of the press that, whatever the weight of their justification, do not seem unduly burdensome. Levying a small fine on journalists who libel anyone from the nearby star system Proxima Centauri could be both content-based and only a modest burden on the press. The institution of the free press could endure.

The assumption remains, though, that content-based restrictions generally are worse than content-neutral restrictions. The Supreme Court has written that content-based regulations pose greater "inherent dangers to free expression" (Turner Broad. Sys. v. FCC, 1996 (quoting Turner Broad. Sys. v. FCC, 1994)) than do content-neutral regulations. The "inherent risk," according to the Court, is "that the Government seeks not to advance a legitimate regulatory goal, but to suppress unpopular ideas or information or manipulate the public debate through coercion rather than persuasion." (Turner Broad. Sys. v. FCC, 1994) According to one commentator, "[c]ontent-based restrictions are more likely than content-neutral restrictions to distort public debate, to be tainted by improper motivation, and to be defended with constitutionally disfavored justifications."[7] The Court has concluded that content-based restrictions more commonly risk stifling debate, suppressing unpopular or disfavored ideas, manipulating public discussion and artificially driving particular points of view from the marketplace of ideas. (See Turner Broad. Sys. v. FCC, 1994)

As a general rule, therefore, content-based restrictions are more judicially disfavored than content-neutral restrictions. The judicial tests of content-based and content-neutral regulations differ in their stringency. Content-based restrictions typically receive "the most exacting" judicial scrutiny. (Turner Broad. Sys. v. FCC, 1994) Given the risk of a government's seeking to suppress a disfavored idea or viewpoint, (See, e.g., Simon & Schuster, Inc. v. Members of the N.Y. State Crime Victims Bd., 1991 (citing Leathers v. Medlock, 1991)) content-based restrictions are presumptively unconstitutional[8] and subject to strict judicial scrutiny. Specifically, content-based restrictions are upheld only where the government discharges its "heavy burden" (Arkansas Writers' Project v. Ragland, 1987) of showing that its regulation is "necessary to serve a compelling state interest and is narrowly drawn to achieve that end." (Arkansas Writers' Project v. Ragland, 1987 (citing Minneapolis Star & Tribune Co. v. Minnesota Comm'r of Revenue, 1983); See also Dept. of Revenue v. Magazine Publ'g, 1992)

In contrast to content-based restrictions, content-neutral restrictions receive only "an intermediate level of scrutiny." The exact requirements of intermediate scrutiny vary depending on the context in which the restriction is entered. However, as a general rule, a content-neutral restriction that burdens press freedom is unconstitutional unless the restriction at issue: (1) furthers an important or substantial governmental interest, (2) the governmental interest is unrelated to the suppression of free expression, and (3) the incidental restriction on alleged First Amendment freedoms is no greater than is essential to the furtherance of that interest. (Turner Broad. Sys. v. FCC, 1994 (quoting United States v. O'Brien, 1968))

The second part of this test is often described as the requirement that a regulation be "narrowly tailored" to advance its stated interest. The Supreme Court has clarified the degree of tailoring required under a content-neutral restriction test. Specifically, the "tailoring" or degree of fit between the scope of the regulation and the regulatory purpose need only be reasonable or proportionate in a practical sense. Some over-inclusiveness and some under-inclusiveness of the restriction may be tolerated. The content-neutral standard is a far easier standard for the government to meet than strict scrutiny, which means that the initial categorization of a restriction as either content-based or content-neutral often determines whether a restriction on press freedom will be upheld.

SOME INITIAL COMPLICATIONS OF THE DISTINCTION

Thus far, the idea of a content-based regulation, and of its judicial testing, seems clear and uncontroversial. But as we will gradually see, the law of content-based regulations is disturbingly unclear. Indeed, while the Supreme Court sometimes has seemed to focus on improper legislative motives as the hallmark of a content-based restrictions, at other times the Court has given more weight to whether the language of a restriction is neutral on its face or whether the effect of the restriction disproportionately burdens speech with a particular content. Thus, the very idea of a content-based restriction, the judicial tests applied thereto, and the logic underlying those tests are all, in practice, slippery and complex.

To begin with, the Supreme Court's understanding of a content-based restriction itself has varied in significant ways.[9] Let us first consider a single illustrative case, and then we will broaden the focus to include some of the complications introduced by other cases. Probably the most useful case for these purposes is actually not a distinctly free press case, but a more general media speech case, City of Renton v. Playtime Theatres. *Renton* involved a restrictive zoning ordinance focusing on movie theaters showing sexually explicit films. In the absence of any free press case posing similar problems, we must draw our lessons for free press law indirectly.

If we ask, naively, whether a restriction focusing on sexually explicit movies is content-based, we are likely to think that we have enough information already to say that it is. Whether we would be legally right in so thinking is, however, unclear. The category of the content-based turns out, in *Renton*, to be more complex than we might imagine.

The *Renton* Court crucially noted that the City did not seek to justify its restrictive ordinance by claiming that sexually explicit commercial films are immoral. Nor did the City claim that such movies seek to communicate ideas with which the City disagreed. Instead, the City referred to alleged indirect and secondary effects of such theaters on the urban social ecology, of a sort often targeted by state police power. The Court assumed that reduced neighborhood property values and certain sorts of criminality such as assaults, littering, public disorderliness, and such are separable from any official or popular dislike of the content of the films in question. Thus, the restrictive ordinance was justified not on the basis of any disapproval of the films' content, but on the distinct basis of the presumed secondary social effects of such theaters.

Such an approach raises a number of questions. An initial question is whether the Court in *Renton* and in similar cases is really denying that such regulations are based on the content of the speech in question. Even this preliminary point is disputed. Some courts (See Tunick v. Safir, 2000) and commentators[10] have concluded that the *Renton* Court considered the zoning ordinance to be content-neutral in character, rather than content-based. Other courts (See, e.g., Richland Bookmart, Inc. v. Nichols, 1988; *see also* DiMa Corp. v. Town of Hallie, 1999) and commentators[11] interpret the Court in *Renton* as treating an obviously content-based restriction as though it were content-neutral, through a sort of legal fiction. (See Richland Bookmart, Inc. v. Nichols, 1988) The Court itself has characterized its analysis in *Renton* as recognizing that "the ordinance did not fall neatly into the 'content-based' or 'content-neutral' category . . . ." (City of Cincinnati v. Discovery Network, Inc., 1993; but *cf.* City of Los Angeles v. Alameda Books, Inc., 2002)

In any event, determining whether a regulation is justified, if at all, on the basis of the secondary effects of the speech, and not by reference to the speech's content, poses serious problems. For example, it is unclear that reduced neighborhood property values are really independent of the public's reaction to the content of the speech in question. Certainly, in other contexts, the Court has been willing to conclude that reduced property values may reflect disapproving or hostile public attitudes. (See, e.g., City of Cleburne v. Cleburne Living Center, 1985; Linmark Associates v. Township of Willingboro, 1977; but see DiMa Corp. v. Town of Hallie, 1999)

More broadly, the very process of determining how a regulation is thought to be justified may itself be controversial. The justification for any given regulation may not be clear. A reviewing court might, for example, look to some combination of the regulation's text, legislative history (if any), and the actual or foreseeable effects of the regulation in practice.[12] (See, e.g., Turner Broad. Sys. v. FCC, 1994) Inevitably, problems of mixed motives, of after the fact justifications, and of the legitimacy of implausible or empirically weak justifications arise.

Among the most interesting problems in determining how a regulation is justified is that of what weight, if any, to assign to the likely or the actual effects of the regulation. The effects of a regulation may fall much more heavily on some class of speakers, subjects, or even points of view than others, whether such effects are noticed or intended or not.[13] By analogy, a rule prohibiting all persons from all economic classes from sleeping under bridges is realistically not neutral in its economic class effects. To the extent that a court downplays or ignores such effects,[14] regulations with severe impact on speech and the press would be treated as merely content-neutral and therefore subjected only to reduced judicial scrutiny.

VIEWPOINT DIVERSITY AS A PUBLIC INTEREST

A recurring problem of special interest to the media is that of the relationship between the idea of content-based regulation and governmental attempts to foster diversity of viewpoints expressed. There is, no doubt, some sense in which any government promotion of viewpoint diversity is content-based. (See Turner Broad. Sys. v. FCC, 1994 (O'Connor, J., concurring in part and dissenting in part)) But to treat all official promotion of viewpoint diversity as content-based, and therefore especially suspect, is to risk missing the First Amendment forest for the doctrinal trees. Viewpoint diversity is often desirable from the standpoint of the very purposes underlying the First Amendment. As many commentators have argued,[15] First Amendment values are advanced rather than threatened when the government attempts to guarantee that all viewpoints can be heard, as opposed to promoting one viewpoint over another.

Clearly, a desire for more viewpoint diversity need not reflect hostility toward any specific views or subjects. Promoting viewpoint diversity can certainly be benignly intended. Not all benignly intended regulations, certainly, are content-neutral.[16] But some governmental attempts to promote diversity of viewpoints also promote the very aims and values normally thought to underlie the First Amendment itself.[17] These attempts should not be classified as content-based and subject to the rigors of strict judicial scrutiny. Promoting diversity in the range of viewpoints expressed may crucially promote the values underlying freedom of speech itself. There is a danger to freedom of the press if it is the government itself that decides which under represented values should be encouraged or subsidized. But in an era of concentrated media ownership, a policy of encouraging new or additional voices, as determined largely by local community interest, is less suspicious and less subject to government abuse. Some mechanisms, such as lotteries, can expand the range of voices without greatly increasing government discretion and control. The primary intent and effect of promoting viewpoint diversity may be to promote values such as the search for truth, the value of self-realization, and the process of genuinely democratic government. These are typically considered the primary values or purposes underlying the First Amendment itself.[18]

Of course, expanding the range of views expressed may to some degree actually undercut those same basic free speech values, if the new voices themselves undercut expression by those who are already socially disadvantaged.[19] But there is no reason to be constitutionally suspicious of genuine expansion of viewpoint diversity. There is something deeply paradoxical about a doctrine of content-based restrictions that treats promoting a diversity of voices in the marketplace of ideas as itself constitutionally suspect.[20]

A TEST CASE OF CONTENT-BASED REGULATION OF THE PRESS

Let us consider an important content-based regulation of special interest to the press. In Simon & Schuster, Inc. v. Members of the New York State Crime Victims' Board,[21] the Supreme Court considered the constitutionality of a statute intended to prevent criminals from profiting from their crime by selling their story to the media. This statute had obvious emotional appeal. To simplify, the New York statute prevented a criminal (or his beneficiary) from receiving the proceeds from the criminal's description of his crimes before the victims of those crimes received compensation.

The Court classified the statute as a content-based restriction on speech, and therefore required the state to show "that its regulation [was] necessary to serve a compelling governmental interest and [was] narrowly drawn to achieve that end."[22] The Court recognized that there may be a compelling state interest in the classic principle that no one should be permitted to profit from his or her own crime. But as the Court pointed out, the New York statute did not, in effect or intent, carry out this broad principle. The statute made no attempt to divert other sorts of income, including, for example, ordinary wages. Instead, the statute focused narrowly on writings referring to criminal activity and on the proceeds of those writings. The Supreme Court found no compelling governmental interest in classifying the proceeds of writings differently than other sorts of income.

The New York statute doubtless was content-based on its face. Speech relating to criminal activity fell within the scope of the statute; speech on other subjects did not. The Court admitted that the statute did not facially target particular ideas or viewpoints. While the statute covered speech glorifying or glamorizing crime, it equally covered speech of bitter repentance and repudiation of crimes. The crucial concerns underlying the rigorous test of content-based restrictions may not have been fully implicated in this case because there was no message, no general viewpoint, no ideology, no point of view threatened by the regulation, however burdensome the speech regulation may have been. The Court responded to this concern by pointing out that First Amendment violations, and presumably the application of strict judicial scrutiny, need not involve any illicit legislative intent. The Court did not go on, however, to discuss the actual effects of the statute, as opposed to its intent, except to say that the statute would apply to great works of literature, such as Martin Luther King's *Letter from Birmingham Jail*, or Malcolm X's *Autobiography*, and might apply for a time to persons not convicted or to persons not likely to face civil tort claims. The scope of the statute thus outran its legitimate purpose.

The Court's analysis in *Simon & Schuster* thus illustrates the slipperiness of the content-based/content-neutral distinction. The case illustrates as well that a statute's ability to pass the content-based restriction test may depend upon how the relevant government interest is formulated. It is certainly reasonable, for example, to characterize the state interest in *Simon & Schuster* in broad, familiar, uncontroversially compelling terms. But the statute might have come closer to passing strict scrutiny, or at least the standards for content-neutral regulations, if the state interest had been formulated in a somewhat more nuanced, interest-sensitive way. Any loss in the interest's compelling character might have been made up for in more narrow tailoring.

Suppose, for example, that New York had argued not for a broad, very general equitable interest underlying the statute, but for a narrower interest that more appropriately balanced the legitimate interests of all affected parties. It might then have been possible to suggest why income from describing one's crime, as opposed to other sources of income, was statutorily singled out.

Consider the hypothetical case of a getaway driver for a gang of juvenile thieves. Among the fruits of his criminal activity, let us assume, are material for an autobiography and, in addition, the knowledge and skills required for a new career as a cab driver. Couldn't a legislature recognize a strong state interest in preventing or delaying the getaway driver, or his publisher, from profiting from his crime descriptions, but little interest in discouraging him from using his admittedly ill-gotten experience in his new, legitimate line of work as a cab driver?

In such a case, the criminal autobiography and the cab driving skills could equally flow from one's criminal activities. But it is certainly reasonable, balancing the relevant interests, to find profiting from the criminal description to be generally more galling, brazen, or offensive to victims[23] (Cf. e.g., Cohen v. California, 1970) than earning a living driving a cab.[24] The particular interest in preventing this narrower kind of moral offense, arguably without censoring any particular ideas or viewpoints, might still be compelling, and the New York statute would at least be somewhat more tailored to this narrower interest.

Admittedly, courts should not assume that the actual effects of a statute are always just the intended effects, and that those effects must inevitably reflect some genuinely compelling governmental interest. But courts also should not formulate the relevant governmental interest too broadly and as a result find insufficiently narrow tailoring. Neither should courts state the relevant governmental interest too narrowly and as a result find it insufficiently compelling. Finally, courts should not seize upon a legislature's responsible attempt to accommodate several conflicting interests as a failure to seriously promote any single interest.

The narrow tailoring requirement actually poses the most serious problem in the Simon & Schuster case. After all, the roster of those who have written about their own presumed criminal history includes figures such as Augustine, Thoreau, Reverend Martin Luther King, Jr., and Bertrand Russell. That a particular crime was victimless,[25] merely symbolic or political, or unconstitutionally prosecuted may well have been irrelevant under the New York statute. This creates serious tailoring problems on any level of scrutiny, especially strict scrutiny. Some writers may have nobler motives than personal financial profit in describing their presumed crimes, and can write influential works without mentioning their own presumed crimes. But some of the works of the distinguished writers listed above would be disfigured by removing references to presumed personal criminality. And the wide dissemination of those works may realistically require a publisher whose motives are at least in part economic.

Perhaps only a minority of personally committed crimes described in print are victimless or political. But there may also be value in, say, claiming one's innocence of other sorts of crimes. There is no sufficient justification for burdening, hypothetically, the widespread publication of Thoreau's *Civil Disobedience* or King's *Letter From Birmingham Jail.*[26] Any statute hypothetically burdening the publication of classic political literature would normally be found insufficiently narrowly tailored, even given a sufficient state interest. The statute in *Simon and Schuster* could quite readily have been written to take more directly into account victimless crimes or the passage of time.[27]

THE CONTENT-BASED REGULATION DISTINCTION ACROSS MEDIA

Not all cases in which the government restricts speech on the basis of content involve the generic content-based strict scrutiny test. For some kinds of cases, the Court applies a more specialized judicial test thought to be better adapted to the particular type of speech. As we refer below to content-based restrictions on several types of communications media, we shall see examples of both the generic strict scrutiny test and the more specifically adapted tests. At work as well in these cases are themes such as: (1) standards appropriate for adults versus those appropriate for minors, (2) intrusiveness versus the right to seek out a willing audience, (3) the manipulability of the "narrow tailoring" requirement in content-based restriction cases, and (4) the role of "community standards" in an age of globalization.

Among the classic instances of a specialized constitutional test for content-based restrictions is the well-known test for obscenity in any of various media established in Miller v. California. According to *Miller*, in an obscenity prosecution the burden is on the government to prove beyond a reasonable doubt each of the elements of the offense. These include:

(a) [W]hether the average person, applying contemporary community standards would find that the work, taken as a whole, appeals to the prurient interest, . . . (b) whether the work depicts or describes, in a patently offensive way, sexual conduct specifically defined by the applicable state law; and (c) whether the work, taken as a whole, lacks serious literary, artistic, political, or scientific value. (internal quotations omitted)

The Court specified that "[w]e do not adopt as a constitutional standard the 'utterly without redeeming social value' test . . . ." (Miller v. California, 1973 (referring to Memoirs v. Massachusetts, 1966))

The *Miller* test recognizes the diversity of tastes across the country in requiring appeal to community standards with regard to the first two elements. The Court, however, explicitly permitted treating the entire state of California as but a single community, even though it is easy to suppose that California itself harbors a rich diversity of altitudes toward explicit sexual expression.

It bears emphasis that prosecutions based on limited segments of a work are discouraged, considering the work as a whole, particularly in conjunction with the Court's later determination that the third, or "serious value" element is to be determined not by local community standards of value, but on an objective or subject-matter expert basis. (See Pope v. Illinois, 1987) It should also be borne in mind that the *Miller* standards are not to be straightforwardly applied in cases of alleged child pornography (See New York v. Ferber, 1982) involving the use of actual minors as participants. (But *cf.* Ashcroft v. Free Speech Coalition, 2002; see also United States v. Playboy Ent'm't Group, 2000; Sable Communications v. FCC, 1989; Reno v. ACLU, 1997; but *cf.* United States v. American Library Ass'n, 2003) More generally, there is a recurring tension in the case law between regulations intended to protect the interests of minors and the limiting principle that subject matter available to adults should not be limited to what is deemed suitable for minors.

In another arguably more intrusive media context, the Court has addressed non-obscene but allegedly indecent radio broadcasts. In FCC v. Pacifica, the Court upheld an FCC regulatory penalty imposed on the owner of a radio station that broadcast, at two o'clock on a weekday afternoon, a recording of George Carlin's *Filthy Words* monologue. The Court recognized that the restriction was content-based, but asserted as well that "[a] requirement that indecent language be avoided will have its primary effect on the form, rather than the content, of serious communication."[28]

It is possible to characterize any restriction on sexually explicit speech as merely a restriction on the manner of speaking, with the speaker permitted to adopt other means of expressing the same idea or content. But this approach would threaten the usefulness of the content-based versus the content-neutral distinction in general. As the Court has also said, in a non-media case, "words are often chosen as much for their emotive as their cognitive force." (Cohen v. California, 1971)

In *Pacifica,* the Court took note of the characteristics of broadcast radio in general, including (1) the difficulty of providing warnings or disclaimers to those changing stations, (2) the possible immediacy of offensive effects, (3) audience captivity, (4) privacy and the social and physical context of listening, (5) the station and programming context, (6) the hour of day, and (7) accessibility to children. Each medium, as well, may also be subdivided according to the presence or absence of devices such as filters, blocking or scrambling mechanisms, credit card use, special access codes, subscription, or even the requirement of literacy.

Most of these devices, in turn, may be more or less effective, and to one degree or another underinclusive or overinclusive in their screening.

The Court in *Pacifica*, based on its overall examination, upheld the FCC penalty. In other media contexts, and under different circumstances, the Court might have determined the overall balance of interests differently, and left any offended parties to "avoid further bombardment of their sensibilities." (Cohen v. California, 1971; United States v. Playboy Ent'm't Group, 2000) The Court did in fact distinguish *Pacifica* in the context of "indecent" commercial telephone messages in Sable Communications v. FCC.

The Court in *Sable* applied strict scrutiny and recognized a compelling governmental interest in shielding minors from indecent, if not obscene speech. The basic problem, however, was lack of narrow tailoring of the complete prohibition, unlike the time of day restriction sought in *Pacifica*. As a practical matter, expansive telephone indecency is less of a trap for the unwary than comparable commercial radio broadcasts. Problems of a captive audience and privacy invasion loomed less large in *Sable*.

The *Sable* Court focused on available and less restrictive alternatives to the complete ban, such as requiring credit card use or access codes, and pronounced such more narrowly tailored means constitutionally preferable. The Court considered the claim that any technology-based limitation on access might be somewhat less effective than a flat prohibition in promoting the compelling governmental interest in the welfare of minors. But in the absence of a better and more decisive record in that regard, the Court was again unwilling to reduce adult listening to what is fit for children.

The courts have also emphasized that different media have different ways of geographically targeting their messages. Magazines and books can be sold by zip code. Telephone-based enterprises can block particular area codes or individual numbers at the initiative of the speaker or the customer. A radio transmitter has only a limited range under typical circumstances, whereas a posting on the World Wide Web may be available unpredictably to unreceptive cultures. And even where technological attempts to limit access to willing recipients are made, those efforts may be only partially successful.

An example of the latter is United States v. Playboy Entertainment Group. This case involved a statutory response to cable television "signal bleed," in which the visual scrambling of, in this case, sexually explicit programming can become temporarily ineffective. A federal statute required such programming to be either fully and effectively scrambled or else broadcast only at certain hours. The Court determined the rule to be content-based, as only sexually oriented programming was thus regulated. While the case bore some resemblance to the *Pacifica* radio broadcast, the Court emphasized that access to any particular cable channel can be completely and effectively blocked at the request of the individual subscriber. In the absence of sufficient evidence of the ineffectiveness of voluntary individualized channel blocking, and even of the scope and severity of the signal bleed problem, this less restrictive alternative regulatory mechanism was constitutionally required.

Subject to even greater public concern, though, are the technological and constitutional differences between traditional book acquisition and maintenance policies by public libraries, or by public school libraries, and public library access to and screening of Internet texts and images. Some forms of the traditional scarcity and selectivity arguments may no longer be as meaningful as formerly.

In the pre-Internet era *Pico* case, a divided Court recognized that school systems often lack the resources to screen library books for suitability in advance, so the real screening often takes the form of a removal decision, rather than a less visible refusal to purchase decision. Justice Brennan for the plurality concluded that such book removal decisions could not be taken on narrowly partisan or ideological grounds. Looking to motivation and intent underlying the book removal, Justice Brennan attempted to distinguish between impermissible public school library book removals based on disagreement with the ideas presented in the book, as distinguished from a permissible judgment that the book was "pervasively vulgar" or educationally unsuitable. (See Mainstream Loudoun v. Bd. of Trustees, 1998) While there may be arguable overlap between these two characterizations, the Court's task in *Pico* was unenviably difficult.

The Court's main Internet-era content-based restriction case involving public libraries is United States v. American Library Association. The federal statute in question was enacted pursuant to the Spending Clause, and denied federal financial assistance to public libraries' Internet access where a library failed to install filters intended to block flexibly defined pornographic images or similar material deemed harmful to minors. This statute provided for unblocking the site or disabling the filter in any cases of "overblocking" of legitimately useful sites at the patron's request.

While the Spending Clause aspect of the case tends to loosen the restraints on the First Amendment (See, e.g., NEA v. Finley, 1998), the plurality reasoned that:

A library's need to exercise judgment in making collection decisions depends on its traditional role in identifying suitable and worthwhile material; it is no less entitled to play that role when it collects material from the Internet than when it collects material from any other source. Most libraries already exclude pornography from their print collections because they deem it inappropriate for inclusion. We do not subject these decisions to heightened scrutiny; it would make little sense to treat libraries' judgments to block online pornography any differently, when these judgments are made for just the same reason.[29]

It is also worth noting that the plurality chose not to rely on public forum doctrine, concluding that "a public library does not acquire Internet terminals in order to create a public forum for Web publishers to express themselves, any more than it collects books in order to provide a public forum for the authors of books to speak."

Outside of the Spending Clause context, congressional attempts to limit access to non-obscene but sexually explicit material for the sake of minors has often met with limited success, usually on the strict scrutiny test imposed on content-based restrictions. Problems of lack of narrow tailoring, in light of inappropriately over-inclusive and underinclusive filtering software, overbreadth, insufficiently well-defined terms such as "indecent" or "patently offensive," and the general disinclination to subject adults to standards fit for minors tend to arise. (See Reno v. ACLU, 1997; but *cf.* Ashcroft v. ACLU, 2002)

In general, technological advances, as in the case of ideal filtering software, might legitimize previously unconstitutional regulations. Sometimes, though, the opposite can occur. A previously narrowly tailored content-based regulation can be rendered far less narrowly tailored by new technological developments as well. Consider, for example, the content-based restriction upheld in Crawford v. Lungren. A California statute prohibited the sale of explicitly sexually oriented material from unsupervised vending machines, except where minors were excluded from the place of sale. The Ninth Circuit Court of Appeals considered the statute to be content-based because it was "designed to prevent the materials from provoking harmful reactions in minor readers," as opposed to some secondary effect, including harm to minors, that is not mediated by agreement or disagreement with the content of the material.[30] The court found a sufficiently compelling governmental interest in shielding minors from the regulated material, and then addressed the crucial requirement of narrow tailoring.

The state was required to use the least restrictive means available to promote the compelling interest at stake. The court observed that "if a plaintiff or the court can imagine and allude to other means, the state has the ultimate burden of showing that the means in question are not effective." The courts have, however, not mandated some single way in which this burden is to be discharged. What would be effective, to whatever degree, can be contested. Common sense, legislative findings, history, social science evidence, intuition, and judicial instinct may all play some role.

The court in *Crawford* could imagine no realistically effective less restrictive regulation. Plaintiffs in the case had suggested the possibility of placing "warning" labels on the unattended vending machines, or prohibiting such machines near schools. The court concluded, however, that there was no reason to think that these less restrictive alternatives would effectively promote the governmental interest at stake. Children do not, for example, invariably find themselves near schools. Given the relatively modest burden of the statute on adults seeking to obtain sexually explicit printed material, the statute was held to be narrowly tailored and, even though content-based, constitutionally sound. But consider possible technological developments. If it becomes possible for vending machines to recognize the identity, or at least the age, of purchasers, the broadly restrictive rule in *Crawford* would then be no longer narrowly tailored.

The court, and especially the concurring opinion of Judge Tashima, were commendably forthright in recognizing the non-mechanical nature of the judicial inquiry into narrow tailoring. But the narrow tailoring inquiry, by its own logic, is actually more complex than even the *Crawford* court was willing to recognize.

Let us assume, for example, that the government has one and only one interest that it seeks to pursue by a given regulation, and that it is somehow possible to measure the extent to which the regulation, and any alternative rule, would actually promote that single interest. Realistically, there will often be a range of alternative, diminishingly restrictive alternative means of promoting the interest in question. Many government interests, after all, can only be achieved to one degree or another, and not finally and absolutely. There is, for example, a government interest in reducing perjury, but we do not do literally all we can to minimize, let alone abolish, perjury. But these diminishingly restrictive alternatives may, correspondingly, promote the single government interest with diminishing degrees of effectiveness. Should a state be required to adopt a slightly less restrictive alternative if, somehow, we can be sure that it would be only slightly less effective in promoting that single government interest? How, more generally, should courts trade off degrees of regulatory effectiveness and restrictiveness? Is any increase in effectiveness in achieving the government aim worth any necessary and unavoidable additional degree of restriction?

Not all costs, further, are costs in terms of First Amendment values. Not all financial costs to publishers are directly relevant to a speaker's First Amendment rights. How, then, should the courts factor in the sheer financial costs of complying with a regulation? How, as well, can a court reasonably anticipate the effects of some allegedly less restrictive alternative regulation on differently situated parties not before the court? Couldn't a hypothetical alternative regulation be less burdensome on the speech of other sorts of publishers?

Are the courts thus to seek out alternative regulations that are less restrictive in some sort of global, overall sense? How can the effects of alternative rules on third parties be determined? Can the courts rely on complete candor from the regulated parties before the court? Why wouldn't some publishers be tempted to downplay less restrictive alternatives that conflicted with other corporate goals? Will all regulated parties admit that an apparently viable alternative regulation could, in practice, be blocked or evaded?

Finally, an alternative speech regulation might be less restrictive as to some single regulated party, in some respects, but more burdensome to that very party in other respects. A speaker's freedom of speech comes not only in different degrees, but along different and often conflicting dimensions. For example, publishers care not only about the financial costs of publishing, but the size of the audience for the publication, and what might be referred to as the 'suitability' of that audience, including their disposable income, their circumstances, ability to

understand and sympathize with the message, the malleability of audience opinion and spending habits, chronological age of the audience and so on.

Of course, these latter factors describing presumed audience 'suitability' can
conflict among themselves. Certainly, audience suitability may conflict with audience size. Audience size may conflict with the financial cost of the speech (the
speech itself, or its necessary promotion). The open-mindedness of one's audience may vary inversely with its ability to spend. The best educated or most
understanding audience may be the least subject to one's persuasive techniques.
For some messages, the most formally educated audience may actually be among
the least comprehending.

These complications could be multiplied indefinitely. Even if all the affected
parties are represented in the case, and they present their circumstances with complete knowledge and candor, a judicial decision as to the existence and likely via-
bility of some overall less restrictive regulatory alternative will require guesswork,
controversial valuations, and sheer luck. As it is formulated in the content-based
restriction cases, the narrow tailoring inquiry is often realistically beyond judicial
capacities. That courts can verbally formulate the narrow tailoring inquiry in
superficially simple terms does not change this bleaker underlying reality.

Some of these complexities appear in the *Crawford* adult material vending
machine case discussed above. The *Crawford* court should also have addressed
the First Amendment principle that a government must not restrict one's speech in
one presumably proper place on the grounds that one's speech rights may still be
exercised in other places. (*Cf.* Schneider v. State, 1939) And the court even today
might also have inquired into the feasibility of credit card or other technology to
limit minors' access to the vending machines in question.[31] With more sophisticated technology, it is unlikely that the statute would remain narrowly tailored.

Let us apply a few of these considerations to a standard, low-tech, content-
based publishing regulation case, that of Richland Bookmart v. Nichols. The Tennessee statute in *Richland Bookmart* limited the days and hours adult bookstores
and similar facilities could be open to the public. The Sixth Circuit began by holding the regulation to be content-based. But because the legislature was said to be
motivated by the *Renton*-like secondary effects of the speech, and because sexually explicit materials were said to fall into a unique category, the court declined
to apply content-based strict scrutiny. The court then determined that:

[U]nder present First Amendment principles governing regulation of sex literature, the real
question is one of reasonableness. The appropriate inquiry is whether the Tennessee law is
designed to serve a substantial government interest and allows for alternative avenues of
communication. Does the law in question unduly restrict "sexually explicit" or "hardcore"
erotic expression?

The court in *Richland Bookmart* found this diminished constitutional test to be
met. An underlying problem, however, is that the above test really comprises

three distinct tests, all vulnerable to subjective manipulation. A mere reasonableness inquiry, first, is ordinarily among the least stringent known to the law. The second formulation, requiring a substantial government interest and alternative channels for conveying one's message, is more demanding and more readily contestable. If a court is so inclined, it may find either that no substantial government interest is genuinely promoted effectively by the statute, or that the alternative speech channels realistically available to the speaker are somehow insufficient, or of far lesser quality. The court's third formulation, that of undue restrictiveness, seems to call not so much for a reasonableness inquiry, or a focused inquiry as in the second formulation, but for a broad interest balancing inquiry. Plainly, this sort of generalized "undue restrictiveness" inquiry is open to judicial manipulation.

Richland Bookmart thus opens the door to judicial subjectivity at two distinct levels. Any given court can, with suitable supporting language from Supreme Court cases, choose from among these three distinct test formulations. And then, at least the latter two, if not all three formulations, are further subject to judicial arbitrariness and subjectivity, depending upon one's sympathy either for the government regulatory efforts on the one hand, or for the publishers on the other.

THE CONTENT-BASED RESTRICTION DISTINCTION IN A SPECIAL CONTEXT

As it happens, sexually oriented material is not the only context in which courts may apply somewhat reduced judicial scrutiny to content-based regulations. Under the Supreme Court's case law, prisons may reasonably regulate the subscription publications received by prison inmates on the basis of the content of those publications. The Supreme Court in the prison magazine case of Thornburgh v. Abbott first asked "whether the governmental objective underlying the prison regulations at issue is legitimate and neutral, and [whether] . . . the regulations are rationally related to that objective." The Court was quick to specify that their use of the term 'neutral' did not import the full idea of content-neutrality, and that all that was needed was merely a "substantial government interest unrelated to the suppression of expression." The regulations in *Abbott* were deemed to be rationally related to the substantial penological interest in promoting prison security. The Court continued its mere reasonableness inquiry in *Abbott* by asking whether alternative means of communication, in some contexts, remained available to the inmates. This amounted to an unusually relaxed alternative speech channel inquiry. This consideration was held satisfied in *Abbott* on the grounds that "a broad range of publications" could still be sent and received by inmates, even if no direct substitute for the actually regulated material was available.

The Court then considered the presumably favorable effects of the regulation on the safety and security of guards and inmates generally, and concluded its broad reasonableness inquiry with a relaxed "narrow tailoring" inquiry. The Court asked at this final stage only whether the regulations on publications could be replaced by "obvious, easy" less restrictive alternative rules, and were thus likely an "exaggerated response" to security concerns. Finding no such obvious and easy alternative rules, and in light of the other elements of its rather complex reasonableness inquiry, the Court upheld the restriction in question as facially valid.

Overall, it is difficult to escape the impression that the law of content-based restrictions in general involves substantial room for judicial subjectivity, of an occasionally conscious, but typically unconscious, sort. Commonly, there will be prior case language available to provide the underpinnings for either a press-restrictive or a press-accommodating case law outcome. Despite the superficial rigor of most content-based restriction tests, the classification and testing of content-based restrictions actually leaves much room for play in the joints.

A CONCLUDING CONTRAST

Consider, as one final example, the relationship between two interesting claims made in the *Turner I* and *Turner II* media regulation cases, which dealt with whether Congress could require cable operators to carry the signals of local broadcasters. Consider first the language from *Turner I*: "Deciding whether a particular regulation is content based or content neutral is not always a simple task. We have said that the 'principal inquiry . . . is whether the government has adopted a regulation of speech because of . . . disagreement with the message it conveys.'" (quoting Ward v. Rock Against Racism, 1989) A positive finding that the government adopted a regulation of speech because it objected to its message would thus suggest the presence of a content-based speech restriction. The primary focus here appears to be whether the government's motive was to advance or hinder speech of a particular content.

In *Turner I*, the majority emphasized that the extent of the restriction on cable owner speech did not depend on the content of either the cable owner's or the local broadcaster's speech. In contrast, Justice O'Connor would have held the "must carry" rules content-based partly on the grounds that one (benign) purpose for the rules was to increase diversity of viewpoint expression. The attempt to increase the range of ideas expressed thus called for a rigorous, heightened constitutional test, on Justice O'Connor's logic.

The majority's language clearly links the content-based/content-neutral decision to the message or viewpoint of the regulated speech. Admittedly, this is merely the 'principal' inquiry in such cases. But contrast the claim in *Turner II* by Justice O'Connor, dissenting on behalf of Justices Ginsburg, Scalia, and Thomas, citing earlier cases for the proposition that: "Whether a provision is viewpoint neutral is irrelevant to the question whether it is also content-neutral." For these justices, the critical inquiry seems to be whether Congress has attempted to benefit speakers (in this case, local broadcasters) on the basis of the content of their speech. Even if the Congressional motives are benign, the dissenters suggest, a content-based distinction still raises grave First Amendment difficulties. The point is not whether these two dramatically different claims about the relationship between viewpoint-based and content-based restrictions can technically be reconciled; perhaps they can.

Instead, the point is that if there is respectable legal authority for holding viewpoint-basis crucial to content-basis as in *Turner I* and, as well, for holding the two ideas to be logically irrelevant to each other, as in *Turner II*, there is obviously room in practice for play in the joints at a basic doctrinal level. On the merits of the two claims, it seems more dubious to claim that viewpoint neutrality and content neutrality are really unrelated. That a restriction is based on hostility to the message or viewpoint of the speech naturally evokes the basic purposes and values[32] (See Turner Broad. Sys. v. FCC, 1994 (O'Connor, J., concurring in part and dissenting in part)) sought to be protected by the stringent content-based restriction test. But the crucial point is not to decide which of these two contrasting approaches is sounder. It is instead to notice the broad scope available for the play of subjective judicial discretion.

Some additional thinking is also needed about the proper degree of scrutiny to apply to speech restrictions that are content-based but not viewpoint-based. A rigorous test should be applied if, let us say, Congress decreed that magazines should abstain from discussing the subject of abortion for a year, regardless of viewpoint. But does the obvious need for a rigorous test in such a case reflect merely that the rule is content-based, though not viewpoint-based, or does it reflect the gravity of restricting debate on an entire subject?[33]

NOTES

1. See, e.g., Geoffrey R. Stone, "Content-Neutral Restrictions," 54 *U. Chi. L. Rev.* (1987) 46, 46 ("[t]he content-based/content-neutral distinction plays a central role in contemporary first amendment jurisprudence"); Mark Tushnet, "The Supreme Court and Its First Amendment Constituency," 44 *Hastings L.J.* (1993) 881, 882 ("[t]oday the central organizing concept of First Amendment doctrine is the distinction between content-based regulations and content-neutral ones"); Susan H. Williams, "Content Discrimination and the First Amendment," 139 *U. Pa. L. Rev.* (1991) 615, 616 (among large organizing principles of free speech jurisprudence, "[o]ne of the most important . . . is the distinction between content-based and content-neutral regulations of speech").

2. One distinguished commentator, for example, has argued that "[b]y defining the context in one way, virtually any regulation can become content-based, while defining the context in another way can make virtually any regulation seem content-neutral." Tushnet, "The Supreme Court and Its First Amendment Constituency," 883. Compare the observation from the bench that "[i]n the sensitive area of First Amendment strict scrutiny, contrary to . . . all conventional wisdom on the scope of judicial review, judges sometimes are

required to rely 'on their own instinct or experience.'" Crawford v. Lungren, 96 F.3d 380, 389 (9ᵗʰ Cir. 1996)(Tashima, J., concurring) (quoting Geary v. Rennie, 911 F.2d 280, 305 (9ᵗʰ Cir. 1990)(en banc)(Rymer, J., dissenting)).

3. Geoffrey R. Stone, "Content Regulation and the First Amendment," 25 *Wm. & Mary L. Rev.* (1983) 189, 190.

4. Stone, "Content Regulation and the First Amendment," 189. This formulation is actually deeply unclear. Consider, for example, a broad prohibition on publishing any language "offensive" to any reader. Such a rule could hold across the political spectrum, and thus without regard to content. But the rule equally depends upon a reader's negative cognitive reaction to the content of the expression.

5. See Stone, "Content-Neutral Restrictions," 54.

6. See Stone, "Content-Neutral Restrictions," 58.

7. See Stone, "Content-Neutral Restrictions," 72.

8. See Stone, "Content Regulation and the First Amendment," 194–97.

9. See, e.g., Mark Tushnet, "The Supreme Court and Its First Amendment Constituency," 883 n.6 (distinguishing between cases focusing on restricting speech "on the basis of its content," on governmental justifications apart from or "without regard" to content, and on a government's concern for the speech's "likely communicative impact"). Such an ambiguity is significant if the outcome of the case could realistically depend on how the ambiguity is resolved in that case. We should also bear in mind that depending upon how we interpret the idea of a content-based regulation, a case outcome may seem more, or less, justified.

10. See, e.g., Susan H. Williams, "Content Discrimination and the First Amendment," 631–32 (despite the Renton ordinance's facial content discrimination, "the Court explicitly found the law to be content-neutral").

11. See, e.g., Geoffrey R. Stone, "Content-Neutral Restrictions," 115 (*Renton* as "treating an expressly content-based restriction as if it were content-neutral").

12. For discussion, see Clay Calvert, "Free Speech and Content-Neutrality: Inconsistent Applications of an Increasingly Malleable Doctrine," 29 *McGeorge L. Rev.* (1997) 69, 81.

13. Consider, for example, a regulation that burdened relatively cheap means of communication, such as leaflets and posters, but not expensive electronic media such as network television time, on grounds of, say, preventing litter. See, e.g., Schneider v. State, 308 U.S. 147 (1939). Whether we classify such a regulation as content-neutral or not, the economic class-based effect of such a regulation is clear. Or consider a noise or sound volume restriction's effect on the content or messages associated with chamber music and with heavy metal. *See* Ward v. Rock Against Racism, 491 U.S. 781 (1989); Kovacs v. Cooper, 336 U.S. 77 (1949); Ofer Raban, "Content-Based, Secondary Effects and Expressive Conduct: What In the World Do They Mean (And What Do They Mean to the United States Supreme Court)?," 30 *Seton Hall L. Rev.* (2000) 551.

14. *Cf.* Clay Calvert, "Free Speech and Content-Neutrality: Inconsistent Applications of an Increasingly Malleable Doctrine," 75 (noting that the Court "may consider or ignore either or both the intent and impact of the laws in question").

15. See, e.g., Owen M. Fiss, "Why the State?," 100 *Harv. L. Rev.* (1987) 781.

16. See Fiss, "Why the State?," (citing cases).

17. The classic elaboration of the most basic purposes underlying the institution of freedom of speech is John Stuart Mill, *On Liberty* (David Spitz ed. 1975) (1859).

18. See, e.g., Thomas Emerson, *The System of Freedom of Expression* (New York: Random House, 1970) 3–7.

19. For background see Richard Delgado, "Words That Wound: A Tort Action For Racial Insults, Epithets and Name-Calling," 1982 *Harv. C.R.—C.L. L. Rev.* 133.

20. Justice O'Connor apparently assumes that attempts to increase speech diversity will be based, at least in part, on the idea that underrepresented or novel views encouraged by the regulation are assumed by the government to be in some way more intrinsically valuable than other sorts of speech. See *Turner I*, 512 U.S. at 677–78. Certainly, though, attempts to increase viewpoint diversity need not be based on any such assumption. A teacher who seeks to draw out a reticent student need not assume that such a student's speech is more likely to be correct, or otherwise valuable, than that of the more eager students.

21. The New York statute involved was widely referred to as the "Son of Sam" statute.

22. The Court concluded, actually, that it need not decide whether the statutory restriction was content-based or content-neutral, as the statute was so overinclusive that it could not pass even the looser constitutional standard appropriate for content-neutral regulations of speech. For further discussion of this test, and of narrow tailoring in particular, see, e.g., United States v. Playboy Ent'm't Group, 529 U.S. 803, 811–18 (2000); Sable Communications v. FCC, 492 U.S. 115, 126–31 (1989).

23. Admittedly, some such accounts may express regret and contrition, but our example assumes that the author or publisher proposes, however contritely, to keep the monetary proceeds. And while it is clear that mere offensiveness of speech does not justify restricting debate, the offensiveness in question here is not of disfavored ideas, but of one form of the act of profiting from crime.

24. Nor would driving a cab, in such a case, typically seem more galling or offensive to victims than earning a living in some way unrelated to one's prior criminal activity.

25. As drafted, the statute operated to the benefit not only of victims or their relatives, but other sorts of creditors as well.

26. Again, as drafted, the running of all relevant statutes of limitation, civil or criminal, was irrelevant to the operation of the statute. No doubt the offense of profiting from recounting one's crime is not always erased by the passing of a statute of limitations, but some account should be taken of the tendency of the wounding effect of such profiting to diminish with the passage of time.

27. The Court has said that "[w]hen a plausible, less restrictive alternative is offered to a content-based speech restriction, it is the Government's obligation to prove that the alternative will be ineffective to achieve its goals." *Playboy Ent'm't Group*, 529 U.S. at 816 (Kennedy, J., for the plurality).

28. Recall also that the Court has characterized their crucial concern in *Ferber* not as with the content or message of, but with the harms of the production of child pornography.

29. On the other hand, historically, the opportunity cost of a library's subscription to a pornographic magazine would have been something like the cost or space required by a general sort of magazine. But, in cyberspace, there is less scarcity, in that free pornography does not reduce the library's budget or physical space available for other materials.

30. We shall simply assume that the relevant material conveyed an idea sufficient to trigger the free press or free speech clause.

31. Of course, even if some high-tech solution appeared practical, some percentage of adult consumers might well be reluctant to use any payment system allowing someone to

track their actual identity. This reluctance would count as a diminution in the size of the publisher's realistically available audience.

32. See Fiss, "Why the State?" and accompanying text.

33. For general background, see Geoffrey R. Stone, "Restrictions on Speech Because of Its Content: The Peculiar Case of Subject-Matter Restrictions," 46 *U. Chi. L. Rev.* (1978) 81.

5

Content-Neutral Regulation
of the Press

The press is an important institution for First Amendment purposes, but it is also a business. As such, the First Amendment does not exempt the media from the types of regulations to which other businesses must adhere, at least where these regulations apply in the same manner to the media as to any other business. For example, if city inspectors determine that a building owned by the *New York Times* does not comply with the fire code, the First Amendment does not prevent the inspectors from issuing a citation or shutting the building down to protect public safety. The fire code is a content-neutral regulation which applies to the *New York Times* in precisely the same way it applies to other businesses, even though application of the fire code might have an effect on publication.

Occasionally, however, content-neutral regulations (and those that are ostensibly content-neutral) do raise First Amendment issues. A regulation imposing heavy taxes on ink, for example, will burden the press more than other businesses, and this differential impact may raise First Amendment concerns. An ostensibly content-neutral regulation that imposes heavier burdens on selected segments of the media may also raise First Amendment concerns. A regulation, for example, that taxes large newspapers more heavily than small ones may be facially content-neutral, but when it just "coincidentally" happens that the large newspapers all favor Republicans and the small ones all favor Democrats, government censorship based on content may well be afoot.

As a general rule, content-neutral regulations of the media receive intermediate scrutiny. In other words, a content-neutral regulation of the media will satisfy the First Amendment if it furthers an important or substantial governmental interest without restricting speech more than necessary to achieve that interest. That said, there is tremendous variation in how content-neutral regulations are treated in various contexts. This chapter gives a sampling of the various contexts in which content-neutral regulations of the media trigger First Amendment concerns and illustrates the different ways in which the Supreme Court has addressed these concerns.

TAXATION OF THE MEDIA

Not all taxation schemes affecting the media will run afoul of the First Amendment. Like other businesses, the media must pay taxes. As a rule, taxes of general application, such as a state sales tax on all goods sold, do not offend the First Amendment. Yet the power to tax is the power to destroy, and the government may sometimes use its taxing power to silence speakers with whom it disagrees or to punish their speech. When a tax singles out the media for special treatment, or when it discriminates among different types of media, enhanced scrutiny is sometimes warranted.[1]

The first Supreme Court decision on differential (that is, discriminatory) taxation of the media was Grosjean v. American Press Co. A Louisiana statute imposed a two percent "license tax" on the business of selling advertisements to be "printed or published, in any newspaper, magazine, periodical or publication whatever." However, the tax applied only to publications "having a circulation of more than 20,000 copies per week." Only thirteen daily newspapers in Louisiana were subject to this special license tax. Four daily newspapers and 120 weeklies were exempt from the tax.

The Supreme Court held that the license tax violated the First Amendment because the Louisiana legislature had given preferential tax treatment to small newspapers. The Court noted that one of the grievances of the American colonists against the British Crown was the Crown's attempt to silence critical newspapers through the imposition of stamp duties. The Court then analogized the license tax to a prior restraint, since it encouraged publishers to keep circulation low to avoid the tax. However, the main defect of the tax was that it was "a deliberate and calculated device in the guise of a tax to limit the circulation of information to which the public is entitled in virtue of the constitutional guaranties." It was not incidental that the tax affected only a small number of urban dailies. The legislators who proposed and enacted the tax were supporters of the infamous Senator Huey P. Long, and the purpose of the tax was to punish urban dailies for opposing Senator Long's state tax proposal.[2] Although the Supreme Court never made explicit note of this fact, it seems clear that it influenced their decision.

Perhaps because *Grosjean* was such a transparent case of content-based censorship of the press, it left many issues unresolved. Specifically, it did not clarify whether differential taxation of the media violated the First Amendment only when it resulted from improper censorial motives. The Supreme Court addressed this question in Minneapolis Star & Tribune Co. v. Minnesota Commissioner of Revenue. At issue in the case was the constitutionality of a "use tax" on "the cost of paper and ink products" used for purposes of publication. The statute exempted the first $100,000 of paper and ink consumed, making only eleven of the state's 388 paid circulation newspapers liable to pay the tax in its first year of operation. A single newspaper, *The Minneapolis Star & Tribune*, paid about two-thirds of the total revenue raised by the use tax.

The Supreme Court declared the use tax unconstitutional for two reasons. First, the use tax was presumptively unconstitutional because it singled out the press for taxation. As the Court explained, a tax that singles out the press is subject to less "political constraint" than a generally applicable tax. This is so because legislators will think twice before generating public hostility by raising taxes for a broad segment of the population. The second reason that the Court found the use tax to be unconstitutional was that it targeted a small group of newspapers to bear the bulk of the tax burden. As the majority opinion noted, "only a handful of publishers pay any tax at all, and even fewer pay any significant amount of tax." This targeting of a small group of publishers thus "begins to resemble . . . a penalty for a few of the largest newspapers."

The Court made clear that its decision hinged on the facially discriminatory form that the use tax took rather than on any finding of illicit legislative motive. The Court found no evidence, "apart from the structure of the tax itself, of any impermissible or censorial motive on the part of the legislature." (Minnesota Star & Tribune Co. v. Minnesota Comm'r of Revenue, 1983) Even so, the *potential* for legislative abuse justified striking it down. As the Court concluded, "[d]ifferential taxation of the press . . . places such a burden on the interests protected by the First Amendment that we cannot countenance such treatment unless the State asserts a counterbalancing interest of compelling importance that it cannot achieve without differential taxation." (Minnesota Star & Tribune Co. v. Minnesota Comm'r of Revenue, 1983) In other words, differential taxation of the press leads to the imposition of strict scrutiny, a standard that the Minnesota use tax could not meet.[3]

Minnesota Star was not the Court's last word on taxation of the media,[4] and indeed its later decision in Leathers v. Medlock pulled back from *Minnesota Star*'s broad condemnation of differential taxation. *Leathers* involved an Arkansas tax that discriminated between different types of media. Specifically, the statute at issue exempted the sale of newspapers, magazines and home antenna satellite services from Arkansas' general sales tax but did not exempt cable television services. After the failure to exempt cable was challenged on First Amendment grounds, the legislature amended the statute to remove the exemption from satellite service, but continued to tax cable. The Arkansas Supreme Court held that discriminating between different media (cable and print) did not violate the First Amendment; however, discriminating between the same media (cable and satellite) was unconstitutional.

In a surprising decision, the Supreme Court held that neither the discrimination between different media, nor the discrimination between the substantially similar media of cable and satellite violated the First Amendment. In reaching this conclusion, the Court read its prior decisions to stand for the principle "that differential taxation of First Amendment speakers is constitutionally suspect when it threatens to suppress the expression of particular ideas or viewpoints." (Leathers

v. Medlock, 1991) Or, to put it in the negative, differential taxation of the media does not violate the First Amendment unless it threatens content-based or viewpoint-based discrimination. According to the Court, the Arkansas sales tax at issue in *Leathers* did not trigger strict scrutiny. Unlike the tax schemes struck down as unconstitutional by prior decisions, the Arkansas sales tax: (1) was generally applicable to all state businesses and did not "single out the press," (2) was not a "purposeful attempt" to censor the press, (3) did not, by targeting a small number of speakers, raise the "suspicion" of censorship, and (4) did not define tax eligibility based on content. The Court found it significant that the tax applied to roughly 100 cable systems, thereby reducing the risk that it might be used to "distort the market for ideas." The Court concluded that nothing in the record before it "indicate[s] that Arkansas' broad-based, content-neutral sales tax is likely to stifle the free exchange of idea," and therefore upheld the state's tax scheme.

The *Leathers*' opinion represents a retrenchment from its prior decisions on differential taxation of the media. As the dissent in *Leathers*' pointed out, the prior decisions seemed to indicate that differential taxation of the media, standing alone, was enough to trigger strict scrutiny. The *Leathers* opinion, in contrast, holds that differential treatment must be coupled with some other indicia of content-based or viewpoint-based discrimination before strict scrutiny is warranted. *Leathers* highlights once more the importance of the distinction between content-based and content-neutral regulation and suggests that it is only the unusual case in which content-neutral regulation of the media will violate the First Amendment.

LABOR AND EMPLOYMENT LAWS

It is nonetheless worthwhile to look at some of the special contexts in which content-neutral regulation of the media may touch upon First Amendment interests. One of these contexts is in the area of labor and employment laws. Labor and employment laws ordinarily bind the press just as they do other employers. Indeed, a 1937 Supreme Court decision held that application of federal labor law to the press does not violate the First Amendment. (Associated Press v. NLRB, 1937) The press, declared the Court, has "no special immunity from the application of general laws." (Associated Press v. NLRB, 1937) However, lower courts have struggled with what to do when this principle comes into conflict with the principle that the government may not interfere with editorial discretion or control.

Consider the following scenario: A columnist is fired for union organizing activity. The remedy for this unlawful firing is reinstatement with back pay. Yet if a court orders reinstatement of a columnist, the court is interfering with the newspaper's editorial control. (see Associated Press v. NLRB., 1937; Passaic Daily News v. NLRB, 1984; see also Newspaper Guild of Greater Phila. v. NLRB, 1980) Does the First Amendment allow such interference? Or consider the analogous scenario that arose in Nelson v. McClatchy Newspapers, Inc. Nelson was an education reporter for *The News Tribune*. *The News Tribune* demoted her from her position as an education reporter because she engaged in highly visible political activism in her spare time. *The News Tribune* argued that the demotion was justified because Nelson's partisan activities violated its code of ethics and comprimised its appearance of objectivity in the eyes of its readers. Nelson claimed that the demotion violated "her statutory right to avoid workplace discrimination based on her politics." The Washington Supreme Court agreed that her rights had been violated and yet refused to reinstate her. To do so, said the court, would violate the First Amendment. The court deemed *The News Tribune* to have "implemented a code of ethics which it designed in good faith to foster the newspaper's integrity and credibility." To order resinstatement of a columnist would interfere with the newspaper's choice of editorial staff—"a core function"—and would compel the newspaper to publish that which it would prefer to withold. As the court concluded, "[f]reedom of the press leaves such decisions to the press, not the legislature or courts." (Nelson v. McClatchy Newspapers, Inc., 1997) The lesson to be drawn from this and similar cases is that generally applicable labor and employment laws do apply to the press when it acts as an employer, but the remedies for violation of these laws cannot include compelled publication.

MEDIA DIVERSITY: ANTITRUST LAW APPLIED TO NEWSPAPERS

The Supreme Court has applied similar logic in the antitrust context. In 1945, the Supreme Court rejected the argument that newspapers were immune from antitrust laws, stating that "[t]he First Amendment affords not the slightest support for the contention that a combination to restrain trade in news and views has any constitutional immunity." (Associated Press v. United States, 1945) In Citizen Publishing Co. v. United States, the Supreme Court specifically held the First Amendment did not prevent application of antitrust laws to "joint operating agreements" between competing newspapers. Joint operating agreements (JOAs) are arrangements between two newspapers in which the newspapers combine their business operations in order to save money. They share the resulting profits, but retain separate identities and separate news departments. The Supreme Court held that JOAs, as they are called, constitute unfair competition under antitrust law, and specifically condemned the profit-pooling and price-fixing aspect of JOAs. (Citizen Publ'g Co. v. United States, 1969) The Court therefore affirmed the principle that applying "generally applicable" law to the press does not offend the First Amendment.

However, Congress essentially "overruled" this decision by passing the Newspaper Preservation Act in 1970. This act retroactively validated existing joint operating agreements and allowed the formation of new ones when one of the newspapers involved in the arrangement was a "failing newspaper." The idea behind creating an antitrust exemption for newspapers is that entering a JOA may prevent a "failing newspaper" from going out of business, and may thereby preserve that newspaper as an independent editorial voice. However, the Newspaper Preservation Act has not resulted in the preservation of diverse editorial voices. Indeed, JOAs commonly result in one paper gaining a monopoly by refusing to renew a JOA or by simply buying out its competitor. Today, newspaper ownership is concentrated in the hands of a small group of newspaper chains, and most cities in the United States are served by only one daily newspaper.[5] Yet it is not the First Amendment but power politics that has insulated newspapers from the reach of at least some generally applicable antitrust laws designed to prevent anti-competitive behavior.

MEDIA DIVERSITY AND MUST-CARRY RULES: *TURNER I* AND *TURNER II*

In the broadcasting and cable context, Congress and the Federal Communications Commission (FCC) traditionally have taken more affirmative steps to prevent anti-competitive behavior through content-neutral restrictions. The FCC, for example, is charged by statute to issue licenses to broadcasters in a manner that fosters a diversity of voices on the airways. However, the FCC often appears to be uncomfortable promoting media diversity. Indeed, the most recent controversy over the FCC's role in preserving diversity on the airways involved its decision to loosen restrictions on the number of television stations a network can own and to drop restrictions preventing companies from owning both a newspaper and radio or television stations serving the same city. Public outcry over the FCC decision has prompted Congress to consider legislation that would reverse it, indicating that the public still believes that media diversity is an important value that should be mandated by law.

As we saw in Chapter 1, the First Amendment allows government to play a role in promoting diversity on the airwaves, even to the extent of forcing broadcasters to carry certain specific content they might prefer to withhold. The government may not, however, ordinarily force the print media or cable operators or other non-broadcast media to air specific content, even in the name of promoting diversity. Nonetheless, the Supreme Court has held that the First Amendment permits content-*neutral* regulation whose purpose is to promote diversity by quelling anti-competitive behavior by cable operators.[6] In Turner Broadcasting System, Inc. v. Federal Communications Commission ("Turner I"), the Supreme Court addressed the issue of whether provisions in the Cable Television Consumer Protection Act requiring cable operators to carry the signals of local broadcasters were content-based or content-neutral. The Court concluded, over strenuous dissent by four justices, that the must-carry provisions were content-neutral and did not trigger strict scrutiny. First, the must-carry provisions were content-neutral on their face. They were triggered "only upon the manner in which speakers transmit their messages to viewers [that is, by broadcasting them], and not upon the messages they carry." Second, Congress enacted the provisions for the content-neutral purpose of preventing cable operators from destroying their broadcast competitors by refusing to carry their signals. Because cable operates via a physical connection between the subscriber's television and the cable, cable operators control all programming coming into the home: If they choose not to carry a broadcast station, the subscriber will not receive that station. Thus, "[a] cable operator, unlike speakers in other media, can . . . silence the voice of competing speakers with a mere flick of the switch." (Turner Broad. Sys. v. FCC, 1994) It was these "special characteristics of the cable medium" rather than any preference for broadcast content that justified forcing "all cable systems in the country" to carry the signals of local broadcasters.

The Court's decision is contestable. Congress clearly enacted the rules because they believed broadcast television makes a valuable contribution to an informed citizenry, a belief surely premised on the notion that broadcasters provide unique content not otherwise available.[7] The majority opinion was willing to overlook this fact, probably because the application of strict scrutiny would have surely doomed the must-carry provisions to unconstitutionality.

The Court instead deemed intermediate scrutiny to be the appropriate standard by which to evaluate the must-carry provisions. Intermediate scrutiny was warranted because the effect of the provisions was to burden (at least potentially) cable operators by displacing content of their choosing with content they might prefer to withhold. Applying this standard, the Court in *Turner II* upheld the must-carry provisions. The Court had initially rejected the argument that the must-carry provisions "were no more than industry-specific antitrust and fair trade legislation." A majority in *Turner II* agreed that must-carry served two important governmental interests—"preserving the benefits of free, over-the-air local broadcast television" and "promoting the widespread dissemination of information from a multiplicity of sources." In addition, at least four justices believed that must-carry also sever a third, "interrelated" interest in "promoting fair competition in the market for television programming."[8] The Court further concluded that the threat to these interests was real: substantial evidence supported Congress' prediction that cable operators might exploit their economic power to the detriment of broadcasters. The Court then assessed the "fit" between the governmental interests and the legislative solution and determined that "must-carry serves the government's interests 'in a direct and effective way.'" (Turner Broad. Sys. v. FCC, 1996 (quoting Ward v. Rock Against Racism, 1989)) Although the Court conceded that "broadcast stations gained carriage on 5,880 [cable] channels as a result of must-carry," the Court concluded that must-carry was narrowly tailored because the the burden it imposed on cable operators "is congruent to the benefits it affords." (Turner Broad. Sys. v. FCC, 1996) Or, in the words of Justice Breyer's concurring opinion, must-carry's "speech-restricting" consequences were more than offset by its "speech-enhancing" consequences.[9]

Again, the majority's conclusions are contestable. Justice O'Connor, joined by Justices Scalia, Thomas, and Ginsburg, argued that the must-carry provisions were not "a narrowly tailored means of addressing anticompetitive behavior" by cable operators. The dissent pointed out that the only broadcast stations protected by must-carry are "marginal" stations and that the only basis for giving them preferential treatment was the improper basis of their content. Whatever one's opinion of this highly complex decision, it surely reconfirms the importance of the threshold decision of whether to label a regulation content-based or content-neutral. It also reaffirms that even content-neutral laws may be subject to enhanced scrutiny, at least where their effect is to place an "incidental burden" on speech. Taken together, *Turner I* and *Turner II* demonstrate that the First Amendment allows the government to enact regulations to preserve a "multiplicity of voices," at least where such content-neutral regulations are justified by the specific technological characteristics of the medium regulated.

DISTRIBUTION OF NEWSPAPERS VIA NEWSRACKS

The First Amendment protects the right to distribute news and information. However, it is not clear to what extent the First Amendment permits content-neutral regulation of the distribution of news via newsracks. Consider the following sample of Supreme Court decisions dealing with distribution.

The Court decided as early as 1938 that states may not prohibit door-to-door solicitation without a permit issued by a government official; such a scheme, the Court said "strikes at the very foundation of the freedom of the press by subjecting it to license and censorship." (Lovell v. City of Griffin, 1938) Five years later, the Court likewise held that a state may not "restrict the dissemination of ideas" by forbidding door-to-door distribution of religious pamphlets. (Martin v. Struthers, 1943). Although these cases established the right of newspapers and other publications to distribute news and information in public spaces, they did not resolve the specific issues posed by distribution via newsracks.

Newsracks commandeer public space for distribution purposes. Due to their semipermanent nature, newsracks present aesthetic and safety concerns not presented by distribution in person. The Supreme Court dealt with a content-neutral regulation of newsracks in Lakewood v. Plain Dealer Publishing Co. In that case, a Cleveland suburb required those wishing to place a newsrack on public property to obtain a permit from the mayor. The ordinance required the mayor to specify the reasons for denying a permit. The grant of a permit was conditioned on having the newsrack design approved by an Architectural Review Board and providing a $100,000 liability insurance policy. The Cleveland Plain Dealer challenged the constitutionality of the ordinance. The Supreme Court held, by a 4-3 vote, that the ordinance was unconstitutional. The dissenters argued that a newspaper's First Amendment right to distribute information does not entail the right to "appropriate [city property] for its own exclusive use, on a semi permanent basis, by means of the erection of a newsbox." The majority opinion, in contrast, seemed to view the right to distribute via newsrack as inseparable from its right to distribute more generally. The majority opinion labelled the distinction between distribution by hand and distribution by newsrack "meaningless," particularly in light of the "effectiveness of the newsrack as a means of distribution . . . for low-budget, controversial neighborhood newspapers." This decision is a fragile basis for constructing a general constititutional right to distribute newspapers by placing newsracks on public property, since only one vote separated the majority from the dissenters, and two justices did not participate in the case. (See also Cincinnati v. Discovery Network, Inc., 1993) Perhaps, then, it is not surprising that lower courts have generally permitted content-neutral regulation of newsrack appearance and placement. (See, e.g., Jacobsen v. Harris, 1989)

What is the conclusion to be drawn from all of this? Perhaps the best that can be said is, as the Supreme Court has stated, that "the enforcement of a generally applicable law may or may not be subject to heightened scrutiny under the First Amendment." (Turner Broad. Sys. v. FCC, 1994) As we have seen in this chapter, the level of scrutiny applied to content-neutral regulations hinges at least in part on the context in which they arise.

NOTES

1. An in-depth treatise of this subject is Randall P. Bezanson, *Taxes on Knowledge In America: Exactions on the Press from Colonial Times to the Present* (Philadelphia: University of Pennsylvania Press, 1994). An excellent historical analysis is found in Collet Dobson Collet, *History of the Taxes on Knowledge: Their Origin and Repeal* (1933).

2. For discussion see Samuel R. Olken, "The Business of Expression: Economic Liberty, Political Factions and the Forgotten First Amendment Legacy of Justice George Sutherland," 10 *Wm. & Mary Bill of Rts. J.* (2002) 249, 284–90.

3. For very critical treatment of this decision, see Bezanson, *Taxes on Knowledge In America: Exactions on the Press from Colonial Times to the Present*, 253–67. See also Jerry R. Parkinson, "Minneapolis Star & Tribune v. Minnesota Commissioner of Revenue: Differential Taxation of the Press Violates the First Amendment," 69 *Iowa L. Rev.* (1984) 1103, 1117–18

4. In the interim, however, the Court decided a relatively easy case of differential taxation, *Arkansas Writers' Project, Inc. v. Ragland*, 481 U.S. 221 (1987). The Arkansas tax statute at issue in Ragland exempted from a generally applicable sales tax newspapers and "religious, professional, trade and sports journals and/or publication." The publishers of a general interest magazine deemed by the Arkansas Commissioner of Revenue to be ineligible for the exemption challenged the constitutionality of the sales tax scheme.

The Supreme Court held that the tax scheme was unconstitutional. The Court found the tax scheme "particularly repugnant to First Amendment principles" because "a magazine's tax status depends entirely on its *content*." *Id.* at 229. Indeed, the statute required that a government official scrutinize the content of a publication as a basis for imposing the sales tax, making it "entirely incompatible with the First Amendment's guarantee of freedom of the press." The tax scheme was also objectionable because of its differential treatment of a particular subset of the media (in this case, special interest publications). This differential treatment triggered a presumption of unconstitutionality independently of the content discrimination. The Court applied strict scrutiny to the Arkansas tax scheme. The state failed to meet this high burden. Neither the State's interest in raising revenue, nor its interests in "encourag[ing] 'fledgling' publishers" and "fostering communications"—ostensibly values supported by the First Amendment—were weighty enough to justify a content-based discrimination among different members of the press.

5. See C. Edwin Baker, "Media Concentration: Giving up on Democracy," 54 *Fla. L. Rev.* (2002) 839, 839.

6. Only four justices found that there was sufficient evidence of anti-competitive behavior to justify must-carry. Justice Breyer concurred in the majority opinion, "except insofar as [the part examining the evidence relied on by Congress in passing the must-carry rules] relies on an anti-competitive rationale."

7. See Susan H. Williams, "Content Discrimination and the First Amendment," 139 *U. Pa. L. Rev.* (1991) 615; Susan Dente Ross, "Today, the First Amendment has become a first line of legal attack," 50 *Fed. Comm. L.J.* (1998) 281; Geoffrey R. Stone, "Content-Neutral Restrictions," 54 *U. Chi. L. Rev.* (1987) 46.

8. Note that the four dissenting justices "agree[d] that promoting fair competition is a legitimate and substantial Government goal." *Id.* at 232 (O'Connor, J., dissenting).

9. Justice Breyer joined in the Court's opinion "except insofar as Part II-A-1 [which discussed the evidence Congress relied on in predicting a threat to broadcasters] relies on an anticompetitive rationale."

6

Defamation

THE CONSTITUTIONALIZATION OF THE TORTS OF LIBEL AND SLANDER

The term "defamation" encompasses the twin torts of libel and slander. Defamation in written or any other relatively permanent form is libel; defamation in spoken or any other "impermanent" form is slander. In defamation actions, private litigants bring suit to recover monetary damages for harm to their reputations caused by speech. For obvious reasons, the press is often a target of defamation (libel) actions, and verdicts can run into the millions of dollars. Even paying the legal fees necessary to defend against a defamation action can put a small press operation out of business. Thus, editorial judgments about what, how, and even whether to publish are inevitably shaped by the prospect of having to defend against defamation actions, even though most defamation actions are ultimately unsuccessful.

Until 1964, the tort of defamation was purely a matter of state law; defamatory speech was thought to be outside the scope of First Amendment protection. (Beauharnais v. Illinois, 1952) In 1964, the Supreme Court held in the landmark case New York Times Co. v. Sullivan that the First Amendment placed limits on the ability of states to award monetary damages against the press for harming reputations. The Court recognized that the threat of libel actions may chill the media from criticizing government officials. The Court therefore held that the First Amendment would not allow government officials to bring defamation suits against the media unless they published defamatory statements with knowledge or reckless disregard of their falsity. New York Times Co. v. Sullivan was only the beginning of the "constitutionalization" of defamation law. In the past forty years, the Supreme Court's decisions have placed additional First Amendment limits on the tort of defamation, an area of law that was already "perplexed with minute and barren distinctions," "filled with technicalities and traps for the unwary," and riddled with "anomalies and absurdities" even before 1964. Even so, the goal of this chapter is not to present all of the intricacies of the underlying tort law. Instead, the goal is to show the changes the First Amendment has wrought on the tort of defamation, and to explain the meaning of those changes for freedom of the press.

SEDITIOUS LIBEL IN THE UNITED STATES

The modern defamation tort originated in the common-law crime of seditious libel. A person committed a seditious libel by publishing anything that would lower the regard in which government officials or government institutions were held. If a newspaper published that a government official was taking bribes, the editor could be prosecuted and jailed even if the charge was absolutely true. Indeed, it was said that the "greater the truth, the greater the libel," for truthful charges would bring the government into even more disrepute than false ones. Seditious libel was a powerful tool for suppressing public criticism of government, and prosecutions were common in seventeenth and eighteenth century England.

Punishing criticism of government as a crime may strike us as a hallmark of despotism, but it is not clear that the Framers of the First Amendment saw it in this light. Although prosecutions for seditious libel were rare in colonial America, they still occurred. Moreover, some of the very men who framed the First Amendment passed the Alien and Sedition Act of 1798, making it a crime, punishable by up to two years in prison, to criticize the President or Congress, "with intent to defame . . . or to bring them . . . into contempt or disrepute." Support for the Sedition Act fell entirely along partisan lines. The Federalists, who controlled the presidency and both houses of Congress, passed the Act to undercut the rising popularity of their rivals, the Jeffersonian Republicans, by targeting Republican newspaper editors for prosecution.

The passage of the Sedition Act sparked vigorous debate about the scope of the First Amendment's guarantee of press freedom. Federalists argued that the First Amendment forbade only prior restraints on the press. Republicans (particularly James Madison and Thomas Jefferson) argued that the First Amendment also forbade prosecutions for seditious libel. Although the debate was never resolved in the Supreme Court, it was resolved in the court of public opinion. The Republicans swept the Congress and the Presidency in the elections of 1800, and they allowed the Alien and Sedition Act to expire. This resolution of the controversy indicated that criminal prosecutions for seditious libel of the federal government had no place in a country committed to freedom of the press.

The debate gained new urgency in the early twentieth century, when the United States began prosecuting hundreds of Americans who protested this country's entry into World War I. The Espionage Act of 1917 made it a crime to "cause or attempt to cause insubordination, disloyalty, mutiny, or refusal of duty in the military or naval forces." The Espionage Act was no more and no less than a modern form of seditious libel. Yet the Supreme Court upheld prosecutions under the Act on the ground that criticism of the war by socialists, pacifists, and other radicals might hinder recruiting. (See, e.g., Frohwerk v. United States, 1919) Out of the Espionage Act cases, however, emerged a new vision of the First Amendment. Justices Holmes and Brandeis, in a series of dissenting opinions, sketched out a comprehensive theory of the role of free expression in democracy. Prosecutions for seditious libel offended the core notions of our democracy, because the government is representative of the people, and the people have a right to make their voices heard, even in the form of harsh and scathing criticism. Holmes wrote, "History seems to me against the notion . . . that the First Amendment left the common law as to seditious libel in force." (Abrams v. United States, 1919) For Holmes and Brandeis, the right to criticize government officials is so important that only when there is a clear and present danger of imminent harm can such criticism be suppressed. The Holmes-Brandeis view of the First Amendment and of the relationship between citizens and their government ultimately became the theoretical underpinning of the modern First Amendment, and the Supreme Court explicitly disavowed its Espionage Act decisions.

Even so, in 1964 it still was not clear that the First Amendment put any restraints at all on private civil libel actions. Prior to that time, there was no indication in any Supreme Court case that civil libel actions were constrained by the First Amendment. That all changed with New York Times Co. v. Sullivan.

SEDITIOUS LIBEL AND PUBLIC OFFICIALS: NEW YORK TIMES CO. V. SULLIVAN

New York Times Co. v. Sullivan began with a paid political advertisement in the March 29, 1960 issue of the *New York Times*. The advertisement, titled "Heed Their Rising Voices," was designed to solicit support for the Civil Rights Movement in the South. The ad decried the "wave of terror" used to intimidate "Southern Negro students" demonstrating for civil rights. The ad specifically stated that in Montgomery, Alabama, student leaders of a demonstration were expelled, and police armed with shotguns and tear-gas ringed their campus. The ad also stated that "Southern violators . . . bombed [Dr. Martin Luther King's] home, . . . assaulted his person [and] arrested him seven times." The ad did not mention any public official by name.

That did not stop a City Commissioner from Montgomery, Alabama from suing the *New York Times* and four Alabama ministers named in the ad for libel. Sullivan sought half a million dollars in damages. In addition to Sullivan's libel action, the Times also faced suits by other Montgomery officials and the Governor of Alabama, asking for damages of $2.5 million. It was very clear that the Alabama politicians were using these libel actions to silence a "Northern" newspaper, the *New York Times*, and prevent further reporting on the Civil Rights Movement. Alabama public officials had found a way to use supposedly "private" civil actions to intimidate and punish those who truthfully described the injustices

suffered by African Americans in the segregated South. The fact that the case was
not truly about repairing Commissioner Sullivan's reputation is demonstrated by
the fact that even his own witnesses could not testify that they thought less of him
after reading the ad. How then could an Alabama jury award him $500,000 in
damages—the largest libel verdict ever at that point—for supposed injury to his
reputation?

The Common Law Tort Elements of Defamation

The answer lies in the "anomalies and absurdities" in the common law tort of
defamation. Alabama libel law, like that of most other states, required a libel
plaintiff to prove: (1) the existence of a defamatory communication; (2) publication of the communication to at least one third party, and (3) identification of the
plaintiff to a third party. These were the common law elements of libel as they
existed in 1960, and indeed they are the common law elements of libel as they
exist today in many states.

Commissioner Sullivan had no problem establishing "publication." Nor did he
have trouble establishing that the ad's criticisms of the Alabama police were
defamatory. A defamatory statement is a statement that tends to harm an individual's reputation in the eyes of his or her community. It is ordinarily defamatory,
for example, to state that an individual is a liar, a crook, or a murderer. These
statements harm reputation by diminishing their target in the eyes of his or her
community. In the Sullivan case, the jury accepted Sullivan's argument that the
advertisement called into question his ability as a City Commissioner to maintain
"good order" in the police force.

It is important to note here that the statements at issue were defamatory
because they would "tend" to harm Sullivan's reputation, not because he proved
that they actually did harm his reputation. In fact, Sullivan's witnesses testified
that they did not really believe the defamatory statements. Why then was Sullivan
able to recover such a large judgment? In most tort cases a plaintiff must prove he
suffered objectively verifiable dollar losses. But because harm to reputation is so
difficult to establish with certainty, libel law has long allowed juries to award
"presumed damages" based solely on the nature of the defamatory statement. The
practical implications of the presumed damages rule allowed the Sullivan jury to
award the largest libel verdict ever prior to that time based merely on the "presumed" effect of the *New York Times* advertisement. The trial judge also
instructed the jury that it could award punitive damages "even though the amount
of actual damages is neither found nor shown."

The hardest part of Sullivan's case was proving that the ad referred to him,
since he was never explicitly mentioned by name. To do this, the trial court
allowed Sullivan to bring witnesses who testified that they understood the refer-

ences to the Montgomery police as a reference to Sullivan's performance as police commissioner. The practical import was to allow Sullivan to transform the advertisement's criticism of government activities into a personal libel. The *New York Times* could not even assert truth as a defense because of minor inaccuracies[1] such as the following: Dr. King was arrested four times rather than seven, the students were expelled for demanding service at a lunch counter rather than for leading a demonstration on campus, and the police did not "ring" the campus but were merely deployed in large numbers.

The defendants asserted their First Amendment rights, but their arguments fell on deaf ears in both the trial court and in the Alabama Supreme Court. The United States Supreme Court immediately cast the case as a modern form of seditious libel "brought by a public official against critics of his official conduct." Indeed, the Court pointed to the repeal of the Sedition Act of 1798 by the victorious Jeffersonian Republicans as evidence of a "broad consensus" that the First Amendment forbade undue restraint "upon criticism of government and public officials." The Court therefore struck down Alabama's libel law as unconstitutional as applied to a public official's suit for criticism of his official conduct.

A Breathing Space for Free Expression: The Actual Malice Rule

Even so, the Court was unwilling to give the press absolute immunity from libel actions by public officials. The Court recognized that factual errors were inevitable in free debate; indeed, one of the primary justifications for the Court's decision was the fear that defamation actions would have a chilling effect on vigorous reporting of governmental affairs. Nevertheless, the Court did not want to protect publishers of outright lies or reckless falsehoods.[2] Thus the Court held that the Constitution demands public officials to prove "actual malice" in order to recover for libel. "Actual malice" is a term of art meaning that the publisher knows of the falsity of the statement published (that is, knows it is a lie) or recklessly disregards the falsity of the statement. (New York Times Co. v. Sullivan, 1964) The actual malice rule protects merely negligent falsehoods in order to create "breathing space" for the press to engage in "uninhibited, robust, and wide open" debate on public affairs.

The actual malice rule was a tremendous boon to media defendants in libel actions, but it was not the only protection extended by the Court. The essential first step in the constitutionalization of defamation law was the Supreme Court's decision that a state's application of its libel law was a form of state action. If the Court had viewed the case as merely a matter between two private litigants, it could not have intervened. Moreover, the Court created several procedural protections to bolster the actual malice rule. First, the Court required that actual malice be shown with clear and convincing clarity, a higher standard than simply the normal preponderance of the evidence standard. Second, appellate courts must independently review the trial court record to ensure that the evidence establishes actual malice with clear and convincing clarity. Third, the Court effectively shifted to public official plaintiffs the burden of proving falsity; truth was no longer a defense that had to be pleaded and proved by the defendant. These additional procedural protections have been as important in shielding the media from defamation liability as the actual malice rule itself.

Consider, for example, what would have happened in the *Sullivan* case if the Supreme Court had simply sent the case back down to the Alabama courts with an instruction that the jury must make a determination of actual malice. No doubt the jury would have found that the *New York Times* and the ministers recklessly disregarded the falsity of the published statements. To avoid this result, the Supreme Court independently reviewed the record and determined that "the proof presented to show actual malice lacks the convincing clarity which the constitutional standard demands." The Court also found the evidence constitutionally inadequate to prove that the ad was "of and concerning" Sullivan. The First Amendment does not allow "criticism of government, however impersonal it may seem" to be transmuted into a personal libel of "the officials of whom the government is composed."

New York Times Co. v. Sullivan was a victory both for the Civil Rights movement and for press freedom. It forever put to rest the notion that the First Amendment was merely a prohibition on prior restraints. It also reflected the theory that political speech lies at the core of the First Amendment's protection. This theory, often associated with Alexander Meiklejohn, assumes that the First Amendment's primary role in our constitutional system is to foster democratic self-governance. In order to work effectively, the democratic process requires a free flow of information about government representatives to the citizens who elect them and a free flow of information from those same citizens to make their wishes known to their representatives. The press plays a vital role both by gathering the information citizens need to make informed decisions and by reflecting the popular will and communicating it back to government officials. Although the modern First Amendment protects far more than merely political speech, it is still the case that infringements on political speech trigger the highest level of constitutional solicitude, thanks in part to the Court's decision in New York Times Co. v. Sullivan.

As significant as the *Sullivan* decision was at the time, it was just the beginning of the constitutionalization of defamation law. *Sullivan* gave the press protection from crippling defamation liability in order to allow the press to report on public officials, that is, those who hold positions in government such "that the public has an independent interest in the qualifications and performance of the person who holds [them]." (Rosenblatt v. Baer, 1966) Enhanced scrutiny of these officials was crucial because of their ability to shape public policy and to wield political power to make their voices heard. But public officials are not the only people who wield power and influence to shape public policy. Thus, the logic of *Sullivan* demanded extension if the press was to engage in uninhibited, robust and wide-open debate on matters of public concern.

THE EXTENSION OF *SULLIVAN* TO PUBLIC FIGURES

The first part of that extension came in Curtis Publishing Co v. Butts, which was decided in conjunction with Associated Press v. Walker. These two cases both involved plaintiffs who had gained prominence in their selected spheres of influence. Wally Butts was prominent largely by virtue of his position as the athletic director and former football coach of the University of Georgia. In fact, it was this prominence that made the ensuing defamatory story about him so newsworthy. The story stated that he had "fixed" a football game by telling a rival coach his secret plays. Walker, on the other hand, was prominent partly by virtue of his former position as a U.S. Army general, but more pertinently by virtue of his activism. Walker resigned from the military to protest federal intervention in the South to support civil rights. Walker sued for defamation after a news wire report stated that he had instigated and participated in a riot against the federal marshals supporting the registration of James Meredith, an African-American, at the University of Mississippi. The question before the Supreme Court was whether the *New York Times'* actual malice rule should apply to Butts and Walker. In a fractured opinion, a majority of the Court said yes.[3]

Chief Justice Warren's opinion, which was joined by four other justices, justified application of the actual malice rule to public figures by pointing to the significant public interest in both of the plaintiffs. Warren explained that "what we have commonly considered to be the private sector" has become increasingly powerful and has even taken over some governmental functions. This shift of power to the private sector means that "many who do not hold public office at the moment are nevertheless intimately involved in the resolution of important public questions or, by reason of their fame, shape events in areas of concern to society at large." (Curtis Publ'g Co. v. Butts, 1967)

The political power and influence wielded by public figures gives the public a "legitimate and substantial interest in the[ir] conduct." This alone might justify treating them like public officials for purposes of defamation law. Yet the Court also reasoned that it was fair to subject public figures to the actual malice rule because public figures, like public officials, have "ready access" to the media "both to influence policy and to counter criticism of their views and activities." (Curtis Publ'g Co. v. Butts, 1967) In other words, public figures have tools other than tort law to deal with defamatory falsehoods. In fact, public scrutiny of public figures may be even more important than public scrutiny of public officials, precisely because public figures are not subject to the political process. Thus, the proper balance between protecting "uninhibited debate" about public figures and safeguarding individual reputation is properly struck by adoption of the actual malice rule.

The Court did not just extend the actual malice rule itself to public figures. It also extended the other procedural protections of press freedom developed in New York Times Co. v. Sullivan. Public figures, like public officials, must prove both actual malice by clear and convincing evidence, and they must prove falsity. And courts must independently review cases in which public figures are involved to ensure the plaintiff has adduced adequate evidence of actual malice to justify a judgment in his or her favor. As we shall see in the following sections, application of these "heightened substantive and evidentiary standards for all public persons suing as to matters of public interest"[4] has dramatically reduced defamation recoveries for a broad class of plaintiffs.

PRIVATE FIGURE PLAINTIFFS AND MATTERS OF PUBLIC CONCERN: GERTZ V. ROBERT WELCH

The Supreme Court's extension of *Sullivan* to public figures left uncertain whether there were any constitutional limits on defamation actions brought by private figures. The Court definitively resolved this uncertainty in Gertz v. Robert Welch, Inc. The plaintiff in that case was an attorney of some local prominence who had been hired to represent the family of a young man murdered by a Chicago policeman. A publication put out by the conservative John Birch Society described the plaintiff as the "major architect" of a plot against the police officer, called him a "Leninist" and "Communist-fronter," and falsely stated that he had a long police record. In the plaintiff's subsequent defamation action, the trial court decided that since a matter of public concern was involved, the plaintiff should be required to prove actual malice by clear and convincing evidence. The trial judge found the evidence insufficient to support the jury's verdict of $50,000 for the plaintiff and entered a judgment notwithstanding the verdict.

Despite the plaintiff's involvement in "community and professional affairs" in the Chicago area, the Supreme Court determined that he was not a public official or public figure. Although he had previously served on a Chicago housing committee by mayoral appointment, he had never held paid government office. And although he had been active in civic groups and had written books and articles on legal topics, he did not enjoy "pervasive fame or notoriety." Nor had he "voluntarily inject[ed] himself . . . into a particular public controversy" by virtue of his representation of the family of the youth murdered by the police officer. (Gertz v. Robert Welch, Inc., 1974) Although the murder was a newsworthy incident, the plaintiff's participation did not go beyond representation of his clients. He did not attempt to use the press to influence the case; indeed, "he never discussed either the criminal or civil litigation with the press and was never quoted as having done so." The Court therefore labeled Gertz a private figure.

His status as a private figure gave the Supreme Court an opportunity to reassert the important value of protecting reputation. Quoting Justice Stewart, the Court stated that "the individual's right to protection of his own good name 'reflects no more than our basic concept of the essential dignity and worth of every human being—a concept at the root of any decent system of ordered liberty.'" (Gertz v. Robert Welch, Inc., 1974 (quoting Rosenblatt v. Baer, 1966 (Stewart, J., concurring))) In cases involving public figures and public officials, the balance between protecting reputation and protecting expression tips strongly in favor of the latter. But where private figures are involved, the state has a stronger interest in protecting reputation, and the balance must be struck differently. Not only are private persons "more vulnerable to injury" than public officials or public figures, private persons are also "more deserving" of defamation recovery because they have not voluntarily thrust themselves into public affairs or attempted to influence public policy. Moreover, private figures must rely more on legal recourse to protect their reputations because they have less access to the media to rebut defamatory falsehoods.[5]

Even in cases involving private figure plaintiffs, however, the Supreme Court was unwilling to return to the strict liability of the common law tort of defamation, at least in cases like *Gertz*, which involved commentary on a matter of public concern. The Court, voting 5-4, held that "so long as they do not impose liability without fault, the States may define for themselves the appropriate standard of liability for a publisher or broadcaster of defamatory falsehood injurious to a private individual." (Gertz v. Robert Welch, Inc., 1974) The Court further held though, that even in the case of private figure plaintiffs, "States may not permit recovery of presumed or punitive damages at least when liability is not based on a showing of knowledge of falsity or reckless disregard for the truth."

In practical terms, the Court's holding meant that in order to recover for defamation, private figure plaintiffs must ordinarily prove that the publisher of a defamatory statement was at least negligent. However, states can require an even higher standard of fault if they wish. For example, although the majority of states requires plaintiffs to prove negligence,[6] New York requires them to prove gross irresponsibility, (See, e.g., First United Fund, Ltd. v. Am. Banker, Inc., 1985) and some even require them to prove actual malice. (See, e.g., Reddick v. Craig, 1985; Kitco, Inc. v. Corp. for Gen. Trade, 1999; Schwartz v. Worrall Publ'ns, 1992)

Moreover, the way in which plaintiffs go about proving negligence may vary from state to state. Some states have required plaintiffs to back up their claim by providing expert testimony to establish professional journalistic negligence; in essence, they must show journalistic "malpractice" in publishing the defamatory statement.[7] (See, e.g., Lansdowne v. Beacon Journal Pub. Co., 1987; Martin v. Griffin Television, Inc., 1976; Seegmiller v. KSL, Inc., 1981) More commonly, states have simply allowed the jury to determine, based on the evidence presented, whether the publisher used reasonable care (that is, was not negligent) before publishing the defamatory statement. (See, e.g., Troman v. Wood, 1975)

Even though most states allow private figure plaintiffs to proceed with a defamation action by proving negligence, many private figure plaintiffs who sue the press will choose to prove the higher standard of actual malice. The explanation for this seeming anomaly stems from the second part of *Gertz*'s holding. If a plaintiff proves only negligence, the plaintiff cannot recover unless he also shows "actual injury." A plaintiff can prove actual injury by showing, for example, that his business has lost customers because of the defamation, or he can merely show that he has suffered "personal humiliation, and mental anguish and suffering." (Gertz v. Robert Welch, Inc., 1974) Nonetheless, a plaintiff will often want to prove actual malice to open the door to recovery of presumed and punitive damages. Presumed damages are based on the nature of the defamatory statement itself; the jury does not need to benchmark them to any actual loss to the plaintiff. And punitive damages, which are not available without proof of actual malice, may be the extra incentive necessary to persuade a plaintiff's attorney to pursue a notoriously difficult defamation action against a media defendant. Thus, even though *Gertz* allows private figure plaintiffs to recover if the defendant's negligently published defamatory communication caused the plaintiff actual injury, many private figure plaintiffs will choose to prove the defendant acted with actual malice.

PRIVATE FIGURE PLAINTIFFS AND MATTERS OF PRIVATE CONCERN: DUN & BRADSTREET V. GREENMOSS BUILDERS

The Court's decision in Gertz v. Robert Welch, Inc. left at least two important questions unsettled. The first question was whether *all* defamation actions were now subject to First Amendment limitations. The second question was whether the constitutional privileges developed in *Sullivan*, *Curtis*, and *Gertz* applied only to benefit publishers and broadcasters or whether they protected non-media defendants as well. In Dun & Bradstreet v. Greenmoss Builders, the Court appeared to answer "no" to both questions.

In *Dun & Bradstreet*, a construction contractor sued for defamation after five of its creditors received a false credit report stating that the contractor had filed for bankruptcy. The defamation occurred because a 17-year-old employee of the credit reporting agency, who had been paid to review state bankruptcy petitions, mistakenly attributed the bankruptcy of one of the plaintiff's former employees to the plaintiff itself. The credit reporting agency made no attempt to verify the information before reporting it to five subscribers to its credit report, who were contractually bound not to reveal the contents to anyone else. The plaintiff won a verdict of $50,000 in compensatory or presumed damages and $300,000 in punitive damages on its defamation claim. The defendant, Dun & Bradstreet, moved for a new trial on the grounds that the trial court did not properly instruct the jury that punitive damages could not be awarded without proof of actual malice. In other words, the basis for the motion was that the constitutional requirements set forth in Gertz v. Robert Welch, Inc., had not been met. In reviewing the case, the Vermont Supreme Court held that Dun & Bradstreet was not entitled to "the media protections outlined in Gertz" because it was a "non-media" defendant.

In a plurality decision, the United States Supreme Court agreed that Dun & Bradstreet was not entitled to the protections of *Gertz*, although not because it was a non-media defendant. Instead, the Court based its decision on the conclusion that the case involved "speech on matters of purely *private* concern," and distinguished *Gertz* as involving a matter of undoubted *public* concern. In a case involving a private figure plaintiff and a matter of merely private concern, the plurality opinion held that "permitting recovery of presumed and punitive damages . . . absent a showing of 'actual malice' does not violate the First Amendment."

The plurality's rationale was that a different balance must be struck in cases where the type of speech involves only matters of private concern. The speech at issue in these cases is less vital, from a First Amendment standpoint, than speech on matters of public concern. In other words, private concern speech is not as essential to the "free and robust debate of public issues," nor to a "meaningful dialogue of ideas concerning self-government," as public concern speech is. On the other side of the balance, the state interest in awarding presumed and punitive damages as an "effective" remedy for defamation is higher in cases involving matters of private concern, given the difficulties plaintiffs face in proving actual damages even where "'it is all but certain that serious harm has resulted in fact.'"

Although the plurality did not spell out the practical implications of this decision, its reasoning suggested that states may impose strict liability on defendants who defame private plaintiffs concerning matters of private concern. In other words, the *Dun & Bradstreet* decision may mean that in a limited class of cases, the states may simply require a plaintiff to prove the traditional common law elements of defamation—the publication of a defamatory statement of and concerning the plaintiff—without regard to fault.

However, the reach of the Court's decision is limited because its analysis indicated that cases involving purely private concern speech will be rare. The Court indicated that "content, form and context" are determinative in deciding whether speech is of public concern or of private concern. (drawing on Connick v. Myers, 1983) Based on these factors, Dun & Bradstreet's credit report was private because it was "solely in the individual interest of the speaker and its specific business audience." Almost by definition, the credit report made no contribution to "the free flow of commercial information" because the audience for the speech consisted only of the five paid subscribers who were contractually bound not to disseminate the information more widely. The Court also emphasized that the speech deserved no special constitutional protection due to the allegedly "hardy" nature of commercial speech in general. Because credit reporting agencies will have powerful market incentives to continue publishing and to verify the accuracy of reports, they will presumably not be unduly chilled by the imposition of defamation liability for false reports.

As far as members of the media are concerned, *Dun & Bradstreet*'s reach is limited simply by the fact that the media ordinarily have little interest in reporting on matters of private concern. It is significant, however, that six of the justices who decided the case rejected a distinction between media and non-media defendants. (Dun & Bradstreet v. Greenmoss Builders, 1985 (Brennan, J., dissenting)) This did not definitively resolve the issue because the case was decided on other grounds. Since that time, the Supreme Court has gone out of its way to state that the media/non-media issue remains unresolved. (See Milkovich v. Lorain Journal Co., 1990; Philadelphia Newspapers, Inc. v. Hepps, 1986) However, the "best educated guess"[8] of most commentators (including the authors of this book) and most lower courts[9] is that non-media defendants should receive the same level of constitutional protections as media defendants. A media/non-media distinction would draw unworkable status distinctions between the institutional media and other speakers, particularly in light of the new technology that allows single individuals to reach and influence a mass audience. In a poignant but now obsolete metaphor, the Supreme Court recognized that the "lonely pamphleteer's" contribution to public debate may be just as important as that of the most powerful media speaker. (See Branzburg v. Hayes, 1972) Thus, a revival of the media/non-media distinction seems unlikely and unwise.

THE FALSITY REQUIREMENT: PHILADELPHIA NEWSPAPERS, INC. V. HEPPS

At common law truth was a defense to libel, to be pleaded and proved by the defendant. New York Times Co. v. Sullivan implied that public official plaintiffs must bear the burden of proving falsity. The Supreme Court, in Philadelphia Newspapers, Inc. v. Hepps, cleared up any lingering doubt on this point by stating clearly that public officials and public figures must prove falsity in order to recover for defamation. More surprisingly, in *Hepps*, the Court held that private figure plaintiffs suing over speech on a matter of public concern must also prove falsity. In other words, in the common situation where such speech cannot be proved true or false, the plaintiff will lose. The rationale for putting the burden of proving falsity on the plaintiff was that where the evidence is ambiguous as to whether particular speech is true or false, the balance should tip "in favor of protecting true speech." Thus, the media will not be chilled from publishing speech on matters of public concern just because they fear they will not be able to later prove its truth to a jury's satisfaction.

A SUMMARY OF CONSTITUTIONAL STANDARDS

The preceding discussion gives some idea of the complexity the Supreme Court has imposed on the already complex common-law tort of defamation. The following chart should help sort out some of this complexity:

The Constitutional Minimum Fault Standard

Status of Plaintiff	Minimum Fault Standard	Damages Available	Burden on Truth/Falsity Issue
Public Official or Public Figure/ Matter of Public Concern	Actual Malice, by Clear and Convincing Evidence	Presumed and Punitive Damages	Plaintiff must prove falsity
Private Figure/ Matter of Public Concern	Negligence	Compensatory Damages for "actual injury" upon proof of negligence; Presumed and Punitive Damages if actual malice is proved	Plaintiff must prove falsity*
Private Figure/Matter of Private Concern	Probably Strict Liability†	Presumed and Punitive Damages	State may probably make truth a defense to be proved by defendant‡

*at least in cases involving media defendants and probably in all cases: issue is unresolved

†not fully resolved by *Dun & Bradstreet*

‡not resolved by *Hepps*

APPLYING THE STATUS CATEGORIES

As we have seen above, the status of the plaintiff is a crucial determinant of what the plaintiff must prove in order to succeed in a defamation action. However, the court rather than a jury must decide this crucial question of whether a plaintiff is a public official, public figure, or private figure. There is an extensive body of case law to assist courts in this determination.

WHO IS A PUBLIC OFFICIAL?

As the Supreme Court stated in Rosenblatt v. Baer, the rationale for protecting commentary about public officials even at the expense of having individual reputations is the "strong interest in debate about those persons who are in a position significantly to influence the resolution of [public] issues." The Supreme Court defined the parameters of the public official category in *Rosenblatt*, stating that "the 'public official' designation applies at the very least to those among the hierarchy of government employees who have, or appear to the public to have, substantial responsibility for or control over the conduct of governmental affairs." In other words, government employees in high-level positions are almost certain to be deemed public officials. The Court made this point more explicitly by saying that a person will be deemed a public official (and thus subject to the actual malice rule) "[w]here [that person's] position in government has such apparent importance that the public has an independent interest in the qualifications and performance of the person who holds it, beyond the general public interest in the qualifications and performance of all government employees." A low-level government employee does not become a public official simply because a news story about him attracts public attention; he must be a public official by virtue of his position or potential influence over governmental policy.

The Court's comparison of public figures and public officials in Curtis Publ'g Co. v. Butts is instructive in this regard. Public figures are subject to actual malice rules because, *like public officials*, they have access to the media to influence policy and to rebut defamatory falsehoods about them. Also, public figures, *like public officials*, assume the risk of public scrutiny and media criticism by virtue of the role they have chosen to play in influencing public debates. (See e.g., Kassell v. Gannett Co., 1989)

Elected officials are the prototypical public officials. Even candidates who have not yet attained elective office will be treated like public officials because the public has a paramount interest in candidates' fitness for office. Indeed, the Court has defined quite broadly the scope of legitimate commentary about candidates to include "anything which might touch on an official's fitness for office." (Garrison v. Louisiana, 1964; Monitor Patriot Co. v. Roy, 1971) In Monitor Patriot Co. v. Roy, for example, the Court held that a false accusation that a candidate had committed a crime many years earlier was not actionable unless published with actual malice. The Court declared that a "charge of criminal conduct, no matter how remote in time or place, can never be irrelevant to an official's or a candidate's fitness for office." (See also Ocala Star-Banner Co. v. Damron, 1971) In fact, the

Court stated, it is "by no means easy to see what statements about a candidate might be altogether without relevance to his fitness for the office he seeks." This essentially opens up the candidate's whole life to public scrutiny: Nothing is too remote in time to be relevant; no detail of her private life is too trivial or too personal to reflect on her fitness for office. (See also Ocala Star-Banner Co. v. Damron, 1971; Harte-Hanks Communications, Inc. v. Connaughton, 1989) Even former public officials remain public officials for life, at least for purposes of commentary on their prior job performance.

Although it is easy to apply the rule that elected officials and candidates for elective office at all levels will be treated as public officials, the determination of public official status becomes much more fact-intensive in other contexts, with a chief determinant being the level of responsibility exercised by the government employee.[10] Consider, for example, whether police officers are public officials. It is clear that the chief of police should be a public official, given his or her role in shaping the policy of an entire police department. But what about an ordinary patrol officer?

As David Elder has argued, this type of low-ranking government employee has not in any real sense assumed the risk of intensive public scrutiny merely by taking his job, nor does he have meaningful access to the media to rebut defamatory falsehoods. On the other hand, some courts have noted that the decision whether to arrest is essentially the first "policy" decision that brings someone into the criminal justice system, and the public does have a significant interest in how police officers perform their duties. (See Britton v. Koep, 1991) Courts face similar difficulties when dealing with other low-ranking government employees. Public school teachers are usually not treated as public officials, but an elementary school principal might or might not be treated as one, depending on the specific facts and how expansively lower courts construe the Supreme Court's decision. The same is also true for the infinite variety of public functionaries in the middle ranks of the government, making it difficult to predict in advance which of these plaintiffs are public officials for purpose of the *Times* rules. (Gertz v. Robert Welch, Inc., 1974)

PUBLIC FIGURES VERSUS PRIVATE FIGURES

Public figures come in three different types, all of which have additional defining criteria. These three different types are: (1) "general" public figures, who have achieved such "pervasive fame or notoriety" that they are public figures "for all purposes and in all contexts," (2) limited-purpose public figures, who are public figures only for purposes of discussion of a particular controversy in which they have become involved, and (3) "involuntary" public figures, who are thrust into a controversy through no action of their own and become public figures only for purposes of discussion of that controversy. (Gertz v. Robert Welch, Inc., 1974) As we shall see in this section, the determination of whether a plaintiff is a private figure becomes simply a matter of ruling out public figure status.

GENERAL-PURPOSE PUBLIC FIGURES

Of the public figure categories, the first is the easiest to apply. If the plaintiff has achieved "such pervasive fame or notoriety" that her name is a household word, she will be a general-purpose public figure. Cher, Madonna, Brad Pitt, Jennifer Aniston, Jennifer Lopez—all are general-purpose public figures. The Supreme Court has reasoned that it is fair to label them public figures "for all purposes and in all contexts" because they "occupy positions of such persuasive power and influence." (Gertz v. Robert Welch, Inc., 1974) This logic makes sense for activist-type public figures, like Ralph Nader or the Reverend Jerry Falwell, who have tried to exert influence in the public sphere, but it is questionable as applied to the average celebrity, who lacks power and influence in the political sense. The notion that such individuals can "transfer their recognition from one field to another" is questionable. (Waldbaum v. Fairchild Publ'ns, Inc., 1980) Still, the Supreme Court is correct in asserting that celebrity-type public figures may have unusual media access to tell their story and "invite attention and comment" through their own voluntary activities. (Waldbaum v. Fairchild Publ'ns, Inc., 1980) In a sense, if they live by the sword, they must die by the sword: It is publicity that makes them celebrities, and it is the fact that they are celebrities that makes the public so interested in their affairs.

Harder issues arise when the plaintiff is a local or regional "celebrity" but is not nationally known. In Curtis Publishing Co v. Butts, the Supreme Court concluded that the athletic director and former head football coach of the University of Georgia was a public figure who "may have attained that status by position alone" Yet in Time, Inc. v. Firestone, the Court found that a Palm Beach socialite was not a public figure (even for limited purposes) when defamed in a nationally circulated publication, despite a degree of local prominence. Likewise, the plaintiff in Gertz v. Robert Welch, Inc., had some prominence as an attorney in the Chicago legal community but was still a private figure due to his lack of "general fame or notoriety in the community." This language suggests that a relevant factor in determining public figure status is whether the audience of the defamatory statement is the same audience in which the plaintiff has prominence or notoriety, and this approach has prevailed in some lower courts.[11] Nonetheless, these cases present difficult issues for lower courts, and one can certainly find discrepancies in the case law regarding how prominent a plaintiff must be before he or she is labeled an all-purpose public figure.

LIMITED-PURPOSE PUBLIC FIGURES

The most difficult and also the largest category of public figure is undoubtedly the limited-purpose public figure. Limited-purpose public figures receive less protection from libel than private figures do because they have "thrust themselves to the forefront of particular public controversies in order to influence the resolution of issues involved." (Gertz v. Robert Welch, Inc., 1974) They become public figures only for the limited purposes of discussion of those issues. The Supreme Court laid out the two most important determinants of limited-purpose public figure status in Gertz v. Robert Welch, Inc. These determinants are: (1) whether the plaintiff has access to channels of effective communication to rebut defamatory falsehoods, and (2) whether the plaintiff voluntarily assumed a prominent role in a public controversy and the attendant risk of enhanced public scrutiny.

Ironically, the best evidence of which plaintiffs will qualify as limited-purpose public figures comes from Supreme Court cases in which the Court determined that the plaintiffs were not public figures. In *Gertz*, the plaintiff was a private figure because he had done nothing to "thrust himself into the vortex of th[e] public issue" surrounding a murder by a Chicago police officer, "nor did he engage the public's attention in an attempt to influence its outcome." Thus, the Court's analysis suggests that a lawyer involved in a high-profile case who attempts to "try the case in the media" might receive very different treatment. But the simple act of representing clients indirectly connected to a high-profile case is insufficient to make the lawyer a public figure (although F. Lee Bailey and Johnnie Cochran almost certainly became general public figures while representing O.J. Simpson in his high-profile murder trial).

The Court's analysis in Time, Inc. v. Firestone was similar to that used in *Gertz*. *Time* magazine published that the heir to the Firestone fortune had received a divorce due to his wife's adultery. Although the Supreme Court ultimately vacated and remanded the plaintiff's $100,000 libel judgment, Justice Rehnquist, writing on behalf of himself and four other justices, determined that Mrs. Firestone was not a public figure. Justice Rehnquist conceded the public interest in "the marital difficulties" of the Firestones, but he found that there was no "public controversy" of the sort required to transform Mrs. Firestone into a public figure. Mrs. Firestone did not voluntarily open her private life to public scrutiny but was instead required to participate in the judicial process in order to obtain a divorce. Justice Rehnquist's opinion even dismissed the fact that Mrs. Firestone had held press conferences about her divorce, on the grounds that she was only trying to get her side of events out to the public rather than attempting to influence the outcome of a public issue. This analysis indicates the lengths to which a plaintiff must go before she will be deemed to have voluntarily injected herself into a public controversy. Mere public interest in a plaintiff is not enough to make her a limited-purpose public figure.

The Supreme Court confirmed this point in Wolston v. Reader's Digest Ass'n, Inc. and Hutchinson v. Proxmire. In *Wolston*, the plaintiff sued after a 1974 book falsely accused him of being a Soviet agent with an espionage conviction. In fact, the plaintiff had been convicted in 1958 of contempt of court for failing to respond to a grand jury investigation of Soviet agents in the United States. The Court held that, despite the publicity the contempt conviction had received in 1958, Wolston was not a public figure. The Court conceded Wolston "voluntarily" failed to appear before the grand jury, knowing it might attract media attention. However, his reason for failing to appear was his poor mental health, rather than any desire for publicity. Moreover, he "never discussed [the] matter with the press and limited his involvement to that necessary to defend himself against the contempt charge."

The plaintiff in Hutchinson v. Proxmire likewise had limited media contact only for the purposes of responding to the defendant's criticism. The plaintiff was a research scientist receiving a federal grant. He sued for defamation after a U.S. Senator derided his research as an example of wasteful government spending. The Supreme Court held that the plaintiff was not a limited-purpose public figure even for purposes of comment on his receipt of federal funds. The Court found that the only reason plaintiff's research became a matter of controversy was because of the Senator's remarks about it. Moreover, although the plaintiff was able to respond in the press to the Senator's remarks, "his access, such as it was, came after the alleged libel." In other words, the plaintiff must be a public figure prior to the alleged libel. The defendant cannot transform a private figure into a public figure merely by making accusations about the plaintiff that garner media attention.

Relying on these decisions, lower courts have developed various multi-factor tests for determining whether a plaintiff is a limited-purpose public figure. For example, the Fourth Circuit Court of Appeals has held that a defendant must prove the following in order to establish that the plaintiff is a limited-purpose public figure: (1) the plaintiff has access to channels of effective communication, (2) the plaintiff voluntarily assumed a role of special prominence in the public controversy, (3) the plaintiff sought to influence the resolution or outcome of the controversy, (4) the controversy existed prior to the publication of the defamatory statement, and (5) the plaintiff retained public figure status at the time of the alleged defamation. (Reuber v. Food Chemical News, Inc., 1991) This multi-factor test represents a reasonable and necessary attempt to synthesize the Supreme Court's sometimes confusing case law on limited-purpose public figures.

INVOLUNTARY PUBLIC FIGURES

The last category of public figure is the involuntary public figure. This category comes from dicta in the *Gertz* case, in which the Supreme Court speculated: "Hypothetically it may be possible for someone to become a public figure through no purposeful action of his own." The Supreme Court has thus far left the definition of the category to the lower courts. Yet the lower courts have split on how to define involuntary public figures and, indeed, whether the category even continues to exist. (Compare, for example, Clyburn v. News World Communications, Inc., 1990; Marcone v. Penthouse Int'l Magazine, 1985; Schultz v. Readers Digest Ass'n, 1979) One approach is represented by Dameron v. Washington Magazine, Inc. A plane crashed when Dameron was the sole air-traffic controller on duty, although subsequent investigations absolved him of any blame for the crash. Eight years later, however, a magazine article attributed the crash to controller error. The District of Columbia Circuit Court of Appeals held that Dameron was an involuntary public figure for purposes of discussion of the crash, and therefore his libel action failed for lack of proof of actual malice on the part of the magazine. The D.C. Circuit concluded that even though Dameron had taken no voluntary actions, "[t]here was indisputably a public controversy" in which "Dameron played a central role." Thus, the court concluded that a person may become a public figure simply by being in the wrong place at the wrong time.

This logic applies to people like Richard Jewell, who was falsely reported to have planted the bomb that killed two and injured 110 during the 1996 Olympics. Jewell, far from being the culprit, was actually a hero. He was the security guard who spotted the bomb and prevented more people from being injured. Nonetheless, the mere fact that he happened to become caught up in a newsworthy event would make him an involuntary public figure under the logic of *Dameron*. However, a Georgia appellate court went even further and determined that Jewell was a "voluntary limited-purpose public figure," basing the decision in part on his willingness to be interviewed by the media after the bombing. (Atlanta Journal-Constitution v. Jewell, 2001)

Wells v. Liddy, a recent case from the Fourth Circuit Court of Appeals, takes issue with the *Dameron* approach on the grounds that it "rest[s] involuntary public figure status upon 'sheer bad luck.'" According to the Fourth Circuit, the relevant factors in determining involuntary public figure status are (1) whether the allegedly defamatory statement arose in the context of a discussion of a "significant public controversy" in which the plaintiff was a "central figure," and (2) whether the plaintiff "assumed the risk of publicity." A plaintiff assumes the risk of publicity by "pursu[ing] a course of conduct from which it was reasonably foreseeable, at the time of the conduct, that public interest would arise." The court also demanded that, as in the case of limited-purpose public figures, the controversy must pre-exist the defamation, and the plaintiff must "retain public figure status at the time of the alleged defamation." The *Liddy* court was thus much more careful than the *Dameron* court not to conflate public interest in an individual with that individual's involvement in a public controversy. As of yet, however, the number of cases dealing with involuntary public figures is so small that it makes it impossible to say which approach will win more adherents.

THE CONSTITUTIONAL STANDARDS IN ACTION

To understand the effects of these decisions on modern defamation law, one must appreciate the difficulties that plaintiffs face in proving actual malice and falsity. The actual malice standard is designed to prevent juries from imposing crippling liability on unpopular defendants for minor mistakes of fact. Negligent, and even grossly negligent, publication of defamatory falsehoods is protected in cases involving public officials and public figures. It is only intentional or reckless falsehoods that subject a defendant to liability. Without "breathing space" around erroneous statements of fact, the threat of libel actions would unduly chill speakers who fear they may not be able to prove the truth of their statements or fear "the expense of having to do so." (New York Times Co. v. Sullivan, 1964)

In order for a plaintiff to establish actual malice, the Supreme Court has said that "[t]here must be sufficient evidence to permit the conclusion that the defendant in fact entertained serious doubts as to the truth of his publication." (St. Amant v. Thompson, 1968) In other words, actual malice focuses on the mental state of the defendant at the time of publication, his subjective awareness of falsity. Actual malice may be found, for example, where the defendant invents a story, bases it on "an unverified anonymous telephone call," publishes information "so inherently improbable that only a reckless man would have put [it] in circulation," or where the defendant publishes despite "obvious reasons to doubt the veracity of [an] informant or the accuracy of his reports." (St. Amant v. Thompson, 1968)

In addition to these examples of when actual malice may be found, the Supreme Court has given many examples of when it may not. First, a plaintiff cannot prove actual malice merely by showing that the defendant failed to investigate fully before publication; however, "the purposeful avoidance of the truth is in a different category." (Harte-Hanks Communications, Inc. v. Connaughton, 1989) Thus, the plaintiff may be able to show actual malice by showing that the defendant failed to confirm a story provided by a known liar when the sources that would confirm or deny the story were readily available. Second, the plaintiff cannot show actual malice by showing only that the defendant acted out of bad motive, ill will, or spite (i.e., common law malice), though these can be relevant to show knowledge or reckless disregard of falsity when coupled with other evidence. By the same token, the defendant's lack of objectivity, the adoption of a sarcastic tone, the reliance on a single source, or the misinterpretation of available data will not, by themselves, be enough to establish actual malice. (Time, Inc. v. Pape, 1971) Finally, the plaintiff may not show actual malice by establishing that the defendant knew of a mere technical falsehood in the publication. Thus, even a showing that a reporter deliberately altered a direct quotation by the plaintiff is not a showing of actual malice unless the material meaning is changed in a way that is defamatory. (Masson v. New Yorker Magazine, 1991) As this list makes clear, mere professional negligence, or neglect of good journalistic practices, does not equate with actual malice. In fact, the Supreme Court has said that actual malice cannot be shown by proof of even "highly unreasonable conduct constituting an extreme departure from the standards of investigation and reporting ordinarily adhered to by responsible publishers." (Curtis Publ'g Co. v. Butts, 1967)

Despite the formidable hurdle plaintiffs must overcome to prove actual malice, they can sometimes do so by presenting cumulative bits of evidence from which the defendant's subjective awareness of falsity can be inferred. In Curtis Publishing Co. v. Butts, the three Justices who addressed the actual malice issue found sufficient evidence of actual malice to support plaintiff's judgment based on: (1) the defendant's stated intention to "muckrake," (2) its "slipshod and sketchy investigatory techniques," (3) the fact that the piece was not time-sensitive, (4) the source's credibility problems, (5) the journalist's lack of expertise in sports reporting coupled with his failure to consult experts, and (6) the fact that the plaintiff gave notice of the falsity of the piece prior to publication. It was the cumulative effect of these individual pieces of evidence that added up to actual malice; any one of them standing alone would not constitute actual malice. Indeed, even the inclusion of the defendant's stated intention to muckrake as one of the factors is problematic. The D.C. Circuit, for instance, held that evidence that a newspaper encouraged reporters to find sensational stories "cannot, as a matter of law, constitute evidence of actual malice" because "the First Amendment forbids penalizing the press for encouraging its reporters to expose wrongdoing by public corporations and public figures." (Tavoulareas v. Piro, 1987)

Even if a plaintiff has evidence of a defendant's actual malice, that evidence must be sufficient to allow a reasonable jury to find actual malice with convincing clarity. Convincing clarity is a higher standard than preponderance of the evidence, but it is a lower standard than beyond a reasonable doubt, the standard used in criminal cases. The convincing clarity requirement might not be such a benefit to defendants if it were only applied by juries, for it is not clear how much weight juries would give to a slight difference in verbal formulas. Judges, however, give great weight to the standard in independently reviewing the evidence of actual malice, as they are constitutionally compelled to do. Moreover, the Supreme Court has held that federal courts must apply heightened standards of proof, like the convincing clarity standard, when deciding summary judgment motions. (Anderson v. Liberty Lobby, Inc., 1986) The convincing clarity standard thus helps defendants to defeat libel actions before trial and not have to face potentially hostile and unpredictable juries.

Even so, media defendants must often engage in costly and intrusive litigation prior to the entry of summary judgment in their favor.[12] Because actual malice focuses on the mental state of the defendant, it relies heavily on circumstantial evidence. To obtain the relevant facts, the plaintiff is allowed to inquire into editorial discussion and practices that resulted in publication. Not only does this type of discovery disrupt the newsroom and interfere with relationships with sources, it is highly costly as well. Because it is so fact-intensive, it does not lend itself to early resolution. In fact, some libel cases against the media have dragged on for 10 or 15 years before being resolved on the grounds that there was insufficient evidence of actual malice. (See, e.g., Herbert v. Lando, 1979) The practical operation of the actual malice regime therefore threatens to chill freedom of expression, even though media losses in libel suits are quite rare.

Probably the largest source of the chilling effect that libel law imposes on media defendants stems from the prospect, albeit remote, of having to pay a huge verdict. Even though plaintiffs rarely prevail against the media, the damages can be in the millions when they do. Recall that in a case in which plaintiff proves actual malice, which will be most cases against media defendants, damages may be presumed. This allows juries to award damages based on "supposed damage to reputation without any proof that such harm actually occurred," limited only by their own "discretion." (Gertz v. Robert Welch, Inc., 1974) Moreover, the plaintiff who is able to successfully prove actual malice will often be able to seek punitive damages as well, further magnifying the damages. Although the media have applauded the constitutionalization of defamation law, it certainly did not eliminate the threat libel law poses to freedom of expression.

CONSTITUTIONAL PRIVILEGES TO DEFAMATION ACTIONS

A privilege is a defense to a defamation action. If a defendant can successfully plead and prove that his defamatory publication was privileged, he can escape liability for defamation. The common law created a variety of privileges to protect defendants from libel actions. Some of these common law privileges were explicitly designed to protect what we might think of as "First Amendment" values. For example, the fair and accurate report privilege protects the media from liability for defamatory statements made in the course of "a report of an official action or proceeding or of a meeting open to the public that deals with a matter of public concern . . . if the report is accurate and complete or a fair abridgement of the occurrence reported." (Medico v. Time, 1981 (quoting Restatement (Second) of Torts Sec. 611)) The purpose of this privilege is to encourage reporting on the operation of government, and it insulates the media from liability when its actions are consistent with this purpose.

Constitutional privileges operate similarly to common law privileges. The most important constitutional privilege is the "opinion privilege"—the privilege that protects statements that do not imply an assertion of objective fact. This constitutional privilege originated with Gertz v. Robert Welch, Inc., in which the Supreme Court stated: "Under the First Amendment, there is no such thing as a false idea. However pernicious an opinion may seem, we depend for its correction not on the conscience of judges and juries but on the competition of other ideas." Lower courts seized this dictum as evidence that opinion, traditionally protected by a common law privilege called fair comment, deserved expansive First Amendment protection. The opinion privilege soon became a powerful defense to counter the chilling effects of libel actions on the media. Unlike other privileges, the opinion privilege could be deployed by filing a motion to dismiss the plaintiff's complaint. The judge would decide as a matter of law whether the alleged defamatory statements were opinion, and, if so, costly litigation could be avoided.

"Opinion" in its ordinary sense includes statements couched in loose, figurative, or vituperative language, statements that are purely subjective expressions of an author's point of view, and statements that contain "deductions from known data or personal observation.[13] After *Gertz*, it was not clear which of these types of opinion were constitutionally protected. Although the Supreme Court did indicate that hyperbole and vituperation are protected by the First Amendment, its *Gertz* dictum did not give lower courts guidance in separating fact from opinion. Left to their own devices, lower courts adopted various approaches, the most influential of which was that of the D.C. Circuit Court of Appeals in Ollman v. Evans. Writing for the court, then-Judge Ken Starr identified four factors that, when considered along with the "totality of the circumstances," should guide courts in distinguishing fact from opinion: (1) the meaning of the language of the challenged statements, (2) the verifiability of the statements, (3) their linguistic context, and (4) the broader social context. Yet just when courts appeared to be reaching a consensus in applying this eminently reasonable approach, the Supreme Court stepped in and threw the opinion privilege into disarray.

Sixteen years after its delphic dictum in *Gertz*, the Supreme Court addressed the opinion privilege issue in Milkovich v. Lorain Journal Co. The plaintiff in *Milkovich* was a high school wrestling coach from Maple Heights, Ohio, whose team was involved in a fight that broke out during a wrestling match. After a hearing in which the coach and his superintendent testified, the Ohio High School Athletic Association censured Coach Milkovich and placed his team on probation due to their role in the altercation. Several wrestlers and their parents sued the association claiming a lack of due process. The judge agreed, and after a hearing at which Milkovich and his superintendent testified, overturned the association's decision.

The next day, sports columnist Thomas Diadiun harshly criticized Coach Milkovich. The heading for Diadiun's column was, "Maple beat the law with the 'big lie.'" Diadiun made it clear in the column that he had attended both the match at which the brawl had taken place and the subsequent association hearing. Diadiun wrote: "Anyone who attended the meet, whether he be from Maple Heights, Mentor [the rival team], or impartial observer, knows in his heart that Milkovich and [Superintendent] Scott lied at the [court] hearing after each having given his solemn oath to tell the truth." Diadiun concluded with the rhetorical question: "Is that the kind of lesson we want our young people learning from their high school administrators and coaches? I think not." (Milkovich v. Lorain Journal Co., 1990)

Milkovich and Scott brought separate libel actions, both alleging that the column accused them of perjury. The Ohio Supreme Court upheld a grant summary judgment against Scott on the grounds that the sports column was "constitutionally protected opinion." (Scott v. News-Herald, 1986) Subsequently, the Ohio Court of Appeals upheld a summary judgment against Milkovich on the same basis. (Milkovich v. News-Herald, 1989) Both decisions reached this conclusion based on the four-factor test for opinion laid out in Ollman v. Evans.

Milkovich appealed to the Supreme Court, and in a stinging rejection of the *Ollman* approach, the United States Supreme Court reversed. The Supreme Court chastised the lower courts for misreading *Gertz* "to create a wholesale defamation exemption for anything that might be labeled 'opinion.'" For the Court, the operative distinction was not the distinction between fact and opinion, but the distinction between statements that imply an assertion of objective fact and those that do not. The Court rejected the fact/opinion distinction as artificial because a statement of opinion will often imply the existence of objective facts harmful to reputation. Hence, the Court declared, the statement "'In my opinion Jones is a liar,'" can be just as damaging to reputation as the statement "'Jones is a liar.'" The first statement may imply a false assertion of fact because it invites the audience to assume the author is privy to factual information that is defamatory. Even if the author states the underlying facts on which her conclusion is based, she can still be liable for defamation if the underlying facts are incorrect or if she draws erroneous conclusions from them. Therefore, statements clearly denoted as the author's "point of view" can still be defamatory if they imply factual assertions that are defamatory and untrue.

Despite its rejection of the fact/opinion distinction, the Supreme Court did not reject the notion that the First Amendment protects opinion on matters of public concern. Instead, the Court found adequate protection for opinion (defined as statements that do not imply an assertion of objective fact) in existing First Amendment doctrine. Two of the doctrines identified by the Court are relevant to the question of whether a statement implies an assertion of objective fact and thus define, albeit in an indirect manner, what counts as constitutionally protected opinion. First is the doctrine that requires both public figure and private figure plaintiffs to prove falsity in all defamation actions involving matters of public concern. This protects opinion because statements not capable of being proved false are not actionable. In other words, statements that are not provably false are one form of protected opinion. The second doctrine that protects opinion is the requirement that the defendant not be held liable for speech that cannot reasonably be interpreted as stating actual facts. The Court gleaned this requirement from its prior cases protecting rhetorical hyperbole, satire, and parody—all of which the Court characterized as "nonfactual" and therefore another form of protected opinion. The justification for protecting statements that cannot be interpreted as stating actual facts is so "that public debate will not suffer for lack of 'imaginative expression.'"

The *Milkovich* decision thus confirms that the First Amendment protects at least two kinds of opinion: statements that are not capable of being proved false and statements that cannot reasonably be interpreted as asserting actual facts. However, the decision suffers from a critical flaw because it fails to specify the role of context in interpreting whether a statement implies an assertion of objective fact (and is therefore not protected as opinion). Certainly context is relevant to the determination of whether a statement is rhetorical hyperbole, satire, or parody. The statement that "Brutus is an honourable man," standing alone, appears to be complimentary, but every reasonable reader of Shakespeare's *Julius Caesar* knows that, read in context, the statement means just the opposite. Accusing Dr. Smith of murder sounds like a factual statement, unless the audience knows that the statement is made by an abortion protestor criticizing Smith for performing abortions; then, the statement is merely rhetorical hyperbole.

The decisions the Supreme Court relied on in *Milkovich* as a basis for protecting nonfactual expression either implicitly or explicitly recognize the importance of context, but *Milkovich* itself apparently does not. The Court's analysis of *Milkovich* stressed the verifiability of the statements made in the defendant Diadiun's sports column rather than their context. As the Court noted, whether Coach Milkovich committed perjury could be objectively verified "by comparing, inter alia, [his] testimony before the [association] with his subsequent testimony before the trial court." The Court also observed that neither the *language* of the column nor its *general tenor* negated the impression that Diadiun was accusing Milkovich of perjury. Justice Brennan, dissenting, criticized the Court's analysis for failing to take account of the broader social context in which the accusation had been made. Specifically, the fact that the accusations had appeared in a signed editorial sports column, the tone of which was "pointed, exaggerated, and heavily laden with emotional rhetoric and moral outrage," should have signaled that Diadiun's accusations were hyperbole.

Not surprisingly, the *Milkovich* decision has created confusion in lower courts attempting to define the scope of the constitutional privilege for opinion. Some courts continue to rely heavily on context in assessing whether an allegedly defamatory statement implies an assertion of objective fact. Other courts downplay context in favor of verifiability, as the Court did in the *Milkovich* decision itself. Still others have rejected *Milkovich* entirely, holding that their own state constitutions or the common law require an *Ollman*-type "totality of circumstances" (See, e,g., Phantom Touring, Inc. v. Affiliated Publ'ns, 1992) approach to separating opinion from fact. Needless to say, the confusion generated by the *Milkovich* decision makes it difficult to predict in advance what role context will play in the outcome of any particular defamation action.[14]

One final constitutional privilege is worthy of note. In order to understand this rule, however, one must understand the so-called "republication rule." At common law, the person who republishes or repeats a defamatory communication adopts it as his own, for the purposes of defamation liability. Thus, a newspaper that publishes a defamatory letter to the editor can be liable for defamation, as can a broadcaster who broadcasts defamatory accusations by callers to a radio show. The effect of the rule is to treat the repeater of a defamatory statement as if he were the originator of the defamatory statement, thereby preventing the media from defaming at will simply by attributing defamatory statements to a third-party source. Obviously, the actual malice rule helps ameliorate the effects of the republication rule on the media, for it is only when they repeat information that they know to be false, or recklessly disregard its falsity, that they can face liability.

Of course the actual malice rule does not apply in all libel cases, and it is of no help at all in the following scenario: What if a newspaper wants to publish a quote from Vice President Dick Cheney stating that President Bush is fraudulently using campaign funds to hire space aliens to put thoughts in his head? Under the republication rule, the newspaper cannot publish the quote for fear of defamation liability, since the newspaper knows the statement to be both false and defamatory. Nonetheless the accusation itself is newsworthy, suggesting as it does delusional thinking on the part of a high government official.

The neutral reportage privilege seeks to solve this problem. As formulated by the Second Circuit Court of Appeals: "When a responsible, prominent organization . . . makes serious charges against a public figure, the First Amendment protects the accurate and disinterested reporting of those charges, regardless of the reporter's private views regarding their validity." (Edwards v. Nat'l Audubon Soc'y, 1977) In other words, the fact that the statements were made may be highly newsworthy regardless of whether they are true or not. Where the reporter simply relates the accusations, making it clear that he does not support them, he has made a contribution to public debate and should not be liable for republishing the defamatory accusations.

Despite the strength of this argument for protecting the republishing of accusations that are newsworthy in and of themselves, the United States Supreme Court has never held that the First Amendment demands recognition of the neutral reportage privilege. Many jurisdictions have rejected the privilege, while others have varied the elements of the privilege from those first laid out by the Second Circuit Court of Appeals. It seems fair to conclude, however, that the Supreme Court would allow, on First Amendment grounds, a newspaper to report truthfully that Cheney thought Bush was out to get him. Whether the Supreme Court will ever adopt a broader neutral reportage privilege, however, is anybody's guess.

Many jurisdictions allow a libel defendant's retraction of a defamatory statement to help reduce the amount of damages the defendant will have to pay. However, the (partial) defense of retraction tends to be a common law or statutory defense, not a constitutional one. A defendant may also try to reduce the damages he must pay by showing that the plaintiff's reputation was already low prior to the publication of the allegedly defamatory communication. By extension, some courts have allowed defendants to show that the plaintiff's reputation was so bad that he was essentially libel-proof. A related doctrine is the idea of incremental harm; here, the notion is that the false and defamatory part of a publication caused no worse harm than the true or privileged parts of the publication. Again, however, the Supreme Court has never held that these defenses are demanded by the First Amendment. (See, e.g., Masson v. New Yorker Magazine, 1991)

A RETROSPECTIVE: THE LEGACY OF *SULLIVAN*

Forty years after New York Times Co. v. Sullivan began the process of constitutionalizing defamation law, we are left with a system that protects the media, albeit imperfectly, from the chilling effects of the common law tort. Publishers are freer today to report on public affairs and concerns than they were in 1963. A public official or public figure is unlikely to prevail against the media when he or she has been falsely accused of infidelity, criminality, or debauchery, even if the media were grossly negligent in airing the accusation. Whether as a response to the constitutional changes in defamation law, or to larger cultural trends, commentary today seeks to plumb what were once the private depths of the personalities of public people. For example, a president's sexual liaisons before, during, and after his presidency are fair game for commentary; the president's only weapon against false accusations is rebuttal through the media, which is a partial remedy at best for reputational harm. While most First Amendment scholars celebrate the legacy of robust debate spawned by *Sullivan*, others bemoan the coarsening and cheapening of political dialogue that has accompanied it.

NOTES

1. Normally a defendant is allowed to use truth as a defense if something is "substantially true." Here, however, the trial court seems to have required "literal truth," a standard which The *New York Times* could not meet.

2. As the Court later said, "the use of the known lie as a tool is at once at odds with the premises of democratic government and with the orderly manner in which economic, social, or political change is to be effected." (Garrison v. Louisiana, 379 U.S. 64 (1964))

3. A divided Court affirmed the jury's award in favor of Butts by a 5-4 vote, on the grounds that there was adequate proof of actual malice in the trial court record. The Court reversed *Walker* unanimously.

4. The phrase is from David Elder's helpful treatise, *Defamation: A Lawyer's Guide* (Deerfield, Il.: Clark Boardman Callaghan, 1993) § 4:1, at 2.

5. For a discussion of the notion that public plaintiffs assume the risk of defamation by voluntarily participating in public affairs, see Susan M. Gilles, "From Baseball Parks to

the Public Arena: Assumption of the Risk in Tort Law and Constitutional Libel Law," 75 *Temp. L. Rev.* (2002) 231.

6. Gilles, "From Baseball Parks to the Public Arena: Assumption of the Risk in Tort Law and Constitutional Libel Law," § 6:2, p. 4 (listing states).

7. See, e.g., Restatement (Second) of Torts § 580B, cmt. G (1997).

8. Rodney A. Smolla, "Dun & Bradstreet, Hepps and Liberty Lobby: A New Analytic Primer on the Future Course of Defamation," 75 *Geo. L.J.* (1987) 1519, 1564.

9. See Lyrissa Barnett Lidsky, "Silencing John Doe: Defamation and Discourse in Cyberspace," 49 *Duke L.J.* (2000) 855, 906 (citing cases and commentators rejecting the media/non-media distinction).

10. See Gilles, "From Baseball Parks to the Public Arena: Assumption of the Risk in Tort Law and Constitutional Libel Law," 249.

11. See Elder, *Defamation: A Lawyer's Guide* § 5:6 at 44 (citing cases).

12. David A. Anderson, "Is Libel Worth Reforming?," 140 *U. Pa. L. Rev.* (1991) 487, 515 (noting that "legal fees account for about eighty percent of the total cost of libel suits against the press.").

13. Diane Leenheer Zimmerman, "Curbing the High Price of Loose Talk," 18 *U.C. Davis L. Rev.* 359, 398–99 (1985).

14. See Lyrissa Barnett Lidsky, *Silencing John Doe: Defamation & Discourse in Cyberspace*, 49 *Duke L.J.* 855 (2000) for an extensive discussion of the opinion privilege.

7

Liability for Publications that Invade Privacy or Inflict Emotional Distress

PUBLIC DISCLOSURE OF PRIVATE FACTS

Tort law in many states imposes liability on the media for giving unreasonable publicity to embarrassing private facts about an individual, for publicizing information that places the individual in a false light before the public, and for "appropriating" an individual's name or likeness for its own use or benefit. Tort law also imposes liability for the intentional infliction of emotional distress, by publication or otherwise. As with the torts of libel and slander, however, the Supreme Court has imposed constitutional limits on these torts in order to protect press freedom. These limits define how far the media may delve into the intimate lives of the people they cover, how viciously or outrageously they may parody or satirize their targets, and how much they may "use" people for profit. As the reader might glean from a casual perusal of current media fare, the limits set by the Court allow little leeway for tort law to impose liability for invading privacy or inflicting emotional distress.

Unlike the common law tort of defamation, the torts protecting privacy against media invasions are a comparatively recent legal development. Their origin was an 1890 article, "The Right of Privacy," in which Louis D. Brandeis and his law partner Samuel Warren argued for a common law "right to be let alone."[1] In the article, which has been termed "perhaps the most famous and certainly the most influential law review article ever written,"[2] the authors lamented the development of journalism that pandered to the masses by invading privacy:

Gossip is no longer the resource of the idle and of the vicious, but has become a trade which is pursued with industry as well as effrontery. To satisfy a prurient taste the details of sexual relations are spread broadcast in the columns of the daily papers. To occupy the indolent, column upon column is filled with idle gossip, which can only be procured by intrusion upon the domestic circle. . . . When personal gossip attains the dignity of print, and crowds the space available for matters of real interest to the community, what wonder that the ignorant and thoughtless mistake its relative importance.[3]

From a twenty-first century standpoint, the authors' language sounds elitist. It is the "indolent," the "ignorant," and the "thoughtless," who are entertained by "personal gossip" rather than "matters of real interest to the community."[4] Yet they correctly identify the central challenge in striking a balance between privacy and press freedom. Courts that recognize a right of privacy must inevitably make normative judgments about what information the public *ought* to have, and must often curtail the right of the press to provide the public with information it desires.

Despite this challenge, Warren and Brandeis' article inspired many states to begin protecting a "right to be let alone." Indeed, when Professor William L. Prosser surveyed the privacy case law in 1960, he found that states had recognized four distinct torts: (1) intrusion upon an individual's solitude or seclusion, (2) publicity given to embarrassing private facts, (3) publicity that places an individual in a false light in the public eye, and (4) commercial exploitation of an individual's name or likeness.[5] Five years later, the American Law Institute incorporated this four-fold division into its influential summary or synthesis of tort law, the Restatement (Second) of Torts. The *Second Restatement*, which includes definitions, examples, and explanations of all four privacy torts, influenced even more states to either recognize the four torts or to develop their privacy torts consistently with its definitions. (See, e.g., Olan Mills v. Dodd, 1962; Lovgren v. Citizens First Nat'l Bank, 1989; McCormack v. Okla. Publ'g Co., 1980)

Of the four torts—intrusion, private facts, false light, and commercial appropriation—the last three focus on the defendant's *publication* of privacy-invading information. Indeed, mass dissemination to the public at large is a required element of both the private facts tort and the false light tort, and commercial appropriation claims are almost inevitably based on the publication of a plaintiff's name or likeness. These torts, then, were developed specifically to deal with invasions of privacy by the mass media. However, because their formative period was the twentieth century, a concern for press freedom is built into the structure of the torts, rather than being merely superimposed by Supreme Court decisions.

Consider, for example, the private facts tort, which imposes liability on the publication of truthful but privacy-invading information. In order to establish a case for public disclosure of private facts, the Restatement Second specifies that a plaintiff must show that the defendant (1) gave publicity to (2) a matter concerning plaintiff's private life (3) whose publication would be "highly offensive to a reasonable person," and (4) "not of legitimate public concern."[6] As discussed above, simply revealing a private matter to a few individuals is not enough to make a defendant liable for public disclosure of private facts; the tort protects not against water cooler gossips but against widespread exposure. (But *cf.* Beaumont v. Brown, 1977)

Moreover, if liability is to be imposed, the matter publicized must be private. Courts have held that a matter in the public records, such as an arrest record, a conviction, or the fact that an individual was the victim of a crime or the owner of real property, are not ordinarily private matters. By definition, these matters are open to the public if they choose to look. Thus, from an objective standpoint, one has no expectation of privacy in them. By extension of this logic, courts have held that widespread dissemination of information available through public records does not make the media liable for invasion of privacy, even though it is likely to be more objectionable to the person about whom the information is published. (See, e.g., Uganda v. Federated Publ'ns, Inc., 2003) Courts have also held that it is not highly offensive to broadcast or report on matters that occur in public places. (But see Daily Times Democrat v. Graham, 1964) Those who go out in public assume the risk of being observed, and, according to the law, they thereby assume the risk of having their conversations broadcast or pictures disseminated to a mass audience.

In analyzing whether a published matter is private, courts give great weight to the plaintiff's own actions taken to preserve her privacy. If the plaintiff divulged the matter to a large group of friends and acquaintances, the matter can lose its "private" status. On the other hand, simply divulging a private matter—such as the fact that one is HIV positive—to a small group of family and close friends does not make it a public matter. An interesting recent case on this issue was Michaels v. Internet Entertainment Group, which involved the actress Pamela Anderson Lee, known for marketing her sexuality as part of her public persona. The defendant, an adult entertainment corporation, obtained a video of Lee having sex with her boyfriend, who then sued to obtain an injunction to prevent further public disclosure of private facts. A federal district court rejected the contention that Lee had lost her right to privacy because she had appeared nude in magazines and movies and because she had allegedly distributed a different videotape showing her having sex with her then-husband Tommy Lee. The Court stated that it was "not prepared to conclude that public exposure of one sexual encounter forever removes a person's privacy interest in all subsequent and previous encounters." The Court further noted that the "visual and aural details of . . . sexual relations . . . are ordinarily considered private even for celebrities." The Court therefore granted a preliminary injunction against further publication of the videotape. As this case demonstrates, celebrities may have a smaller expectation of privacy than the average citizen, but even celebrities should be free from some forms of unwarranted media invasions.[7]

Even so, determining whether a matter is private is rarely the most difficult element of the private facts tort. The most difficult element is the one that requires the plaintiff to prove the published information was not of public concern. Courts have had great difficulty in formulating standards for determining what sorts of information are of legitimate public concern. (See Schulman v. Group W Prods.,

Inc., 1998) The privilege for matters of legitimate concern rests on the premise that the media should not be punished for publishing information typically considered news. Some courts have recognized that what is newsworthy is "in the last analysis . . . a matter of community mores" and have given great deference to jury determinations on this issue. (See, e.g., Green v. Chicago Tribune Co., 1997; Nobles v. Cartwright, 1995; Montesano v. Donrey Media Group, 1983) The more popular approach, however, is to define newsworthiness descriptively. Under this approach, courts look at whether the public actually is interested in the information, not whether the public ought to be interested.[8] Yet when courts make the "reasonable editor" the standard for determining what is of legitimate public concern, the private facts torts becomes a toothless remedy for plaintiffs whose privacy has been invaded. Courts end up deferring to the media's judgments about newsworthiness, in essence allowing the media to create their "own definition of news."[9] The end result is that only in the extreme case will the standard be met.

Even if a plaintiff could overcome the common law (tort) obstacles to recover, the Supreme Court has made the constitutional obstacles almost insurmountable. In Cox Broadcasting v. Cohn, a television station obtained the name of a deceased teenage rape victim when a court clerk allowed a reporter to see documents containing the victim's name. The station broadcast the girl's name and her father sued. Although actions for invasion of privacy do not usually survive the death of the person whose privacy was invaded, the dead girl's father's tort suit was based on a Georgia statute making it a crime to publish or broadcast the name of a rape victim. The Supreme Court held that states may not award damages based "on the accurate publication of the name of a rape victim obtained from public records." (Cox Broad. v. Cohn, 1975) Once information appears in a public record, the Court reasoned, any privacy interests automatically fade, for "the State must be presumed to have concluded that the public interest was thereby being served" by placing the information in the records in the first place. Not only is it unfair to punish the press for publication of information obtained from government records; the Court also feared imposing liability would chill the press from "inform[ing] citizens about the public business." The rationale appears to be two-fold: Information in the public record is not private by definition, and it is inherently a matter of public concern. Hence, the press is absolutely privileged in accurately publishing information obtained from open court records.

The Court in *Cox Broadcasting* acted as if the reporter obtained the name from an open public record, even though the reporter obtained the name because a clerk decided to reveal it; it is not at all clear that any public citizen could have obtained the name at will. Moreover, the clerk probably showed the reporter the document assuming that the reporter would not publish the name. Nonetheless, it is clear that the decision in *Cox Broadcasting* makes it impossible for plaintiffs to recover in cases in which the media obtain information from open public records. The significance of this absolute privilege has expanded as technology has made more and more public records available via the Internet.[10] Many public records that were once available only by going to a dusty courthouse basement and making a request of the clerk are now available via Internet search engines. Meanwhile, technology also has allowed the government to collect more and more information about its citizens, thereby magnifying the risk that formerly private information will become public.

The Supreme Court's most recent private facts decision makes recovery for public disclosure of private facts even more difficult. In Florida Star v. B.J.F., a rape victim sued after her name mistakenly appeared in the police beat section of a local newspaper. The newspaper had obtained her name from an erroneously released police report. The newspaper then published the name in violation of its own policy guidelines. B.J.F. was a highly sympathetic plaintiff. After her name was published, a man called her mother to say he would rape B.J.F. again. As a result, B.J.F. moved from her home and sought psychiatric counseling. B.J.F. therefore sued, asserting that the newspaper was negligent *per se* in violating a Florida statute prohibiting mass dissemination of a rape victim's name.

The Supreme Court nonetheless denied B.J.F. recovery, holding that where the press "lawfully obtains truthful information about a matter of public significance then state officials may not constitutionally punish publication of the information, absent a need to further a state interest of the highest order." (Florida Star v. B.J.F., 1989 (quoting Smith v. Daily Mail Publ'g Co., 1979)) The Court found the imposition of tort liability to be a form of "punishment" prohibited by the First Amendment. The Court explicitly distinguished the case from Cox Broadcasting v. Cohn because the information was obtained from a police report rather than "courthouse records that were open to public inspection." The fact that the information was lawfully obtained, but not obtained from a public *court* record, led the Court to extend only a conditional privilege, rather than an absolute one, to its publication.[11] (See Smith v. Daily Mail Publ'g Co., 1979; Okla. Publ'g Co. v. District Court of Okla., 1977) Theoretically, the decision leaves open the possibility that a state might impose liability for the publication of truthful information. Practically, however, the decision makes clear that rarely will information be deemed "unlawfully obtained," rarely will privacy be deemed a "state interest of the highest order," and rarely will a private matter fail to be "of public significance."[12]

Consider the application of the announced standard to the facts of *B.J.F.* The Court found that the defendant newspaper lawfully obtained B.J.F.'s name from police records, even though the police department's inadvertent release of her name was tortious and against government policy, and even though Florida law made publication of a rape victim's name a criminal offense. Again, the Court focused on the chilling effect that imposing tort liability might have on coverage of government affairs. (Florida Star v. B.J.F., 1989) The Court reasoned that press self-censorship would result if the press were forced to sort through information it obtains from the government or to make editorial judgments about what information is okay to publish (which, of course, it does all the time). Therefore, the Court concluded that once the government releases information it implicitly represents to the media that "the government consider[s] dissemination lawful, and indeed expect[s] the recipients to disseminate the information further." (Florida Star v. B.J.F., 1989)

The Court also rejected the argument that imposing tort liability on public disclosure of rape victim's name served "a need to further a state interest of the highest order." The Court said that protecting the privacy and safety of rape victims and encouraging them to report rape were "highly significant interests." However, the Court faulted the state for having chosen "too precipitous a means of advancing these interests." The proper way for the state to have solved the problem, said the Court, was to prevent the police from releasing the name in the first place. And even if the state wished to impose tort liability, it would have to require case-by-case findings, similar to those required by the common law private facts tort, and it would also have to require scienter (that is, a culpable mental state) on the part of the defendant. Finally, the method of imposing tort liability in the case was improper because it only prohibited publication of a rape victim's name in an "instrument of mass communication," leaving the interests the statute claimed to protect only partially protected. The Court therefore concluded that the state's "selective ban" on publication was not narrowly tailored to its purposes.

Although the Court claims its decision is limited, it is hard to envision a situation after *B.J.F.* in which a state could impose tort liability for publication of truthful private facts. Although the common law tort of public disclosure of private facts does require individualized factual finding, it does not specifically require scienter. And even if B.J.F. had chosen to sue for public disclosure of private facts, she still would have lost her case because the police department failed in the first instance to protect her name. Moreover, as Professor David Anderson has observed, *B.J.F.* compounds the difficulties plaintiffs face by forcing them to defend the methods that their state has chosen to protect their interest.[13] After all, it was B.J.F. who was required to identify the state interests supporting the Florida statute and to argue that it was narrowly tailored enough to protect those interests.

If this were not enough to deter all but the most determined plaintiffs, the Supreme Court has subsequently defined the parameters of the term "lawfully obtained" even more broadly. Bartnicki v. Vopper confirms that privacy interests often must give way to the First Amendment even when the press knowingly accepts material whose release was illegal or contrary to government policy. Under ordinary legal principles, a person who knowingly accepts stolen property may be criminally liable.[14] But under the Court's recent decision in *Bartnicki*, if the media knowingly accepts information that was illegally obtained by someone else, they cannot be liable for publishing it, at least where the information concerns a matter of public interest. In *Bartnicki* a radio station broadcast a conversation that it allegedly knew had been intercepted and recorded in violation of federal and state wiretapping laws. By *broadcasting* the intercepted information, the radio station itself violated the provisions of the wiretap statutes. Nevertheless, the Supreme Court cast the issue as whether the government could punish the publication of information of public interest that had been obtained "in a manner lawful in itself from a source who has obtained it unlawfully." (Bartnicki v. Vopper, 2001) The Court then held that punishment for publication was unconstitutional. Again the Court found that the proper remedy was to punish the first wrongdoer (in this case, the interceptor) rather than the recipient and subsequent publisher of the information. Even so, it is not clear how broadly the *Bartnicki* decision should be construed. Two of the justices in the majority wrote separate concurrences to emphasize the "special circumstances" in the case that made the Court's holding a narrow one. They noted specifically that the plaintiffs in the case were public figures whose taped conversation involved a "threat of potential physical harm to others" and that the media defendant did not participate in the eavesdropping. (Breyer, J. and O'Connor, J., concurring) Moreover, the Court still refused to reach the question whether imposing tort liability on the publication or broadcast of truthful information of public significance could ever be constitutional, although certainly *Bartnicki* adds to the already long odds against it.

FALSE LIGHT

The tort of false light protects the plaintiff's right to put forth an accurate image of themselves before the public and to not have the image sullied by falsehoods that would be offensive to a reasonable person. In a false light action, therefore, plaintiffs must prove that the defendant has given "publicity to a matter concerning another that places the other before the public in a false light," and that the "false light in which the other was placed would be highly offensive to a reasonable person."[15] As in defamation actions, the First Amendment also requires the plaintiff to prove falsity and fault, although, as we shall see, the Supreme Court has failed to clarify whether all of the constitutional limits on defamation actions apply with equal vigor to false light actions.

The following scenario raises a fairly typical example of false light. *The Hurricane* is a movie which relates the true story of the unjust imprisonment of an African-American boxer, Rubin "Hurricane" Carter, for a murder he did not commit. The movie opens with a "reenactment" of the 1964 boxing match between Carter and Joey Giardello, a Hall of Fame boxer of the 1950s and 1960s.[16] In the movie version, Giardello is unjustly awarded victory because he is white; in reality, Giardello was the clear winner. Upset by his portrayal in the film, Giardello filed suit for false light, claiming the movie inaccurately portrayed him as a poor boxer and beneficiary of a racist decision. It is important to note here that Giardello could not have sued for defamation: There is no reputation-damaging moral opprobrium attached to being a weak fighter or to being the recipient of an unjust award. But Giardello claimed that the film caused him shame and embarrassment and tainted his legacy as a great boxer. The defendant, Universal Pictures, ultimately settled the case and modified the film somewhat to set the record straight in subsequent releases.

As this case demonstrates, fictional embellishments to a true story can lead to false light actions, and this is true even if the light in which the plaintiff is portrayed is largely a positive one. The goal of false light is to protect an individual's right to "inviolate personality." It gives the individual a cause of action when she is falsely associated with views she does not hold; falsely held up as an object of pity or sympathy; falsely associated with a product she does not endorse; or more generally, falsely and offensively depicted as "something or someone she is not." As in defamation, a plaintiff can recover in a false light action for both harm to reputation and for humiliation, shame, and emotional suffering as well as for any concrete monetary losses.

In fact, the false light tort often overlaps with the tort of defamation, a factor leading several state courts to reject false light as unnecessary. (See, e.g., Denver Publ'g Co. v. Bueno, 2002; ELM Medical Lab v. RKO General, Inc., 1989; Renwick v. News & Observer Publ'g Co. 1984) If a newspaper publishes a story falsely labeling Senator Hillary Clinton as a former member of the National Rifle Association, Senator Clinton would likely be aggrieved. Being labeled an NRA member would not ordinarily harm someone's reputation; after all, it is a lawful organization supported by many Americans. But in the case of Senator Clinton, the attribution makes her appear to be a hypocrite, since she has publicly favored gun control. More to the point, the false attribution might very well harm her with the liberal voters who are her core constituents. Could Clinton bring a false light action, a defamation action, or both? Clearly she was portrayed in a false light (that would arguably be highly offensive to a reasonable person), but she could also bring a defamation action claiming that although it is not normally defamatory to say that a person is a member of the NRA, it injured her reputation amongst the voters she most valued and, moreover, created the impression that she was a hypocrite. Even if Clinton chose to bring both a defamation claim and a false light claim, she can only get one full recovery of her damages. So why might she still choose to pursue a false light action?

The answer is that she might choose a false light claim because it lacks some of the constitutional and common law obstacles to plaintiffs' success that plague the defamation tort. In some states, for example, defamation plaintiffs must prove special damages—specific monetary losses that resulted from publication—if the defamatory sting of a publication is not obvious on its face. Moreover, the Supreme Court requires proof of falsity and fault in all defamation cases involving matters of public concern, although the requisite fault depends on the status of the plaintiff. If plaintiffs were able to avoid these requirements simply by choosing to sue for false light rather than defamation, it would encourage an "end run" around the First Amendment.

The United States Supreme Court foresaw and partially prevented this problem in its first false light case, Time, Inc. v. Hill. The plaintiffs in *Time* sued *Life* magazine for violation of New York's statutory "right of privacy." A *Life* article falsely claimed that a new play was a "re-enactment" of a real-life hostage crisis involving the Hills. The hostages in the play were brutalized and degraded. In reality, the Hills had been treated humanely by their captors. Although the suit seemed rather trivial, a jury initially awarded the plaintiffs substantial damages. However, the Supreme Court later reversed, on the ground that states may not award damages "to redress false reports of matters of public interest in the absence of proof that the defendant published the report with knowledge of its falsity or reckless disregard of the truth." In other words, the Court extended New York Times Co. v. Sullivan's actual malice rule to false light cases. The Court's reasoning was parallel to the reasoning being developed in defamation cases: Errors are inevitable in free debate on matters of public interest, and the press must have breathing space to protect it from liability for such "inevitable" errors.

Yet dicta in the Supreme Court's second false light case suggests that, though the logic of Time, Inc. v. Hill is sound, its specific holding may no longer be. In Cantrell v. Forest City Publishing Co., a newspaper article purported to contain an interview with plaintiff Margaret Cantrell, when in fact she had not been at home when the reporter came to her house. Cantrell was the widow of a disaster victim, and the article as a whole discussed the suffering that she and her children had experienced as a result of the disaster. She objected not only to the fabricated interview but also to the reporter's exaggerated descriptions of her family's poverty, claiming she and her son suffered shame and humiliation as a result. A jury agreed.

The timing of the *Cantrell* case is significant, because the Court decided Gertz v. Robert Welch the same term. In *Gertz*, the Court held that in defamation cases involving matters of public concern, states may impose liability based on a lower fault standard than actual malice, so long as they require plaintiffs to show actual injury. Like *Gertz,* the *Cantrell* case involved a matter of public concern (a bridge disaster). By analogy, then, states ought to be able to allow plaintiffs to recover for false light without proof of actual malice. Yet the issue never arose in *Cantrell* because the jury was instructed to apply the actual malice standard, and the litigants raised no objection. The Court went out of its way to state that the *Cantrell* case did not resolve the question of "whether a State may constitutionally apply a more relaxed standard of liability" than actual malice in false light cases involving private individuals. What this has meant is that lower courts can apply either a negligence standard (*Gertz*) or an actual malice standard to false light cases involving private individuals and matters of public concern and can still plausibly claim to be following the dictates of the Supreme Court.[17]

COMMERCIAL APPROPRIATION OF NAME OR LIKENESS

The Restatement (Second) of Torts provides: "One who appropriates to his own use or benefit the name or likeness of another is subject to liability to the other for invasion of privacy."[18] A typical "appropriation" occurs where an advertiser falsely claims that an individual, usually a celebrity, endorses its product in order to increase sales of the product. (See, e.g., Midler v. Ford Motor Co., 1988) By doing so, the advertiser "commercializes" the personality of the plaintiff. (Gautier v. Pro-Football, Inc., 1952) The appropriation thus potentially violates both the plaintiff's privacy interests and property interests. It violates the plaintiff's privacy interest to the extent that it forces him to expose his personal identity in a manner not of his own choosing. Moreover, to the extent the plaintiff's identity has a monetary value (as in the case of a celebrity), it deprives the plaintiff of the ability to exploit this value for his own benefit. In essence, the advertiser has taken the value of the celebrity's endorsement without compensation. Many states give redress—via common law or statute—for appropriations of both types of interest, often referring to the property interest as a "right of publicity" (as opposed to the "right of privacy"). (See, e.g., Comedy III Prods., Inc. v. Gary Saderup, Inc., 2001; People for the Ethical Treatment of Animals v. Bobby Berosini, Ltd., 1995) Indeed, this terminology has even made its way into a separate Restatement, the Restatement (Third) of Unfair Competition sec. 46–49.

The threat that the commercial appropriation tort might otherwise pose to the media's ability to report on public affairs is ameliorated by two privileges: the newsworthiness privilege and the "incidental use" privilege. In his treatise, Privacy Torts, Professor David Elder refers to the newsworthiness privilege as a "hybrid" of tort and constitutional law "for newsworthy matters not involving substantial falsity."[19] This privilege protects not only uses of the names or likeness of individuals in reporting the news, it also protects such uses for entertainment or educational purposes. Publication of an unauthorized biography of George Bush or a photo of Joe Namath in connection with a story on the techniques of famous quarterbacks are not actionable as commercial appropriation torts. In addition, publishing a photo of an actor in connection with a review of his new movie is in no way actionable. Yet the newsworthiness privilege does not only protect reporting on the doings of celebrities. The media often use the names and identities of private individuals in reporting on newsworthy events, and these uses are also protected. The fact that the media use the names and identities of celebrities and ordinary people to make a profit does not deprive them of the benefit of the privilege. After all, most media are not in business for free.

Even so, the newsworthiness privilege does have limits. A famous boxer successfully sued Playgirl magazine for appropriation after it published a nude sketch of him with anatomical "enhancement" in its pages.[20] (Ali v. Playgirl, Inc., 1978) In this case, the sketch was primarily for the purpose of selling magazines and had little if anything to do with commentary on the boxer or his career. Similarly, transparent attempts to camouflage a commercial use of an individual's name or likeness by including some token news items about her will not insulate the media from liability.

Commercial appropriation cases sometimes arise against the media when they are engaged in self-promotion. A magazine may republish a previous cover photo in its advertisements in order to attract new subscribers; courts have held this not to be commercial appropriation, but rather an "incidental use" demonstrating sample content of the magazine. (Fogel v. Forbes, 1980) The media are also not liable for commercial appropriation when they make only limited reference to an individual's name or likeness in the context of a larger broadcast or publication. A single reference to an individual in a long film or book is not actionable. Nor is it actionable to publish photos of public places which happen to include members of the public in the background. In fact, the media will not ordinarily be liable for commercial appropriation even where they use the name or likeness of a member of the public for the "incidental" purpose of illustrating a broader theme, say, homelessness, or unemployment, or the buying habits of Latin American travelers. (See, e.g., Brown v. Twentieth Century Fox Film Corp., 1992; Namath v. Sports Illustrated, 1976; Booth v. Curtis Publ'g Co., 1962) These cases do not involve purposeful exploitation of the names or likeness of the individuals involved. Indeed, the media derive only marginal benefit from these types of uses, and to force them to get consent for each use would unduly burden reporting on newsworthy events.

The incidental use and newsworthiness privileges provide the media substantial protection from being held liable for commercial appropriation or violation of the right of publicity. The only time the Supreme Court has spoken on the subject was to correct a lower court decision which gave *too much* protection to the media in the name of the First Amendment. (Zacchini v. Scripps-Howard Broad. Co., 1977) Zacchini v. Scripps-Howard was, to say the least, an unusual case. Hugo Zacchini was a "human cannonball." A reporter covering a fair videotaped Zacchini's performance over his objection, and the performance—all fifteen seconds of it—was broadcast on the evening news. Thereafter, Zacchini sued under Ohio's right of publicity statute. But the Ohio Supreme Court rejected his claim on the ground that the defendants were constitutionally privileged to include his act in its newscast as "matters of public interest that would otherwise be protected by the right of publicity . . . ." By a 5-4 decision, the U.S. Supreme Court reversed, although its holding was quite narrow. The Court held that the First Amendment does not "immunize the media when they broadcast a performer's entire act without his consent." The Court took pains to state that commentary on the act would have been protected, stressing again and again that the reason the defendants lost that protection was because they broadcast the plaintiff's "entire act." The Court viewed this as a threat to his intellectual property, presenting "a substantial threat to the economic value of [Zacchini's] performance." Presumably the human cannonballs of the world would be deterred from developing their skills if the media could appropriate the value of their labors by such broadcasts. Nonetheless, *Zacchini* should not be read too broadly. It is the unusual case in which the media publish or broadcast an individual's "entire act." Indeed Justice Powell in dissent stated that the majority's "repeated incantation of a single formula: 'a performer's entire act'" was not even clear enough to resolve the *Zacchini* case itself. As Powell noted, if Zacchini's act were preceded by fanfare beforehand, then it would not be fair to say that the defendants had broadcast his "entire act," and the majority's reasoning would not apply. Even if Powell is engaging in overstatement, it is nonetheless fair to say that *Zacchini* provides little guidance in the more typical types of commercial appropriation or right of publicity cases involving the media.

INTENTIONAL INFLICTION OF EMOTIONAL DISTRESS

The purpose of the tort of intentional infliction of emotional distress is to deter antisocial conduct that inflicts excessive and unjustifiable levels of emotional distress on its targets. In order to recover for emotional distress, plaintiffs must ordinarily prove that the defendant's "extreme and outrageous conduct intentionally cause[d] severe emotional distress."[21] In order for liability to be found, it is not enough for the defendant's conduct to be merely offensive; it must be "so outrageous in character, and so extreme in degree, as to go beyond all possible bounds of decency, and to be regarded as atrocious, and utterly intolerable in a civilized community."[22]

It is the rare case in which the media's conduct will rise to the level of outrageousness. Hustler Magazine, Inc. v. Falwell is the rare case. The protagonists in this dramatic case are characters right out of central casting. In fact, director Milos Foreman depicted both in a later movie, *The People vs. Larry Flynt*. Larry Flynt is the sleazy publisher of the sleazy magazine *Hustler*. Jerry Falwell is a fundamentalist preacher, leader of the Moral Majority, and an outspoken commentator on public affairs. In 1983, Hustler published a "parody" of a liquor advertisement in which celebrities talked about their "first time" drinking liquor, but playing on the sexual double entendre of "first time." The *Hustler* parody was made to appear as if it were an interview with Jerry Falwell talking about his "first time." The parody "quoted" him as saying that his first time was in an outhouse with his mother, "drunk off our God-fearing asses."[23] Upon having his attention brought to the parody, Falwell sued for libel, invasion of privacy, and intentional infliction of emotional distress. The jury found that Hustler had not libeled Falwell because the parody could not 'reasonably be understood as describing actual facts about [him] or actual events in which [he] participated.'" (Hustler Magazine, Inc. v. Falwell, 1988) The jury nonetheless awarded Falwell $100,000 in compensatory and $50,000 in punitive damages for intentional infliction of emotional distress. Hustler appealed to the United States Supreme Court.

The Supreme Court framed the case as presenting "the novel question" of whether the First Amendment limits the tort of intentional infliction of emotional distress. The Court held that the First Amendment does limit the tort when invoked to punish commentary on public figures or public officials. Specifically, the Court held that public figures and public officials must show that a "publication contain[ed] a false statement of fact which was made with 'actual malice'" before they can recover for intentional infliction. (Hustler Magazine, Inc., v. Falwell, 1988)

The Court's holding closed the door on plaintiffs hoping to circumvent the strict requirements of libel law by bringing a case for intentional infliction instead. The Court's rationale, too, drew from the principles it had announced in the libel cases. Particularly, the Court thought that breathing space was necessary if the rich tradition of public debate, which includes satire and parody, is to survive. The real heart of the decision, however, was the Court's fear of making *outrageousness* the dividing line between protected and unprotected speech. The "inherent subjectiveness" of the outrageousness standard "would allow a jury to impose liability on the basis of the jurors' tastes or views, or perhaps on the basis of their dislike of a particular expression." (Hustler Magazine, Inc. v. Falwell, 1988) This threat is particularly palpable where the speech in question is satirical and draws its power from its "emotional impact" on its audience.

The Court's reason for its holding was as much negative as positive. The Court feared that punishing the *Hustler* parody would create a slippery slope to suppression of other speech. Although the Court conceded that the caricature of Falwell was "at best a distant cousin" of the famous political cartoons of Thomas Nast and others, it saw no "principled standard to separate the one from the other." (Hustler Magazine, Inc. v. Falwell, 1988) Therefore, the Court concluded that Falwell's intentional infliction claim could not "form a basis for the award of damages when the conduct in question is the publication of a caricature such as the ad parody involved here." By protecting the despicable speech of Hustler, the Court extended the mantle of First Amendment protection to satire, parody, caricature, hyperbole, and other types of imaginative expression that cannot be interpreted as stating actual facts. The case is thus a cornerstone in the protection of colorful, emotional, and other often offensive speech that lends texture and nuance to public discourse in this country.

Even so, Hustler v. Falwell leaves important questions unanswered. Does the actual malice rule apply to intentional infliction cases brought by private figures involved in matters of public concern? If the analogy to libel law holds, private figures should be able to succeed on intentional infliction claims against the press by proving negligence and actual injury. Yet the logic of the opinion, which is rooted in the need to protect imaginative expression, seems equally applicable to speech on matters of public concern as it does to speech about public officials or public figures. The case also does not resolve the question whether plaintiffs may ever sue the media for *negligent* infliction of emotional distress.

What if a television station promises to disguise the identity of an interviewee but negligently fails to do so? That was the issue in Doe v. ABC, in which a TV station took insufficient steps to protect the identity of two rape victims. The court held that the plaintiffs could make a valid claim for negligent infliction of emotional distress and for breach of contract. The First Amendment did not shield the TV station from liability. Even so, it seems clear that the First Amendment *would* shield the media from liability based on negligent publication of false information. Moreover, negligent infliction is a difficult tort to establish even in nonmedia cases. Hence, it is fair to conclude that the media will rarely be held liable for negligently inflicting emotional distress, whether the First Amendment allows it or not.

NOTES

1. Samuel Warren & Louis D. Brandeis, "The Right of Privacy," 4 *Harv. L. Rev.* (1890) 193, 195 (quoting *Cooley On Torts* 29 (2d ed. (1888))).

2. Melville B. Nimmer, "The Right of Publicity," 19 *Law & Contemp. Probs.* (1954) 203, 205.

3. Warren & Brandeis, "The Right of Privacy," 195.

4. Warren & Brandeis, "The Right of Privacy," 195.

5. William L. Prosser, "Privacy," 48 *Cal. L. Rev.* (1960) 383.

6. Restatement (Second) of Torts § 652D (1977).

7. But see Lee v. Penthouse International Ltd., (1997) in which a federal district court in California found that *Penthouse*'s publication of sexually explicit photographs of Pamela Anderson and Tommy Lee did not invade their privacy because the photographs had already appeared in other publications.

8. Linda N. Woito & Patrick McNulty, "The Privacy Disclosure Tort and the First Amendment: Should the Community Decide Newsworthiness?" 64 *Iowa L. Rev.* (1979) 185, 196.

9. See Lyrissa B. Lidsky, "Prying, Spying, and Lying: Intrusive Newsgathering and What the Law Should Do About It," 73 *Tul. L. Rev.* (1998) 173 for further discussion on the extent that the court's have gone to in allowing the media to define newsworthiness.

10. Privacy is becoming even more scarce with advances in computer technology. Byford suggests that to overcome the problems that our western world faces with privacy and cyberspace, "a model of cyberspace privacy must be built from the ground up, based on the specific social and cultural features of an electronic communications environment." Katrin S. Byford, "Privacy in Cyberspace: Constructing A Model of Privacy for the Electronic Communications Environment," 24 *Rutgers Computer & Tech. L.J.* (1998) 1.

11. The Court relied on an alternate line of decisions in which the states attempted to impose criminal sanctions on the media for publishing information obtained through ordinary reporting techniques.

12. Lidsky, "Prying, Spying, and Lying: Intrusive Newsgathering and What the Law Should Do About It," 201.

13. David A. Anderson, "Tortious Speech," 47 *Wash. L. Rev.* (1990) 71, 102–04.

14. 2 W. LaFave & A. Scott, *Substantive Criminal Law* (St. Paul, Minnesota: West Pub. Co., 1986) § 810(a), p. 422.

15. Restatement (Second) of Torts § 652E (1977).

16. For a more extended discussion, see Matthew Stohl, "False Light Invasion in Docudramas: The Oxymoron Which Must Be Solved," 35 *Akron L. Rev.* (2002) 251.

17. Diane L. Zimmerman, "False Light Invasion of Privacy: The Light That Failed," 64 *N.Y.U. L. Rev.* (1989) 364; Gary T. Schwartz, "Explaining and Justifying a Limited Tort of False Light Invasion of Privacy," 41 *Case. W. Res. L. Rev.* (1991) 885.

18. Restatement (Second) of Torts § 652C (1977).

19. David Elder, *Privacy Torts* (Egan, Minnesota: Thomson West, 2002) § 6:13.

20. Compare, *Ali*, with Ann-Margaret v. High Soc'y Magazine, 1980 where a magazine published a photograph of the plaintiff participating in a partially nude scene of a movie to discuss the movie.

21. Restatement (Second) of Torts § 46(1) (1965).

22. Restatement (Second) of Torts § 46, cmt. d (1965).

23. Robert C. Post, "The Constitutional Concept of Public Discourse: Outrageous Opinion, Democratic Deliberation, and Hustler Magazine v. Falwell," 103 *Harv. L. Rev.* (1990) 603, 607.

8

Legal Regulation of Harmful Media Effects on Unconsenting Or Vulnerable Persons

THE EXTREME CASE: RICE V. PALADIN ENTERPRISES, INC.

Rice v. Paladin Enterprises, Inc. (1997) amounts to a legal nightmare for free press advocates. *Rice* involved a civil wrongful death action brought by representatives of three murder victims against a book publisher, the Paladin Press. The suit advanced the startling argument that Paladin was civilly liable for aiding and abetting the murders. Paladin, after all, had done little beyond publishing a book read by the actual murderer. This was not the first time that life had imitated literature. Surely, we can imagine, the publishers of Goethe's 1774 novel *The Sorrows of Young Werther* at some point recognized the unusual number of suicides linked to reading that Romantic classic.[1] Legal liability in such a case, however, seems almost unimaginable under the First Amendment.

Rice dealt with a book aptly entitled *Hit Man: A Technical Manual for Independent Contractors*. Instructed in detail and steeled in his resolve by this book, a contract killer murdered the ex-wife and the 8-year-old quadriplegic son of his employer, along with a nurse employed to assist the son. (See Rice v. Paladin Enterprises, Inc., 1997) The underlying motive for murder, apparently, was a two million dollar settlement fund held in trust for the child and payable tax free to the ex-husband in the event of the demise of both mother and child. (See Rice v. Paladin Enterprises, Inc., 1997) The contract killer, apparently, had carefully studied, been encouraged by, and followed numerous precepts detailed in, the 130-page *Hit Man* book.

What made the *Rice* case especially awkward and troublesome was the defendant publisher's decision to enter into some rather remarkable stipulations. Consider in particular that Paladin stipulated that in marketing *Hit Man*, it "intended to attract and assist criminals and would-be criminals who desire information on how to commit crimes." Paladin also "intended and had knowledge" that *Hit Man* actually "would be used, upon receipt, by criminals and would-be criminals to plan and execute the crime of murder for hire . . . ." Indeed the publisher stipulated that, through publishing and selling *Hit Man*, it assisted the actual murderer in the perpetration of the very murders for which the victims' families now attempted to hold Paladin civilly liable. (Rice v. Paladin Enterprises, Inc., 1997) Given, in part, these extraordinary stipulations, the Fourth Circuit Court of Appeals was willing to deny Paladin's First Amendment-based summary judgment motion on the plaintiff's civil aiding and abetting of murder claim. (See Rice v. Paladin Enterprises, Inc., 1997)

The *Rice* court began its analysis by citing the Ninth Circuit case of United States v. Barnett. In *Barnett*, the court observed generally that "the First Amendment does not provide a defense to a criminal charge simply because the actor uses words to carry out his illegal purpose." Specifically, the *Barnett* court rejected a First Amendment defense to the charge of aiding and abetting the manufacture of the illegal drug phencyclidine by means of publishing and distributing instructions for that process.

Having thus undercut at least the broadest sort of First Amendment absolutism, the *Rice* court observed that a speaker cannot always escape liability by proving that his book was aimed at, and may have reached, a wide audience. (See Rice v. Paladin Enterprises, Inc., 1997) The court then noted that it did not need to resolve all of the deepest issues as to what sorts of intent on the part of a publisher will support tort liability for aiding and abetting. Paladin had actually stipulated, and a reasonable jury could independently find, that Paladin assisted the contract killer in *Rice*, with knowledge and intent that "the book would be immediately used"[2] throughout the course of the murder for hire scheme. (See Rice v. Paladin Enterprises, Inc., 1997)

We might at this point pause to reflect on an unhappy hypothetical vision of Henry David Thoreau being interrogated as to whether his classic work *Civil Disobedience* was specifically intended to promote immediate tax resistance, by persons known or unknown. (For a tax counseling or tax protest criminal liability case, see, e.g., United States v. Freeman, 1985.) Perhaps to forestall the criticism that its decision would chill such works, the *Rice* court understandably invoked the familiar distinction between abstract advocacy on the one hand, and incitement on the other.[3] The First Amendment permits punishment of the latter but protects the former. Whether this distinction between advocacy and incitement by itself would allow recovery against Paladin, while also protecting Thoreau from civil liability for his essay, is uncertain. After all, neither *Hit Man* nor Thoreau's essay is devoid of emotional encouragement.[4] And Thoreau's essay is, surely, the more literally "moving."

The court seemed to appreciate this problem. It noted how relatively easy it is to establish the intent necessary for civil, as opposed to criminal, aiding and abetting. Aiding and abetting for civil liability purposes requires only some sort of advising or encouraging of the underlying tortfeasor. There need be no pre-arrangement or concerted action. And civil, unlike criminal, aiding and abetting requires only that the eventual tort be the natural and probable consequence of the defendant's aiding and abetting. The civil aider and abetter need only foresee the eventual underlying tort; he need not literally intend it. (See Rice v. Paladin Enterprises, Inc., 1997)

The court recognized that the First Amendment may require a more stringent intent requirement than merely the natural and probable consequence standard even in civil cases. But it concluded that the defendant publisher Paladin could not be granted summary judgment on this issue, given its own dramatic stipulations and other evidence from which a reasonable jury could infer the necessary specific intent. (See Rice v. Paladin Enterprises, Inc., 1997) A jury could reasonably conclude that Paladin had the specific purpose of aiding and abetting the underlying murders in question. (See Rice v. Paladin Enterprises, Inc., 1997)

Paladin, by its own admission, was engaged in a "marketing strategy intended to attract and assist criminals and would-be criminals" desiring particularized criminal instruction. Through powerful, imperative prose, Paladin's text not only instructed but specifically motivated its readers with respect to their underlying criminal acts. (Rice v. Paladin Enterprises, Inc., 1997) There is, however, something odd about basing a finding of specific intent to abet some specific crime by a specific actor in part on a "generalized marketing strategy" that makes no reference, express or implied, to the specific criminal act or actor. After all, a marketing strategy is aimed at sales, as opposed to what any or all readers, identified or unidentified, actually do with the book. A marketing strategy is about moving product. It is presumably either successful or unsuccessful apart from how many actual, let alone specifically anticipated, crimes are facilitated by the book in question.

One can imagine a book like *Hit Man* being sold in large measure as a work of perversely transgressive fantasy. Where a less warped sensibility might enjoy a book discussing how to survive alone in the forest, even if such a reader had no intention of actually visiting a forest, so may readers of *Hit Man*, in a loosely analogous way, find some appeal in that work. Similarly, an author conducting research to give realism to his action adventure tale might use the book to find out how contract killers operate. Doubtless *Hit Man* provides much specific, concrete instruction and exhortation. But without these elements, much of the fantasy and the marketability are lost.

The First Amendment will not generally allow a court to hold the rhetorical power, evocativeness, or effectiveness of a book against it in a civil case. A badly written, unmoving version of Thoreau's *Civil Disobedience* is not entitled to greater First Amendment protection than the original. The *Rice* court may have taken the emotional force of *Hit Man* as added evidence of the genuineness of the publisher's intentional aiding and abetting. But it is important not to lose sight of the fact that Paladin was being sued for incidents of which it was never specifically aware, committed by persons of whom it was never aware, against victims it never knew. Paladin could hardly stipulate to the contrary. And it would be difficult for a reasonable jury to find a sufficiently specific intent against a background of such thorough ignorance on the part of the publisher defendant.

The court then, in pursuing the question of specific intent, addressed an explicit disclaimer in the catalogue advertisement for *Hit Man*, which specified that the book was intended "[f]or academic study only!" (See Rice v. Paladin Enterprises, Inc., 1997) The court concluded that a reasonable jury could interpret this disclaimer as a cynical bit of "transparent sarcasm." (Rice v. Paladin Enterprises, Inc., 1997) Of course, a jury might also find the disclaimer to be neither sarcasm nor an invitation for genuine academic study, but as either nervous apprehension in the face of possible legal liability, or, again, as an invitation to fantasy. But this, admittedly, might only create a triable issue of conflicting interpretations for the jury to resolve.

No doubt some or all of these motives may have been operative. But even the plaintiffs' own understanding of the case against Paladin is disturbingly equivocal. The plaintiffs argued that *Hit Man* is devoid of a discussion of ideas, argument, diatribe, propaganda, or even advocacy. (See Rice v. Paladin Enterprises, Inc., 1997; *cf.* Chaplinsky v. New Hampshire, 1942) Plainly, this would, if taken as true, at least reduce if not eliminate the relevance of any First Amendment values[5] to the work in question. (But *cf.* City of Newport v. Fact Concerts, Inc., 1981)

But this inference itself would be double-edged. If *Hit Man* has no such "point" to make, on what basis could a reasonable jury find, in the teeth of the publisher's explicit disclaimers, that the publisher had any preference as to whether anyone was actually murdered or not? If, as the plaintiffs argued, *Hit Man* lacks any relevant "point," could a reasonable jury find not only that Paladin was recklessly indifferent to murder, but actually preferred that some identifiable or unidentifiable person be murdered?[6] (See Rice v. Paladin Enterprises, Inc., 1997)

If we assume that *Hit Man* lacks any social message or point, it becomes unclear why a civil aiding and abetting plaintiff is constitutionally required to prove specific intent on the part of the speaker. A commercial publisher might be recklessly indifferent to some harmful consequences. But the Supreme Court has held that speech that is oriented toward mere entertainment or fantasy is entitled to some degree of First Amendment protection.[7] (See, e.g., Barnes v. Glen Theatre, Inc., 1991; City of Newport v. Fact Concerts, Inc., 1981) However, the Supreme Court has never addressed whether the First Amendment value of pure entertainment, as opposed to a socially pointed "Thoreauvian" essay, is high enough to require that a civil plaintiff show specific intent.

The court in *Rice* acknowledged that the issues presented by the case were novel and concluded in the following terms:

Paladin's astonishing stipulations, coupled with the extraordinary comprehensiveness, detail, and clarity of *Hit Man*'s instructions for criminal activity and murder in particular, the boldness of its palpable exhortation to murder, the alarming power and effectiveness of its peculiar form of instruction, the notable absence from its text of the kind of ideas for the protection of which the First Amendment exists, and the book's evident lack of any even arguably legitimate purpose beyond the promotion and teaching of murder, render this case unique in the law.[8]

The *Rice* case is indeed unique. Citizens in general, whatever their views of the legal merits of the case, can hope that it remains so.

SOLDIERS OF CONTRASTING FORTUNE: THE *EIMANN* AND *BRAUN* CASES

The cases of Eimann v. Soldier of Fortune Magazine and Braun v. Soldier of Fortune Magazine form an instructive legal contrast. Let us first consider them separately, and then briefly reflect on them jointly.

The appellate court in *Eimann* reversed a jury verdict against *Soldier of Fortune* magazine in a Texas wrongful death action brought by survivors of a murder victim. The plaintiffs claimed that the murder victim's husband had contracted for the killing through classified advertisement in the magazine. Plaintiffs' theory was that *Soldier of Fortune* was negligent or grossly negligent in publishing the advertisement in question. (See Eimann v. Soldier of Fortune Magazine, 1989)

The advertisement placed by the eventual contract murderer referred only to a willingness to undertake "high risk assignments," not to a willingness to commit illegal acts. (Eimann v. Soldier of Fortune Magazine, 1989) The contract murderer testified that this phrase was intended to refer only to work "as a bodyguard or security specialist." (Eimann v. Soldier of Fortune Magazine, 1989) At the time the murderer placed the ad, he had neither a criminal record nor a dishonorable discharge, and the name, address, and telephone number he supplied to *Soldier of Fortune* were correct. This evidence undercut the plaintiff's claim that *Soldier of Fortune* should have known that the advertisement was a solicitation of murder for hire and that the magazine was therefore negligent in publishing it.

However, the plaintiffs bolstered their case by presenting evidence of a number of other more lurid or legally questionable personal services classified ads placed with *Soldier of Fortune* over a period of time. A few of these ads referred to the performance of "dirty work," or to a willingness to "do anything, anywhere at the right price." (Eimann v. Soldier of Fortune Magazine, 1989) Apparently, at least seven ads had been tied to criminal plots, five had been linked by major national media to crimes, and *Soldier of Fortune* itself had been contacted by law enforcement officials in connection with two criminal investigations linked to its classified ads. (See Eimann v. Soldier of Fortune Magazine, 1989) An expert witness for the plaintiff testified that all of the personal service classified ads in *Soldier of Fortune* foreseeably could be linked to the eventual commission of crime. The expert admitted, however, that no particular language in the ads could be especially linked to illegal activity, and that the language in a few of the ads actually linked to crimes seemed relatively innocuous. (See Eimann v. Soldier of Fortune Magazine, 1989)

The case was decided by the jury under general Texas negligence principles. The jury presumably found that *Soldier of Fortune* should have known from the text and context of the ad, including the existence of criminal plots linked to other ads, that the ad might actually be a criminal solicitation. A legal duty to refrain from publishing the ad, under the circumstances, was held by the trial court to attach.

The Fifth Circuit Court of Appeals reversed purely on the basis of state tort law, without even reaching the First Amendment issue. The court held on appeal that *Soldier of Fortune* "owed no duty to refrain from publishing a facially innocuous classified advertisement when the ad's context—at most—made its message ambiguous." (Eimann v. Soldier of Fortune Magazine, 1989) The court's analysis of the duty issue made no explicit reference to First Amendment principles. It adopted a balancing approach to resolve the duty issue.[9] (See Eimann v. Soldier of Fortune Magazine, 1989 (citing United States v. Carroll Towing, 1947)) The specific balancing approach used, called "risk-utility balancing," is a common method of resolving the issue of whether a defendant owes a duty. This approach was made famous by the great common law judge Learned Hand in a decision, of all things, about tugboats, called Carroll Towing. Using this approach, the court weighed the probability and gravity of the harm in publishing the ad against the severity of the burden on the publisher of preventing that harm. (See Eimann v. Soldier of Fortune Magazine, 1989) While recognizing the risks of criminal harm, the court was more impressed by the severity of the burden on the defendant publisher in preventing the harm.

The court emphasized that the ad in question was at worst ambiguous in its intent and meaning, given the evidence showing a limited correlation between an ad's language and any resulting criminal act. The court also referred to the "pervasiveness" (See Eimann v. Soldier of Fortune Magazine, 1989) of commercial advertising in our society.[10] (See, e.g., Staples v. CBL & Assoc., Inc., 2000; McClung v. Delta Square Ltd. Partnership, 1996) The ad was thus not shown to be predictably dangerous. And the ad was of substantial social value. The court concluded that the "appreciable risk" of harm from the ad, combined with the gravity of that harm, did not outweigh the "onerous burden" on *Soldier of Fortune*.

Valuable activities, the court explained, inevitably carry certain risks of harm. To ask a publisher to reject all vaguely suspicious, at worst ambiguous,[11] (See, e.g., Fairley v. Peekskill Star Corp., 1981) classified ads is to ask too much. Before a tort duty can be placed on the publisher regarding foreseeable harmful consequences of an ad, there must be greater specific evidence of an underlying illegal intent, precisely because so many kinds of ads might foreseeably be subject to so many kinds of abuse. (See Eimann v. Soldier of Fortune Magazine, 1989)

While the court in Eimann claimed not to reach the First Amendment issue, its interest balancing incorporated something akin to a First Amendment analysis. It is, for example, difficult to fully account for the social value of classified ads, ambiguous or not, unless one considers our constitutional commitment to the values of freedom of speech and of the press. By disclaiming a First Amendment analysis in *Eimann*, however, the court reduced the likelihood of a Supreme Court reversal, since the Supreme Court may not ordinarily dictate the content of state tort law in the absence of any Federal legal issue. In a literal sense, the *Eimann* court followed the Supreme Court's expressed preference for resolving cases on narrow legal grounds[12] without deciding constitutional questions unnecessarily.

In contrast, Braun v. Soldier of Fortune Magazine involved intriguingly similar facts, but different jury instructions and a distinctly different analysis and result on appeal. In *Braun*, the plaintiffs alleged negligence and malice on the part of defendant *Soldier of Fortune* in their wrongful death action brought under Georgia law. The personal services classified ad in *Braun* read as follows: "GUN FOR HIRE: 37 year old professional mercenary desires jobs. Vietnam Veteran. Discrete [sic] and very private. Bodyguard, courier, and other special skills. All jobs considered." (Braun v. Soldier of Fortune Magazine, 1992)

The plaintiffs in *Braun* presented the same evidence of *Soldier of Fortune*'s knowledge, or ability to learn, or prior criminal plots linked to their personal ads as was presented in *Eimann*. More crucially, according to the Eleventh Circuit Court of Appeals, the jury instructions in *Braun* were more protective of the publisher's rights.

The jury instructions in *Braun* required, for liability, that "a reasonable reading of the advertisement in this case would have conveyed to a magazine publisher, such as *Soldier of Fortune*, that this ad presented the clear and present danger of causing serious harm to the public from violent criminal activity." (See Braun v. Soldier of Fortune Magazine, 1992) The risk, according to the jury instructions, must have been "a clearly identifiable unreasonable" risk of such harm. (Braun v. Soldier of Fortune Magazine, 1992) Further, the harm or risk must have been identifiable at the time of placing the ad, not only with the benefit of hindsight. Crucially, the jury instructions specified that *Soldier of Fortune* owed no duty to investigate the ad or its circumstances. The risk posed by the ad must have been reasonably apparent from the face or text of the ad itself. (Braun v. Soldier of Fortune Magazine, 1992) Although this seems to have been the same duty rule applied in *Eimann*, the ultimate outcome of the *Braun* case was very different.

On appeal, the Eleventh Circuit held that the instructions in the case properly stated Georgia state tort law. Certainly, the jury instructions in *Braun* were in some respects more rigorous than in *Eimann*. The ad in *Braun* was to some degree more suggestive of overt criminal soliciation than the ad in *Eimann*. And there is some echo in *Braun* of the First Amendment's classic test for speech that merely advocates, as opposed to inciting, criminal activity. (See, e.g., Brandenburg v. Ohio, 1969)

Braun, however, does not simply track the constitutional requirements imposed by the Court in the subversive advocacy cases. Crucially, in subversive advocacy cases the Supreme Court has required a showing of intent, or of a defendant's mental directedness toward the illegal act, and not merely a showing of "modified" negligence on the part of a defendant in such cases.[13] (See, e.g., Brandenburg v. Ohio, 1969; See also, e.g., White v. Lee, 2000) Yet the court in *Braun* actually required, on the issue of the defendant *Soldier of Fortune*'s state of mind, no more than a finding of "modified" negligence regarding the harm. (See Braun v. Soldier of Fortune Magazine, 1992) This modified negligence standard could not suffice for a criminal prosecution under current Supreme Court case law.[14] Thus, it is certainly open to question whether the modified negligence test in *Braun* was stringent enough to satisfy the requirements of the First Amendment.

It is possible to argue generally that lower liability requirements should be permissible in civil, as opposed to criminal, First Amendment cases. A criminal conviction can be officially stigmatizing in a way in which a civil suit may not. But the Supreme Court has famously recognized the possibility that fear of civil financial liability may discourage more legitimate press speech than modest criminal penalties. (See New York Times Co. v. Sullivan, 1964)

On the other hand, the burden that case law such as *Braun* imposes on the basic values and concerns underlying the First Amendment may actually be rather modest. A publisher need not investigate every classified ad that is submitted for publication lest it be a solicitation for contract murder; it is only those ads that clearly constitute criminal solicitation on their face that will subject a publisher to liability. If one seeks only legitimate employment as a bodyguard or business security consultant, one can presumably clearly say so, at only a modest cost in First Amendment values.[15] Moreover, the outcome in *Braun* may be explained by the fact that the ad at issue was commercial speech, a supposedly "hardy" category of speech that the Supreme Court has not generally accorded full First Amendment protection.

THE SUBTLE VARIETY OF ALLEGED MEDIA TORT VICTIM CASES: SOME EXAMPLES

A number of cases have been brought against media defendants, on behalf of plaintiffs injured at least indirectly by some form of expressive content. Often, a third party unknown to either the media defendant or the victim is the immediate cause of the victim's harm. Such third parties, whether foreseeable or not, were involved in the *Rice*, *Eimann*, and *Braun* cases discussed above. Sometimes, however, the victim causes his own injuries by imitating something depicted by the media defendant or by following instructions provided by the media defendant.

In some cases, the media allegedly endorses, or at least depicts, some sort of violence. In other cases, the media allegedly facilitates a violent act or accident. Even among the cases in which the media defendants win by summary judgment via a First Amendment defense, the cases are interestingly varied. Let us simply illustrate the range and variety of these sorts of cases.

Orozco v. Dallas Morning News, Inc. involved the standard decision of a local newspaper to report the street name and block number, but not the precise address, of an arrested murder suspect. Allegedly, third parties used the general address printed in the newspaper to locate the arrested murder suspect's home and to retaliate against that suspect by shooting two of his family members. (See Orozco v. Dallas Morning News, Inc., 1998) The plaintiffs sued for negligence and argued that the defendant newspaper should have considered the implications of several of its own recent articles detailing the local phenomenon of retaliatory shootings among rival gang members. (See Orozco v. Dallas Morning News, Inc., 1998)

The appellate court in *Orozco* determined as a matter of law, however, that even if considerations of reasonable foreseeability and gravity of the possible harm were weighed, the newspaper owed no duty not to publish the relevant street and block number. (See Orozco v. Dallas Morning News, Inc., 1998) While the gravity of the harm would admittedly be high, any causal link of the harm to the newspaper's publication decisions would seem speculative or unlikely. (See Orozco v. Dallas Morning News, Inc, 1998)

The court in *Orozco*, purportedly without reaching the First Amendment issue, considered the burden on the press of preventing the killings by not publishing the address information in question. The court observed that "[t]he reporting of crimes and arrests is an important newspaper function, and the public has the right under Texas law to be informed about criminal activity and criminal suspects, including where they reside."[16] (Orozco v. Dallas Morning News, Inc., 1998) Balancing the risk and severity of injury against "the social utility of crime reporting," the appellate court located no relevant legal duty on the part of the defendant newspaper. (See Orozco v. Dallas Morning News, Inc., 1998)

More controversial in content were the music lyrics at issue in the case of Davidson v. Time Warner, Inc. In *Davidson*, a state trooper was killed by the driver of a stolen car who had been listening to the lyrics of *2Pacalypse Now*. The lyrics and the album were by Tupac Amaru Shakur, in cooperation with various other media defendants. The Court concluded that:

2Pacalypse Now depicts violence, and a reasonable jury could find that the recording entreats others to act on Shakur's violent message. However, . . . [t]he probability that a listener of *2Pacalypse Now* would act on Shakur's message is substantially less than the chance that a person responding to a *Soldier of Fortune* advertisement would hire a "hit man" for illegal activity. (Davidson v. Time Warner, Inc., 1997)

The Court emphasized the absence of evidence that *2Pacalypse Now* had inspired any (prior) criminal activity, despite sales of 400,000 records. (See Davidson v. Time Warner, Inc., 1997) The Court therefore concluded that the imposition of tort liability was unwarranted because the harm was not reasonably foreseeable.

While thus finding no liability at the level of state tort law, the Court in *Davidson* went on to consider the constitutional requirements imposed by the arguably relevant First Amendment law of incitement. The Court determined that incitement law's requirements of imminence of harm, probability of the harm, and of specific intent to cause such harm were all absent in *Davidson*. This analysis thus merely reinforced the media defendants' non-liability.

In McCollum v. CBS, Inc.,[17] several media entities were sued for damages arising from the suicide of a listener to a particular musical composition allegedly endorsing suicide under specific circumstances. The decedent had listened to that and other related musical albums repeatedly immediately before his suicide. The suicide was by handgun, and the suicide victim was found still wearing headphones, with the stereo system still running. (See McCollum v. CBS, Inc., 1988)

The plaintiffs alleged that the defendants, and the performer Ozzy Osbourne in particular, had often conveyed messages of hopelessness, despair, and the logic of suicide under particular circumstances, to a target audience including vulnerable adolescents, with whom Osbourne's music sought to cultivate a sense of direct communication.[18] (See McCollum v. CBS, Inc., 1988) The California Court of Appeal, however, imposed the constitutionally demanding incitement test. (See McCollum v. CBS, Inc., 1988) This required a showing of a specific intent on the part of the defendants to bring about a suicide, along with the imminent likelihood of such a suicide. No such specific intent, and no such imminent harm, were found. Thus, once again, the defendants could not be held liable.

As with a number of these alleged incitement cases, the result in *McCollum* itself is less troublesome than the steps taken by the court to reach that result. It is true, for example, that the harm in recording a song or writing a poem was not in fact imminent if the first resulting harm occurs only months or years later. But imminence in this literal sense may not entirely track the logic of freedom of speech. We might ask not whether the harm immediately followed the publication, but instead whether there was any realistic opportunity for counter speech in the time between the publication and the harm. (See, classically, Whitney v. California, 1927 (Brandeis, J., concurring)) Candidly, the existence of a realistic opportunity for counter speech may be a jury issue in some of the alleged illegal incitement cases. And at some point, once enough harm linked to a publication has accrued, further harm may realistically be probable, whether we wish to legally admit so or not. This was true with Goethe's *Werther*, and may sometimes be true today.

Sometimes, a harmful publication case analyzed as incitement may thus seem to come down to jury questions as to imminence and probability of the harm, and perhaps even, in a case much more extreme than *McCollum*, a jury question on the publisher's intent. Questions of a defendant's actual subjective intent are typically poorly suited for summary judgment. (See, e.g., Harlow v. Fitzgerald, 1982) Subjective intent is instead often a jury issue. A court determined to protect freedom of the press might, in such a case, choose to carefully narrow what constitutes a jury question over which reasonable persons might disagree. This might prevent the case from going to the jury stage. Or a court might simply hold that an extremely broad range of publications ought to be protected under a broad range of circumstances, without going to a jury, merely as a matter of sound free press law.

The Court in *McCollum* took both of these routes. It argued, a bit broadly, that given the nature of poetry and song lyrics, as opposed to ordinary prose, "[n]o rational person . . . would . . . mistake musical lyrics and poetry for literal commands or directives to immediate action." Actually, we can certainly imagine political lyrics or political poetry that are indeed intended to be acted upon immediately. We are, however, even in such a case inclined to legally protect the publication, given the general importance of the First Amendment as a legal institution. (See McCollum v. CBS, Inc., 1988; Matarazzo v. Aerosmith Productions, Inc., 1989) Much of the value of the First Amendment would be lost if too many cases go to the jury for decision.

A number of different publishing media were targeted in the case of James v. Meow Media, Inc. In *James*, parents of three students murdered at school by a fellow student brought a claim against several media defendants, who published allegedly obscene or violent Internet Web sites, violent computer and video games, or similar movies, including *The Basketball Diaries*. The plaintiffs alleged that the shooter in this case was an active consumer of these media, and that he was profoundly influenced by exposure to such materials.

The Court in *James* wished, as is common, not to unnecessarily reach the First Amendment issues. (Citing Ashwander v. TVA, 1936) Instead it chose to rely on the determination that, as a matter of law, the injuries to the plaintiffs were not reasonably foreseeable by the defendants. (Relying on Watters v. TSR, Inc., 1990) Because the injuries were unforeseeable, the defendants owed no relevant duty of care. Therefore, the case could not be brought to trial.

In this sort of case it is preferable to focus on issues other than that of foreseeability. What is said to be reasonably foreseeable to a media defendant is, after all, to some degree arbitrary and manipulable, depending on how we choose to describe the events in question.[19] Events described generally—for example, a media-connected school shooting—may sound reasonably foreseeable to at least some reasonable persons. We have all heard of some instances of school shootings.

Events described, on the other hand, in all their detailed particularity may sound freakish or literally one in a million. The greater the detail with which we describe such a shooting, the more unique and the less realistically foreseeable it seems.

Of course, this flexibility of the idea of reasonable foreseeability may be attractive to judges committed to the early ending of these sorts of First Amendment cases. But sheer flexibility in any legal doctrine is unlikely to be the consistent ally of a free press. Legal flexibility may be used against the press as well as for the press. And there is no guarantee that cultural trends will always suggest the unforeseeability of media-related torts. If there are thought to be more school shootings today than fifty years ago, and a greater preoccupation with violent media on the part of some young people, this can only increase the foreseeability of media-related violent torts. Courts should instead focus, where possible, on policy grounds for not imposing a legal duty, on the indisputable lack of the media defendant's specific intent, or more broadly on the excessive First Amendment costs of allowing the trial of such cases.

It may be tempting to try to bypass the difficulties with foreseeability by holding that the actual violent act itself underlying these cases is the only cause of harm to the victim, and that the victim's harm is not caused by the media defendants. This would be a legal expression of the belief that the actual violent actor in these cases is much more responsible for the harm than the media defendants. This approach, however, may offer no real improvement over a focus on the reasonable foreseeability of harm. This is because the foreseeability of a later tortious or even criminal act itself often helps determine who bears legal responsibility for the victim's harm. Reasonably foreseeable future acts, generally, do not erase prior responsibility.[20] Thus if media defendants could have reasonably foreseen future torts somehow following from their speech, this would itself be relevant to whether the media defendants bear legal responsibility for later harm to a victim.

A variation on the incitement to violence theme was at work in the California appellate case of Bill v. Superior Court. There, the plaintiff was injured when shot outside a theater showing the allegedly violent movie *Boulevard Nights*. The focus of the complaint was not that the content of the movie provoked an actual viewer of the movie to immediate violence. Instead, the theory was that the movie, given its content relating to gang violence, would have been known to attract, as viewing customers, the gathering of persons especially prone to violence. There was thus in *Bill* something vaguely akin to a content-neutral "secondary effect" claim. (See, e.g., Renton v. Playtime Theatres, 1986; Cf. Bill v. Superior Court, 1982)

Even though the plaintiff in *Bill* argued that the defendant owed merely a duty to warn potential patrons of risk,[21] the court nonetheless rejected plaintiff's theory in light of its "chilling effect." The court observed that:

[F]ilm producers considering a movie about gangs, or about violence, or bearing some resemblance to a movie which attracted violence-prone persons, would be required to take into account the potential for liability to patrons for acts of violence on the part of persons over whom the producers would have no control. (See Bill v. Superior Court, 1982)

Plaintiff's theory in the *Bill* case was thus held to be incompatible with the First Amendment.

Sometimes a claim is made for harms suffered as a result of the victim's attempt to imitate a media performance. A rather direct, literal imitation of an act performed on television was involved in DeFilippo v. National Broadcasting Co. A viewer of *The Tonight Show* in this case attempted to duplicate a hanging stunt performed by a professional stuntman, resulting in the viewer's death. No third parties were involved. The Rhode Island Supreme Court reached the First Amendment merits, holding the suit on behalf of the deceased to be barred. Whether the case should be treated as an illegal incitement case is doubtful. After all, what if anything the defendants were advocating is unclear. But if the case is considered, by a broad stretch, as still within the scope of the incitement cases, it was clear in *DeFilippo* that all the media defendants lacked any specific intent regarding anyone's death, let alone the death of some particular victim. There was no reasonable dispute over the defendants' actual intent, and thus no jury issue on intent. Given the lack of intent to harm, the plaintiffs in *DeFilippo* could not possibly prevail.

Some of the media defendants, in fact, had warned the television audience of the potential serious risks of attempting the hanging stunt. (See DeFilippo v. National Broad. Co., 1982) These warnings could hardly be reasonably interpreted as some sort of sly inducement to nevertheless attempt the stunt. The media defendants would certainly have no contrary financial or political interest at stake. Specific intent to cause harm is as clearly missing in *DeFilippo* as in any case discussed above. If the illegal incitement cases can be stretched to cover this kind of case, the defendants should normally win at the summary judgment stage.

Yet it bears noticing that the repeated warnings against attempting the stunt itself suggests the foreseeability of at least some such attempt among the many viewers of *The Tonight Show*. A plaintiff might argue that repeated warnings suggest that imitating the stunt was not only obviously conceivable to the defendants, but reasonably foreseeable as well. On the other hand, some actual warnings may be against acts that the law would still, despite the warning, not find reasonably foreseeable.

It also bears noting, however, that the protected media speech in *DeFilippo* was far from the central concerns of news, information, analysis, politics and society, or editorializing on any subject. The speech was pure, and otherwise pointless, entertainment, without any intent to convey any recognizable social idea or message. As such, the hanging stunt bears some relation to the kinds of speech the Supreme Court treats as "low value" speech.

It is thus fair to say that in context, the televised hanging stunt was not an attempt to communicate any meaningful social idea. We might therefore ask why the First Amendment is relevant to the case. The courts, however, see full or partial free speech value in various sorts of pure entertainment speech and even in entertaining conduct. The courts often then insulate such speech or conduct from tort liability largely on the grounds of lack of specific harmful intent, on the authority of factually remote illegal incitement cases. Doubtless the courts are concerned that media self-censorship even in areas of only minimal First Amendment relevance may eventually spread to areas of greater relevance. The theory may be that protecting even merely entertaining speech with no intended social message helps insulate more genuinely social or political speech.

A final representative case, Byers v. Edmondson, illustrates some of the limits on the courts' ability to dispose of alleged inspired violence cases before trial. *Byers* involved a shooting victim plaintiff who claimed that several media defendants had, through the movie *Natural Born Killers* and its alleged glorification of violence, intentionally inspired predisposed persons to a violent crime spree resulting in the plaintiff's injury. The combination of the allegation of an actual intent on the part of the defendants that their movie violence be imitated, and the unusually early stage of the lawsuit, led to refusal, at least temporarily, to dismiss the lawsuit. (See Byers v. Edmondson, 1998)

In cases such as *Byers*, there are, however, two important limits on the plaintiff's ability to press a claim against media defendants. First, the plaintiff must have legally sufficient grounds for making the rather dramatic claim that the media defendants actually intended not only to exploitively maximize profits or to glorify violence, but to spur on the actual commission of violence. And second, the chances of surviving a defendant's motion for summary judgment on the specific intent issue are reduced, in comparison to surviving an earlier motion to dismiss, once the defendants can introduce affidavits regarding their intent, or even the full text of the work in question itself. (See Byers v. Edmondson, 1998) Generally, a media defendant's chances of success on a motion seeking to avoid a full trial go up as the media defendant is allowed to offer more kinds of evidence before trial.

Thus, a plaintiff's case brought against media defendants for inspiring violence may survive a defendant's very early-stage motion to dismiss, at which point the defendant's alleged specific intent to cause the victim's harm is legally presumed. But the defendant's later motion for summary judgment on the basis of a somewhat fuller judicial record and friendlier judicial presumptions may then be successful.[22] In either case, the media defendants would, if successful on their motion, avoid the costs and burdens of an actual trial.

NOTES

1. See, e.g., Robert Barry, "The Development of Roman Catholic Teachings on Suicide," 9 *Notre Dame J.L. Ethics & Pub. Pol'y* (1995) 449, 489.

2. An actual finding or stipulation that Paladin's intention was that the book be used immediately for some serious criminal purpose would be important. The immediacy of serious harm is crucial to the classic "clear and present danger" test in subversive advocacy or illegal incitement cases. (See Brandenburg v. Ohio, 1969 (per curiam)). If there is a genuine opportunity to counter the appeal of a speech through rebutting that speech, such counter-speech remedies are generally preferred in the law. (See Whitney v. California, 1927 (Brandeis, J., concurring)).

3. The classic discussion of this distinction is that of Learned Hand in Masses Publ. Co. v. Patten.

4. The court at this point was trying to draw from the *Brandenburg* incitement case. The speech at issue in *Brandenburg* involved only vague threats of future illegal activity of an unspecified sort, and thus could in this respect be contrasted with *Rice*, but the *Brandenburg* case also involved no attempt to convey any sort of technical instruction on how to commit any illegal activity. (See Brandenburg v. Ohio, 1969)

5. See, e.g., Thomas Emerson, *The System of Freedom of Expression* (New York: Random House, 1970) 3–7.

6. Ultimately, the court denied the existence, or at least the legal significance, of any relevant "ideas" in *Hit Man*.

7. It is certainly possible to think of a book publisher's intent, in some given case, as purely commercial, making the book commercial speech from the publisher's standpoint. And commercial speech certainly receives some degree of first amendment protection in general. (See, e.g., 44 Liquormart v. Rhode Island, 1996). But the problem for Paladin Press in characterizing *Hit Man* as commercial speech would be that commercial speech proposing an illegal transaction, such as murder for hire, is clearly unprotected. (See, e.g., Virginia State Bd. of Pharmacy v. VCCC, 1976). The book *Hit Man* might well not count as itself a proposal for a contract killing. But it might be seen as promoting the entering of two persons into such an illegal transaction, thus at least re-raising some of the issues discussed above.

8. For further discussion, see Beth A. Fagan, Note, "Rice v. Paladin Enterprises: Why *Hit Man* Is Beyond the Pale," 76 *Chi.-Kent L. Rev.* (2000) 503; Avital T. Zer-Ilan, "The First Amendment and Murder Manuals," 106 *Yale L.J.* (1997) 2696 (discussing the district court opinion).

9. It bears mention that Judge Hand himself, and the Supreme Court on several occasions, explicitly adopt this negligence calculus for the specific purpose of resolving a First Amendment issue. (See, e.g., Nebraska Press Ass'n v. Stuart, 1976; Dennis v. United States, 1951). This overlap between tort and first amendment doctrine in itself suggests that the court's claim to have not reached the first amendment issue is truer in form than in substance.

10. The social value of an activity is often taken into account in determining the scope of any tort duty associated with that activity.

11. In some tort contexts, such as that of defamation, ambiguous language may be actionable, but it is typically said that the defamatory meaning must actually be entertained by some portion of the relevant community.

12. In the sense that *Eimann* presumably cannot be cited as a First Amendment case. For the classic statement of the Court's preference for narrowness in judicial decision making, see Ashwander v. TVA (1936) (Brandeis, J., concurring).

13. The "modified" negligence standard requires that the unreasonable risk of harm have been apparent from the face of the ad, without further investigation by *Soldier of Fortune*. Thus the modified negligence test excuses some broader range of negligence by the defendant, while still not requiring anything like intent to harm on the part of *Soldier of Fortune*. Actually, it seems unclear that a specific intent to harm can be inferred from the ad, even on the part of the individual placing the ad.

14. The *Braun* Court also adopted the idea that commercial speech is generally less likely to be deterred by overbroad regulation than political speech, because most commercial speech is tied directly to the speaker's economic welfare. The court also concluded that this logic does not apply to paid classified advertising in which the publisher serves as a mere conduit for the commercial ideas of others. At least some of these assumptions have been accepted by the Supreme Court. (See, e.g., Virginia Bd. of Pharmacy, 1976) Whether there is actually any persuasive case for these claims is doubtful. For common sense objections, see "Commercial Speech—Advertising," 110 *Harv. L. Rev.* (1996) 216, 225–26 & 228 n.84. Political activists and religious martyrs are presumably less willing to compromise over the text of their own expression than are major commercial advertisers. See, e.g., the dynamics in Randall Rothenberg, *Where the Suckers Moon: An Advertising Story* (New York, Knopf: Distributed by Random House, 1994).

15. It should be possible to develop a formula or rule that could insure against liability for straightforward language that avoids unnecessary ambiguity or suggestiveness.

16. Of course, as we have briefly argued above, evaluating the burden on the press and the public for when deciding whether to impose a legal duty of care on the media cannot really be disentangled from freedom of the press considerations.

17. The best known individual defendant in the case was the primary performer, John "Ozzy" Osbourne.

18. Such claims, if true, would amount to at least superficial differences from classics like *Anna Karenina* or *Death of a Salesman*. Ironically, though, there would in some ways be less of a difference between some of Ozzy Osbourne's message and the message conveyed, under dramatically different circumstances and for dramatically different reasons, in Plato's *Apology* and *Crito*.

19. For general discussion, see J.M. Balkin, "The Rhetoric of Responsibility," 70 *Va. L. Rev.* (1990) 197. More broadly, see Mark V. Tushnet, "Anti-Formalism in Recent Constitutional Theory," 83 *Mich. L. Rev.* (1985) 1502, 1514.

20. It is fair to suspect that the idea of a superseding cause—turning the media defendants' acts into mere "conditions" as opposed to crucial legal "causes"—is open to judicial subjectivity, but probably no more so than that of reasonable foreseeability.

21. Depending upon context and genre, of course, warnings accompanying movie publicity might have either a favorable or unfavorable net effect on movie patronage. *Cf.* the "not for the faint-hearted" warnings accompanying some 1950s horror films.

22. There is a substantial body of commentary on the law addressed in this chapter. On the Rice/Paladin Press/Hit Man Case, see, e.g., Isaac Molnar, "Comment, Resurrecting the Bad Tendency Test to Combat Instructional Speech: Militias Beware," 59 *Ohio St. L.J.* (1998) 1333; Patricia R. Stembridge, Note, "Adjusting Absolutism: First Amendment Pro-

tection for the Fringe," 80 *B.U. L. Rev.* (2000) 907. On the question of the proper role of the Brandenburg incitement test in these sorts of cases, see, e.g., S. Elizabeth Willborn Malloy & Ronald J. Krotoszynski, Jr., "Recalibrating the Cost of Harm Advocacy: Getting Beyond Brandenburg," 41 *Wm. & Mary L. Rev.* (2000) 1159; Rodney A. Smolla, "Should the Brandenburg v. Ohio Incitement Test Apply in Media Violence Tort Cases?," 27 *N. Ky. L. Rev.* (2000) 1. More broadly, see, e.g., S. Michael Kernan, "Should Motion Picture Studios and Filmmakers Face Tort Liability For the Acts of Individuals Who Watch Their Films?," 21 *Hastings Comm/Ent L.J.* (1999) 695; Bruce W. Sanford & Bruce D. Brown, "Hit Man's Miss Hit," 27 *N. Ky. L. Rev.* (2000) 69.

9

Investigative Newsgathering and "Neutral Limits" on Press Rights

INCIDENTAL RESTRICTIONS ON THE PRESS

The courts have made clear that whatever the scope of investigatory newsgathering rights may be, such rights are not absolute. Rights are limited by what the courts consider neutral, broadly applicable rules not aimed at specially burdening the press.

A leading case in this area is Cohen v. Cowles Media Co. The holding of *Cohen* is narrow, but the case is broadly instructive. In *Cohen*, the Supreme Court rejected a newspaper's claim that the First Amendment barred an informant from receiving damages for the newspaper's breach of its promise, in exchange for information, to keep confidential the informant's identity.[1]

The Court began by recognizing a newspaper's right to publish properly obtained and accurate news stories of public import without fear of punishment. The Court recognized that "if a newspaper lawfully obtains truthful information about a matter of public significance then state officials may not constitutionally punish publication of the information, absent a need to further a state interest of the highest order." (Cohen v. Cowles Media Co., 1991 (quoting Smith v. Daily Mail Publ'g Co., 1979)) The Court, however, found this general rule not to control the case before it in *Cohen*.

The Court instead emphasized the even broader rule that "generally applicable laws do not offend the First Amendment simply because their enforcement against the press has incidental effects on its ability to gather and report the news."[2] Journalists may not, for example, ignore highway speed limits, impersonate police officers, or break into locked safes in order to further the newsgathering process. Nor is there a First Amendment right of a journalist to refuse to answer appropriate questions before a grand jury, even where this would require disclosing a confidential source of information. (See Cohen v. Cowles Media Co., 1991 (quoting Branzburg v. Hayes, 1972))

To further illustrate this "incidental effect" principle, the Court listed a number of neutral, general regulations upheld despite possible adverse effects on news-gathering. In particular, the Court cited the copyright laws, the National Labor Relations Act, the Fair Labor Standards Act, antitrust laws, and general taxation statutes. None of these statutes singles out the press, any more than does the general state law of promissory estoppel.

The *Cohen* case is thus a straightforward application of general state contract law. One might even argue that the media should welcome this type of suit, because their vulnerability to such suits means that their promises of confidentiality are legally enforceable and therefore trustworthy. Courts should, however, consider balancing the interests, or at least controlling damages awards, when the identity of a confidential news source itself unexpectedly becomes a matter of genuine public importance. The public may need to know a source's identity in order to evaluate otherwise unconfirmable claims on an important matter. And this public need may not be apparent at the time the newspaper agrees to confidentiality. The public interest in reasonably full and accurate discussion of important public issues should at least be considered by the courts in a confidentiality case.

GRAND JURY TESTIMONY AND CONFIDENTIAL NEWS SOURCES

The Supreme Court case of Branzburg v. Hayes[3] has much to teach about the scope of constitutional press rights. *Branzburg* actually involved several underlying cases. The common issues focused on possible First Amendment limits on the extent to which journalists could be called before, or required to testify before, state or federal grand juries. Particularly at issue were cases in which journalists had agreed to keep confidential their knowledge of potentially criminal conduct, including conduct personally witnessed by the journalist.

Justice White's opinion in *Branzburg* began by recognizing that "without some protection for seeking out the news, freedom of the press could be eviscerated." But the opinion then emphasized that the press could rightly be subjected to a variety of broadly applicable, incidental legal restrictions. A journalist may, for example, be punished for contempt of court. Nor, more broadly, does the press enjoy rights of access to information superior to that of the general public. Given these sorts of limitations, the opinion continued, "it is not surprising that the great weight of authority is that newsmen are not exempt from the normal duty of appearing before a grand jury and answering questions relevant to a criminal investigation."

The Court was aware that compelling reporters to testify before grand juries might deter some potential confidential informants from furnishing newsworthy information. The Court concluded that it is difficult to show any real loss in the flow of valuable information to the public as a result of such a rule. Judgments as to the inhibiting effect on the communication of valuable information from such a rule were said to be speculative and to vary widely. (Branzburg v. Hayes, 1972)

While the adverse effects of requiring reporters to testify might be significant, the Court emphasized the problems that a constitutional press privilege would create. There would first be the question of who counts as a member of the press. It would sometimes be difficult to determine who would qualify for the privilege and who would not. (See Branzburg v. Hayes, 1972; See, e.g., Lovell v. Griffin, 1938) The "press," after all, is not self-defining, either in formal or functional terms. Academic researchers, pollsters, and artists all may draw upon confidential sources for publicly useful information. (See Branzburg v. Hayes, 1972) Yet such persons might not be thought of as among the press. On the other hand, freelance journalists, Internet publishers, and amateur, as-yet-unpublished journalists might pose additional problems of definition.

Second, according to the Court, any attempt to balance the need for the reporter's testimony, assuming there is no other means of obtaining the substance of what the reporter would testify to, against free press interests would inevitably involve the court in ranking criminal laws in terms of their importance. Would it be more important to effectively pursue a burglary, or an environmental crime? The legislature and the executive branch, rather than judges, are ordinarily assigned the task of deciding which criminal activities are most serious, and any attempt by courts to place press freedom above law enforcement priorities would be arbitrary.

The Court in *Branzburg* concluded with the observation that its ruling need not be the final word. Denying that the First Amendment requires the creation of a constitutional reporter's privilege need not stand in the way of legislatures who wish to pass a statutory reporter's privilege, nor must it stand in the way of state courts interpreting their state constitutions to require such a privilege.[4]

Although the majority seemed to be firmly rejecting a First Amendment reporter's privilege, the seeds of confusion were sown by Justice Powell's "enigmatic" (to quote Justice Stewart) concurrence. Justice Powell joined in the majority opinion, making him the crucial fifth vote, but he also wrote separately to emphasize how "limited" the majority's opinion was. Powell's concurrence seriously undermined the logic of the majority opinion. Whereas the majority emphasized that the press has no special immunity from generally applicable laws, Powell emphasized that reporters do have constitutional rights. He therefore read the majority's opinion to allow for balancing of these rights on a case by case basis. Justice Powell's reading of the majority opinion is misguided. The majority believed that there was no need for such balancing because the press must comply with generally applicable laws. Even if balancing were appropriate, the majority opinion would have balanced in favor of law enforcement interests when reporters are subpoenaed to testify before grand juries.

The true irony of *Branzburg* is that Justice Powell's concurrence ultimately lent weight to the approach favored by the dissenting justices, who developed a detailed balancing analysis to deal with reporter's privilege cases. Justice Stewart, joined by Brennan and Marshall, explicitly advocated a qualified privilege for reporters subpoenaed to testify before grand juries, imposing upon the government a demanding burden in the case of grand jury subpoenas to obtain confidential information from the press. Justice Stewart's basic concern was for the independence of the press as an institution. He feared the possibility that the government, in its prosecutorial function, might seek "to annex the journalistic profession as an investigative arm of government."[5] (See Branzburg v. Hayes, 1972 (Stewart, J., dissenting)) This would threaten the independent contribution of the press to enlightened self-government.

Given this possibility, Justice Stewart would have required the government to show that the grand jury inquiry, insofar as it bears upon free press rights, is of compelling importance, and can be shown to be substantially related to the testimony sought from the reporter.[6] (Branzburg v. Hayes, 1972 (Stewart, J., dissenting)) More fully and specifically, Justice Stewart wrote that:

When a reporter is asked to appear before a grand jury and reveal confidences, I would hold that the government must (1) show that there is probable cause to believe that the newsman has information that is clearly relevant to a specific probable violation of law; (2) demonstrate that the information sought cannot be obtained by alternative means less destructive of First Amendment rights; and (3) demonstrate a compelling and overriding interest in the information.

Justice Stewart recognized that applying these standards would call for some difficult decisions on the part of the courts. But given the broad investigative powers of grand juries, and the lenient standards of legal relevance by which they are bound, he feared that the alternative to making such judicial decisions was worse.

In the final analysis, Justice Stewart's approach has been just as influential as that of the majority. Although the balancing advocated by Stewart was much more protective than that advocated by Powell, together their opinions comprise four votes in favor of a balancing approach. Justice Douglas cast the fifth vote in favor of extending First Amendment protection to subpoenaed reporters, arguing that the First Amendment gave them absolute immunity from grand jury subpoenas. *Branzburg* therefore represents five votes favoring an extraordinarily circumscribed right to gather news (when one considers that Justice Powell joined the majority), and five votes for a more expansive constitutional right (when one adds Justice Powell's concurrence to the dissenting opinions). This strange anomaly has led many lower courts to interpret the case as requiring, rather than rejecting, a federal constitutional privilege.

What, then, should be said today of *Branzburg*? Would the case have been decided differently after the Watergate investigation? One broader element of the problem in *Branzburg*, and in press coverage of accidents, police raids, demonstrations, and even some military actions, has rarely been addressed by the courts.

This problem involves what we might loosely call the "Heisenberg effect" of press activity.[7] The majority and the dissent in *Branzburg* both assume, as courts typically do, that the press, whatever its various biases, simply reports or comments on events. Often, however, this model itself distorts reality.

The press typically does not merely report an event, in more or less biased ways. The event itself does not, in anything like its reported form, preexist the reporting process. Instead, events are actually the co-creation of those who are usually said to report them.

We see this process at work when a supposedly clandestine Marine landing is greeted with enough press illumination for a night baseball game.[8] But this Heisenbergian transforming phenomenon is much broader. A radical underground political group, and even mainstream political actors, tend to talk and act differently in the presence of the media. On the government's own claim, the disciplinary atmosphere of a prison may crucially depend on the availability or unavailability of press interviews of particular inmates. (See, e.g., Pell v. Procunier, 1974; Saxbe v. Washington Post Co., 1974)

Or let us speculate for a moment about the complex circumstances in the neo-Nazi demonstration case of Collin v. Smith.[9] In this case, the neo-Nazi leader Frank Collin announced plans to hold a brief, peaceable demonstration in Skokie, Illinois. Skokie's population at the time was about 70,000, of whom about 40,000 were Jewish, with about 5,000 being survivors of the World War II era Nazi Concentration Camps.[10]

Against the background of a flurry of municipal legislation and litigation in several forums, the Skokie protest was never held. Collin indicated that his tactical point had in fact been to validate his right to demonstrate in Chicago.[11] Doubtless a neo-Nazi demonstration in Skokie, and even the advance public talk of such a demonstration, would, given the historical circumstances, have inflicted pain on a large number of Skokie residents. It is difficult to imagine that a neo-Nazi group would have chosen to demonstrate in Skokie in the belief that Skokie realistically offered more potential converts to the neo-Nazi cause than any other town. It might, on the other hand, be realistically imagined that whether a neo-Nazi protest in Skokie was peaceable or not, favorably covered or not, or even actually held or not, media coverage of the neo-Nazi group would be extensive. Certainly we would expect less media coverage of otherwise similar events where emotions would not run so high.

The Skokie case illustrates how unrealistic it can be to try to locate some press-independent, pre-existing political event that the press then somehow covers. Media coverage is utterly inseparable from the existence, history, content, and meaning of the event itself. This recognition might tempt us to conclude that principled constitutional decisions for or against the press are in a way impossible. If press coverage—whether free, regulated, or non-existent—results in different underlying realities, we can only decide free press questions by comparing the diverse underlying realities themselves. We must inescapably compare different worlds, and not just one underlying world with and without press regulation.

This kind of comparison of alternative worlds can, however, reasonably be done. We can still make intelligent free press clause decisions even if we must compare, for example, actual and hypothetical worlds in which a Marine landing is unobserved, one in which the landing is illuminated by press lights, and one in which the press is used to lure the opposing forces to an irrelevant location. We can also compare a world in which a prisoner is interviewed and becomes influential with a world in which the prisoner is not interviewed and remains unknown. These admittedly difficult considerations can be managed.

The complexities of free press access cases remain. We cannot, for example, even be sure of maximizing the freedom of the press over the long run merely by always ruling in favor of the press. If, for example, granting a press right were to somehow cause a failure to liberate a repressive regime, or to lead to the prompt building and exploding of a hydrogen bomb, (see United States v. The Progressive, Inc., 1979) such a press right might well fail to maximize the values and purposes underlying freedom of the press in the first place.[12] It is fair to say, for example, that protecting the press right to publish nuclear secrets might undermine, rather than promote, the First Amendment ideal of an enlightened citizenry. Less dramatically, the sheltering of criminals or crime-related information by the press may in some cases promote, and in other cases undermine, the values and purposes underlying freedom of the press.

"UNDERCOVER" AND ARGUABLY TORTIOUS PRESS INVESTIGATIONS

Food Lion, Inc. v. Capital Cities/ABC, Inc. involved undercover reporters who posed as ordinary grocery store employees. In *Food Lion*, the grocery store chain was the unwitting subject of a videotaped and sound-recorded clandestine investigation by *Prime Time Live*, a well-known television network news program. Two reporters obtained jobs as a deli clerk and as a meat wrapper trainee at two separate Food Lion stores by means of false resumes. The resumes presumably did not overstate credentials; rather, the resumes crucially failed to indicate the applicants' continuing status as ABC reporters.

The undercover reporters remained on the job for about two weeks. Their reports contributed to a *Prime Time Live* program that was critical of apparently deceptive, unsanitary, and unhealthful meat handling and meat packaging activities of some Food Lion employees. Food Lion pursued fourteen different claims against ABC, including fraud, trespass, and breach of loyalty. Food Lion's case was largely successful at trial, resulting in only modest compensatory damages but in a five million dollar punitive damages judgment, reduced on appeal to $315,000.

The *Food Lion* case is, given the jury's vigorously expressed sentiment on the punitive damages issue, remarkable. The public interest in sanitary meat handling, wrapping, and labeling is obviously substantial. Journalists cannot reliably obtain accurate pictures of such matters by researching public records or by interviewing relevant store personnel. Yet the jury in the case imposed a multi-million dollar punitive damages judgment (later reduced judicially) on the media defendants. Given the rather technical nature of the tortious conduct alleged, it is difficult to escape the possibility that the jury's impression of the media in general was less than favorable.

On appeal, the Fourth Circuit reversed the judgment that the defendants had engaged in fraud and unfair trade practices in pursuing their story, but affirmed the trial court's judgment that the reporters had breached their duty of loyalty to their employer (Food Lion) and had engaged in trespass. The Fourth Circuit also refused to allow Food Lion to prove damages stemming from the news report's publication.

The Fourth Circuit affirmed in particular the trial court's finding of trespass and of a breach of a duty of loyalty to Food Lion on the part of the two undercover reporters. Generally, employees are bound to faithfully promote the interests of their employers throughout the term of their employment. Working simultaneously for two employers does not necessarily violate this loyalty rule, but the court found ABC and Food Lion to have conflicting interests in this case. Crucially, the court concluded that "[e]mployees are disloyal when their acts are 'inconsistent with promoting the best interest of their employer at a time when they were on its payroll.'" (Food Lion, Inc. v. Capital Cities/ABC, Inc., 1999 (quoting Lowndes Prods., Inc. v. Brower, 1972))

Obviously, there is a sense in which the interests of the reporters and of Food Lion were indeed conflicting. A news magazine segment reporting that things are generally fine at Food Lion is not typically a ratings magnet. At the least, ABC's interest was in accurately depicting conditions at Food Lion. Food Lion executives were evidently not pleased by the nature of the story ABC aired, despite their failure to sue for defamation. At least in the short run, Food Lion's interest could not have been to seek or to welcome any unfavorable publicity.

But there is an equally important sense in which it is doubtful that the real best interests of Food Lion were actually disserved by the reporters' conduct. One could easily argue that attempting to prevent the exposure of unsanitary, misleading, or unhealthful practices in the retail sale of food by a major food store chain would not be in the store's genuine best interests. This is particularly so if we imagine that some potential customers may already be suspicious of Food Lion's practices, and that Food Lion's practices have improved as a result of the investigative television program in question. Certainly, there is sound reason in public policy to recognize and emphasize this sense of a store's best interests.

One could, after all, equally say that in some immediate sense, the interests of Food Lion and of any reporter quite openly asking about Food Lion's health practices would be adverse. It is difficult to believe, however, that the law should conclude in such a case that it is really in Food Lion's best long term interests to stonewall, or to somehow persuade the reporter's audience that its practices are better than they actually are.

It may not be appropriate for the federal courts to write something like a "whistleblower" exception, or a public health exception, into state employment or property law. But freedom of the press, as embodied in the First Amendment, may actually call for something to a similar effect. The Supreme Court has certainly been willing to impose First Amendment-based limits on other common law state torts, although these torts deal with publication rather than newsgathering activities by the press. (See, e.g., New York Times Co. v. Sullivan, 1964; Hustler Magazine v. Falwell, 1988) It would not be difficult to carve out an exception to a broad rule of tort liability for the circumstances in *Food Lion*, based on the obvious and substantial public interest in disclosing possible risks to consumers' health.[13]

The Fourth Circuit in *Food Lion* concluded with an attempt to distinguish ABC reporters from the cases of principled "testers," who also misrepresent their real statuses, interests, and purposes in order to gain access to public areas of business offices. Testers do not generally enter business areas to which bona fide customers are denied access. But it is not obvious why the defendant-reporters in *Food Lion* should be said to have actually interfered with Food Lion's ownership property rights any more than testers would. While the defendant-reporters in *Food Lion* had access to employee-only areas, they did not attempt to rifle through files, open drawers, exercise control over objects, or behave in ways beyond what would be expected of ordinary employees.

Ultimately, cases such as *Food Lion* involve consideration not just of standard tort and property law, along with a duty of employee loyalty, but of the constitutional and practical value of a reasonably well-founded private investigation into potentially significant public health or safety concerns.[14] In the absence of real privacy concerns on the part of Food Lion, and of strong reason to believe that the target of the investigation would be entirely candid if merely openly interviewed, the public interest in being informed of potentially important matters of public health would seem decisive.

The Fourth Circuit, however, narrowly saw the torts committed by the reporter defendants essentially as examples of ordinary, garden-variety employee torts. It is certainly true that ordinary, general tort or criminal law may be applied to the press even if such law has an incidental adverse effect on the ability of the press to gather or report the news. (See, e.g., Cohen v. Cowles Media Co., 1991) The press admittedly is not singled out by general state law requiring employee loyalty or prohibiting trespass. The court in *Food Lion* did recognize a possible conflict between the uniform application of presumably neutral tort rules and investigative journalism. The court concluded, however, that "[w]e are convinced that the media can do its important job effectively without resort to the commission of run-of-the-mill torts."

Upon this, reasonable minds could well differ. Some unattractive health and sanitation practices may be difficult to document through ordinary inspections, and may not always be admitted. In some cases, an ex-employee or a present employee can give a revealing, if perhaps anonymous interview. But no such witness may be available. Or such a witness may be portrayed as somehow disgruntled. A professional undercover reporter may be biased in favor of sensation, but may have no grudge against any particular business. Media bias in favor of sensation, if present and relevant, at least can be brought out as part of the judicial process in which the interest in public health is properly balanced.[15]

JOURNALISTIC INVESTIGATION OF ONGOING CRIMINAL ACTIVITIES: MOTIVE, HARM, AND FIRST AMENDMENT VALUES

The Fourth Circuit case of United States v. Matthews involved a journalist who was successfully prosecuted under the federal Protection of Children Against Sexual Exploitation Act.[16] The defendant, Lawrence C. Matthews, had established a reputation as a radio, print, and documentary journalist, in which capacity he had received a Peabody Award in 1983. Some of his journalistic work, including a piece on homelessness for the Washington Post, involved adopting a particular lifestyle in order to do valuable journalistic work. Thus, Matthews' piece on homelessness involved his appearing for a week to be a homeless person.

Matthews had done several radio news reports on the availability of online child pornography, and he had informed the FBI of the particulars of his discoveries, including parental offers of child prostitution. In 1996, Matthews decided to investigate, on a professional but freelance basis, the scope of Internet-related child pornography and child exploitation. Matthews claimed at trial that he was aware that many of his Internet contacts were in fact FBI agents posing as female minors, and that this aspect of law enforcement was itself to be part of the story.

In the course of his activities, Matthews sent or received at least ten photographs over the Internet involving child pornography. Matthews claimed at trial that he did not know that sending or receiving child pornography over the Internet was illegal. He also argued that sending or receiving such materials was necessary for an effective journalistic investigation. Internet pornographers, Matthews argued, would remain inaccessible to journalistic investigation unless Matthews proved his lack of law enforcement association by himself sending pornographic images.

Thus, Matthews argued that his participation in criminal activity was no more extensive than necessary to develop his investigative story. On the other hand,

Matthews was unable to produce much in the way of handwritten notes docu-
menting his conversations and other research focusing on the child pornography
article project.

The Fourth Circuit in *Matthews* began by recognizing the indispensable value,
but limited scope, of press freedom under the First Amendment. In particular, the
court recognized that child pornography has no constitutional value. (See United
States v. Matthews, 2000 (citing Osborne v. Ohio, 1990; New York v. Ferber,
1982)) As the Supreme Court has recognized, the production and recording of
child pornography using actual children inflicts distinctive harms not associated
with adult pornography. Thus, the legal standards adopted by the Supreme Court
to govern obscene adult materials, or adult pornography, do not necessarily govern the law of "actual" child pornography. Following the Supreme Court's lead,
therefore, the Fourth Circuit acknowledged that the occasions on which a legitimate independent purpose will justify sending or receiving of such child pornography will be rare.

The defendant Matthews did not argue primarily that child pornography itself
is of significant constitutional value. In fact, we can better appreciate Matthews'
argument if we take him to be insisting upon, rather than denying, the common
public understanding of the harmfulness of child pornography utilizing actual
children. It is precisely this common public understanding that gives journalistic
value to Matthews' attempt to address genuine uncertainties about the real scope
and frequency of child pornography.

The harmfulness of child pornography does not by itself tell us even vaguely
how common child pornography is. It is hard to tell how high an enforcement pri-
ority should be applied to child pornography laws unless we have at least some
reasonable idea of the actual frequency of the harm. It seems reasonable to allow
a defendant in the position of Matthews to argue, at trial, that reliable information
on the scope of the problem is scarce. It seems equally reasonable to permit such
a defendant to at least argue that there are no reliable ways of determining the real
scope of the problem that do not involve at least some, if carefully minimized,
violation of anti-pornography laws. Of course, some might respond that it is the
job of law enforcement officials, not journalists, to investigate violations of criminal law. Yet undercover journalistic investigations are a valuable adjunct to government enforcement of the criminal law, because the government has neither the
time nor the resources to investigate all private wrongdoing.

If a court is never allowed to answer these questions based on the evidence,
there is a risk of undervaluing the First Amendment interests of the public in
informed decision-making. This is not to suggest that a journalist defendant in
such a case should be acquitted merely upon showing a significant social problem, scarcity of reliable public information, and the unavailability of legal means
of obtaining such information. This would, by contrast, overweight the First
Amendment interests at stake.

The public interest would instead be best served by requiring a journalist defendant to show, as above, the value and necessity of the extent of his otherwise illegal activity, and then asking the court to weigh the First Amendment value of the journalist's work against whatever harms can properly be associated with that work. Part of the problem may be that there is often relatively great First Amendment value in exploring poorly understood but arguably serious public problems. The severity of the problem of child pornography thus enters in on both sides of the legal case.

One additional controlling element, if we wish, could be a legal opportunity, falling short of mandatory self-incrimination, that the journalist formally notify state or federal authorities in advance, and not merely after the fact, of the nature of the journalistic investigation involved, at least where the authorities themselves are not the subjects of the investigation. Such advance notice would of course not immunize the journalist from prosecution. But a journalist's conscientious willingness to identify him or herself to authorities in advance and perhaps offer to cooperate would help both sides build a record for any possible trial, and should certainly weigh into the court's consideration.

Requiring a journalist to show all of the above in order to obtain an acquittal might well discourage some genuinely worthwhile journalistic projects. But imposing such requirements would also go some distance toward meeting the Supreme Court's concerns that the press not simply be granted a license to violate the criminal law, (See United States v. Matthews, 2000 (citing Branzburg v. Hayes, 1972)) and that the press not be exempted from general laws incidentally limiting their ability to gather the news. (See United States v. Matthews, 2000 (citing Cohen v. Cowles Media Co., 1991))

It is difficult to believe that there are no cases in which a journalist's contribution to public understanding of an important public issue could legitimately raise some sort of a defense to a charge of criminal conduct,[17] or that courts cannot recognize such cases as well as they can carry out any number of other tasks. The harm to the public in legally discouraging important contributions to the public understanding in such cases may not be vivid or keenly felt. But this does not mean that such harms are invariably less real than those stemming from a journalist's violation of the law.

Of course, a general criminal statute represents the legislature's official declaration of the harmfulness of the prohibited conduct. But it is also fair to say that the progress of our First Amendment case law is partly a matter of reduced deference by courts to general judgments of social harmfulness made by legislatures. As we have become more sensitive to First Amendment values and interests, we have in some contexts been less willing to rely on general legislative judgments of social danger.

An important example of this phenomenon is the contrast between the Supreme Court free speech case of Gitlow v. New York and Justice Brandeis' classic concurring opinion in Whitney v. California. The Court majority in *Gitlow*, notably excluding Justices Holmes and Brandeis, concluded that there was no need for the trial court to consider whether the defendant's conduct threatened any harm where the legislature itself had "previously determined the danger of substantive evil arising from utterances of a specified character. . . ." Under *Gitlow*, the harm of a specific kind of speech, once generally determined by the legislature, was not to be reconsidered by courts in particular cases under particular circumstances.

In contrast, Justice Brandeis, joined by Justice Holmes in the *Whitney* concurrence, was less deferential to broad legislative judgments of harm. For Justice Brandeis, and for many later observers, the legislature's general finding that a particular kind of speech posed a danger that was clear, imminent, or substantial amounted only to a legal presumption, rebuttable by an individual defendant at trial. (See Whitney v. California, 1927 (Brandeis, J., concurring)) After all, at least some kinds of dangers—gasoline shortages, for example—appear and disappear without immediate legislative acknowledgment. Justice surely requires some attention not only to general tendencies, but to particular and exceptional circumstances as well.

NOTES

1. Actually two newspapers were involved. Each one made an independent decision to publish the name of their source for public court records involving a candidate for Lieutenant Governor of Minnesota.

2. For a similar principle bearing upon the First Amendment's free exercise of religion clause, and for criticism of the use of such a principle in that context, see the opinions in Employment Div., Dep't of Human Resources v. Smith, 494 U.S. 872 (1990)(neutrally intended general state regulation of the use of peyote; regulation upheld as against religiously motivated user).

3. For discussion of *Branzburg*, see Monica Langley & Lee Levine, "Branzburg Revisited: Confidential Sources and First Amendment Values," 57 *Geo. Wash. U. L. Rev.* (1988) 13 (distinguishing anti-establishment sources and "insider" or internal government sources, particularly in cases of reporting on the government); Paul Marcus, "The Reporter's Privilege," 25 *Ariz. L. Rev.* (1984) 815 (arguing for a qualified, limited such privilege, based on appropriate balancing of the interests, in light of the best available evidence).

4. More broadly, see William J. Brennan, Jr., "The Bill of Rights and the States: The Revival of State Constitutions as Guardians of Individual Rights," 61 *N.Y.U. L. Rev.* (1986) 535. For further brief discussion of the logic of the *Branzburg* plurality, see Potter Stewart, "Or of the Press," 26 *Hastings L.J.* 631 (1975)(reprinted in 50 *Hastings L.J.* (1999) 705, 709).

5. Note also that forcing disclosure of a confidential government informant might tend to discourage government whistleblowers who fear retaliation.

6. See id. at 739–40 (Stewart, J., dissenting).

7. For background, see, e.g., Laurence H. Tribe, "The Curvature of Constitutional Space: What Lawyers Can Learn From Modern Physics," 103 *Harv. L. Rev.* (1989) 1,

17–20. See also R. George Wright, "Should the Law Reflect the World? Lessons For Legal Theory From Quantum Mechanics," 18 *Fla. St. U. L. Rev.* (1991) 855.

8. For discussion of the Somalian beach landing press coverage, see, e.g., Michael D. Steger, "Slicing the Gordian Knot: A Proposal to Reform Military Regulation of Media Coverage of Combat Operations," 28 *U. S.F. L. Rev.* (1994) 957, 957; James P. Terry, "Press Access to Combatant Operations in the Post-Peacekeeping Era," 154 *Mil. L. Rev.* (1995) 1; William A. Wilcox, Jr., "Media Coverage of Military Operations: Oplaw Meets the First Amendment," *Army Law.* (1995) 42.

9. The crucial opinion is Collin v. Smith, 578 F.2d 1197 (7th Cir. 1978).

10. See Geoffrey R. Stone, et al., *The First Amendment* (Gaithersburg: Aspen Law & Business, 1999) 84.

11. See Stone, *The First Amendment,* 85.

12. For discussion of the related basic values widely thought to underlie freedom of speech protection, see, e.g., Stone, *The First Amendment,* 9–15.

13. See, for example, Lyrissa Barnett Lidsky, "Prying, Spying and Lying: Intrusive Newsgathering and What the Law Should Do About It," 73 *Tul. L. Rev.* (1998) 173, in which one of the authors of this volume argues for the creation of such a privilege.

14. See, e.g., Thomas M. Devine, "The Whistleblower Protection Act of 1989: Foundation For the Modern Law of Employee Dissent," 51 *Admin. L. Rev.* (1999) 531 (discussing scope of public employee whistleblower protection); Robert G. Vaughan, "State Whistleblower Statutes and the Future of Whistleblower Protection," 51 *Admin. L. Rev.* (1999) 581 (discussing public and private sector whistleblower law).

15. For discussion of additional causes of action that have been brought against investigative media by the targets of their investigation, see Veilleux v. National Broadcasting Co., 206 F.3d 92 (1st Cir. 2000) (addressing claims sounding in defamation, misrepresentation, emotional distress, and invasion of privacy).

16. 18 U.S.C. § 2252 (1994 & Supp. IV 1998).

17. Technically, an investigative journalist who successfully exposes, and perhaps remedies, some serious harm or risk of harm might raise a defense of "necessity," but the necessity defense is generally confined by the courts to narrow circumstances. See, e.g., George C. Christie, "The Defense of Necessity Considered From the Legal and Moral Points of View," 48 *Duke L.J.* (1999) 975; Note, "And Forgive Them Their Trespasses: Applying the Defense of Necessity to the Criminal Conduct of the Newsgatherer," 103 *Harv. L. Rev.* (1990) 890.

10

Police Operations and the Press: Hindrance, Assistance, and the First Amendment

The police, the press, and the public interact in many ways. In some cases, the police hinder newsgathering by excluding the press from the scene of an accident, crash, or other newsworthy event. In other cases, the police invite or allow the press to "ride along" with them, or tip the press off to newsworthy events. Both types of cases involve potential conflicts between the police, the press, public health and safety, privacy, and the public interest in news, gossip, and gore.

STATE V. LASHINSKY: THE CLASSIC CONFLICT BETWEEN PRESS AUTONOMY AND POLICE AUTHORITY

The New Jersey case of State v. Lashinsky is a good illustration of these conflicts. In *Lashinsky*, the defendant was a press photographer for a local newspaper, the *Star-Ledger*. He was convicted of disorderly conduct for refusing to obey a police officer's order to move back from the immediate scene of a "gory, fatal automobile accident" just off the well-traveled Garden State Parkway.

Lashinsky had noticed an overturned car just off the Parkway and had then parked 150 feet away, displaying his official press pass identification in the windshield. He then approached the accident scene and took several photographs. Fifteen to twenty minutes later, a New Jersey State Police Officer arrived on the scene. The timing of the arrivals of Lashinsky and then of the officer suggests that Lashinsky could not possibly have been denied the opportunity to take a number of photographs from a number of angles, and he in fact did so.

By the time of the arrival of the police officer, a crowd of about forty to fifty people had gathered at the accident scene. A first aid squad member already on the scene advised the arriving police officer that there were casualties. In particular, "[a] girl, seriously injured, covered with blood and going into shock, was pinned inside the automobile against the corpse of her mother, who had been decapitated."

After calling for an ambulance and additional police units, the police officer noticed that the automobile was leaking gasoline, oil, and transmission fluid and that the still-connected car battery had fallen and cracked open. Items of personal property were strewn about the crash site. Given the various safety and accident site-preservation concerns, the police officer ordered away from the scene everyone except two first aid squad members. A number of spectators declined to immediately comply, but eventually all the spectators, with the exception of the photographer Lashinsky, began to move some distance away.

Lashinsky showed the police officer his official press card issued by the state police, but the officer again asked Lashinsky to leave the scene. At this point, there was some divergence in the trial court testimony. Lashinsky testified that he was arrested immediately, before being given a chance to respond. In contrast, the police officer and the two first aid squad members testified to a rather heated three- to four-minute argument between Lashinsky and the officer, with Lashinsky's position being that each could do his own job in the presence of the other. Lashinsky did not threaten or touch the officer, but in light of his refusal to leave the scene, Lashinsky was arrested.

One of the first aid squad members testified that she had wanted the officer's assistance in administering first aid, but that the officer's time and attention were occupied by his dispute with Lashinsky. On the other hand, at some point after Lashinsky was arrested, two other photographers, one from the New Jersey Highway Authority and the other from the State Police, were allowed to take photographs.

The New Jersey State Supreme Court, in affirming Lashinsky's conviction, first observed that the state disorderly conduct statute could not be confined merely to actual physical or specifically intended obstruction of physical movement. The court then addressed the applicability under the circumstances of the disorderly conduct statute to a member of the press, particularly when the press representative timely identified himself as such.

The court acknowledged that the general right of journalists to gather news is legally recognized and is indeed "entitled to special constitutional protection." (State v. Lashinsky, 1978 (citing, inter alia, In re Farber, 1978)) The court quoted the United States Supreme Court's decision in Branzburg v. Hayes (1972) for the proposition that "without some protection for seeking out the news, freedom of the press could be eviscerated." Such constitutional protection, however, is not without its limitations. The court determined that "the constitutional prerogatives of the press must yield, under appropriate circumstances, to other important and legitimate government interests." (State v. Lashinsky, 1978 (citing In re Farber, 1978))

In particular, the court noted, the liberty of the press to gather news is not meaningful without a minimally sufficient degree of public order. The value of at least minimal orderliness may apply not just as a general social background requirement, but in specific circumstances as well. Thus, the liberty of the press could be subjected to content-neutral[1] reasonable time, place, and manner restrictions. Presumably, the court's reference merely to orderliness was not intended to thereby exclude the various safety and other public interests potentially at stake in *Lashinsky*.

On the other hand, there are also important public interests underlying the newsgathering and related activities of the press. The press, however defined, may be in a position to serve broad public informational interests better than other observers at an accident scene. There may be cases in which restraints on press access to news sites and sources may be unreasonable, whereas excluding the general, non-journalist public would not be harmful to the public interest and would be constitutionally permissible.

Given the possibility of conflicts among important public interests, the *Lashinsky* court majority concluded that a balancing of the competing values, in context, was required. A recognized member of the press[2] acting within the scope of his or her journalistic responsibilities should, if possible, be accommodated by the police.

The *Lashinsky* court majority, however, held that the defendant's actions could reasonably have been determined to have impeded the officer in the discharge of his own vital responsibilities. Lashinsky's refusal to cooperate by withdrawing was thus unlawful and constitutionally unprotected. The court concluded in particular that:

Lashinsky's obstreperous actions impeded the trooper. The officer, working virtually alone, could not, in his professional judgment, have permitted defendant to remain, even as a member of the press, and still discharge his own paramount responsibilities for the safety and welfare of those who were his immediate concern.

The *Lashinsky* court was, however, not unanimous. Justice Pashman, in particular, emphasized in dissent the distinct constitutional rights accorded the press, as opposed to the more general right of freedom of speech, and the central First Amendment concern for the free flow of information to the public. The news media, Justice Pashman observed, promote democratic self-government and serve as an institutional check upon governmental abuse and error. They make possible enlightened choice by the public on the basis of publicized facts and a range of expressed opinions.

Against this general background, Justice Pashman found insufficient obstruction or interference on the part of the defendant. The prolonged argument between the police officer and the defendant may, indeed, have itself impaired the officer's ability to carry out his responsibilities. But if the original order to leave the scene was itself unreasonable or unconstitutional, the real responsibility for any such impairment would lie chiefly with the police officer himself.

Justice Pashman then focused on the risk to the photographer-defendant himself, conceding that the press need not be granted access to the most dangerous sites. But in the case at bar, Justice Pashman concluded, the risk to the defendant was "not substantial"[3] and was presumably fully understood and appreciated by the defendant, who was capable of taking appropriate steps to minimize the personal risks involved.

Overall, the majority in *Lashinsky* was inclined to apply a particularized fact-sensitive balancing test. Justice Pashman's dissent may have simply weighed the conflicting interests differently. Any fact-sensitive balancing test case may be decided on a mixture of articulated and unarticulated, conscious and unconscious, considerations. In *Lashinsky*, some of the justices were not entirely impressed by the quality of the defendant's conduct. (Clifford, J., dissenting) It is difficult to be sure how any such consideration might have played into the fact-sensitive balancing and into the case outcome.

Two arguably relevant factors were not taken into explicit consideration by the court in *Lashinsky*. One might imagine that under the circumstances of the accident, involving a gruesome fatality and a trapped, injured daughter, the taking and widespread publication of photographs would raise issues of personal privacy.[4] Any privacy interests, even to simply not be photographed under unconsented-to, harrowing, grotesque circumstances, may be amplified when joined with any sense that the photographer acted insensitively. Courts might, of course, differ over the proper weight to be assigned to the victims' privacy interests in *Lashinsky*. But they seem entitled to at least some consideration.

Loosely related to the privacy interests at stake is a second consideration. It may, under the circumstances, actually be surprisingly difficult to argue that photographs of the accident victims or of their car can easily be linked to the noblest purposes underlying freedom of the press. It is all very well to refer generally to the role of the press in promoting democratic self-government, checking governmental error and abuse, and furthering the deliberations of an intelligently informed public. But these values may not inevitably link up to the particular defendant's desire to remain on the accident scene and continue taking photographs.

Of course, the courts should not generally attempt to somehow rank the importance of public concerns in free press cases. If, say, the engineering or design of a particular stretch of highway, or of the guardrail, or automobile and tire safety issues are somehow even arguably implicated, courts should not generally second-guess the public interest in such matters. But there is no reason why devoted proponents of a free press should live by the illusion that every item in every newspaper has some serious purpose somehow bearing on the common welfare. Some of the photographs, we may imagine, might have had only a superficial, sensationalized, titillating, and voyeuristic interest.

It is not obvious that the latter sorts of frivolous, voyeuristic interests are of the highest constitutional order. And we might again consider that the defendant photographer had already taken several photographs before being asked to leave, and finally that the Highway Department and the State Police both had photographers on the scene at a later point. Doubtless there may well be cases in which discouraging private news photography, while allowing official photographs, may bias the flow of public information. But if we set aside the highway or automobile safety possibility, there is no obvious reason to believe that any such scenario was relevant in *Lashinsky*.

Often, we can reasonably distinguish, and weigh differently, potentially useful photographs from the merely gruesome. Realistically, though, courts are reluctant to edge into an area fraught with relativism and subjectivity, or even to appear to distinguish among levels of public taste. In a given case, a court may have some confidence in distinguishing potentially useful information from the pointlessly grotesque, apart from any ideological point of view. But even such a court may be reluctant to discount the status of anything at all that is printed in a general newspaper for which there is apparently some popular market demand. Fact-sensitive balancing tests should still generally allow courts to take such considerations into account, whether implicitly, or even consciously, or not.

Courts recognizing a free press right in cases involving police operations might wish to use the *Lashinsky* case as a useful sort of legal baseline, in the sense that some press conduct is more justified, and some less, than that of *Lashinsky*.[5] All else being equal, mine disasters[6] and major airplane crashes[7] will, for example, tend to be of greater public interest and significance than individual car crashes at random sites. But ongoing rescue operations at a mine cave-in, for example, should not be jeopardized by press insistence, singly or in great numbers, on immediate physical access to trapped victims. Under these hypothetical circumstances, the possibility of saving lives or the minimization of injury will often be worth the less vivid or delayed press coverage, especially if there are no apparent safety issues requiring immediate press access.

Many accident cases, unlike *Lashinsky*, take place on private property, thereby raising a possible trespass issue.[8] Any trespass-related crime or tort committed by the newsgatherer should be weighed against the likely significance of any otherwise unavailable evidence of official error, incompetence, corruption, or other matter of potential public concern. While courts should be generally unwilling to assess the merits of competing views of official competence, they already frequently consider quite explicitly whether a given subject matter bears upon the public interest. (See, e.g., Connick v. Myers, 1983; Gonzalez v. Lee County Housing Auth., 1998; McVey v. Stacy, 1998; Azzaro v. County of Allegheny, 1997; Campbell v. Towse, 1996; Watters v. City of Philadelphia, 1995). Of course, the courts tend to accord no greater constitutional rights to the press than to the general public. Arguably, though, courts should consider the possible significance, or the patent triviality, of the press role in a given case. Admittedly, the public interest or public issue value of a photograph may sometimes be apparent only after the fact and not at the scene itself. But this should not invariably license the trampling of competing concerns for physical safety, or even for privacy.

POLICE ASSISTANCE TO THE PRESS AND THE INTERESTS OF THIRD PARTIES

Sometimes, the relationship between the press and the police is one not of acute confrontation, but more like one of mutual assistance. The sort of private "media ride-along" involved in the police raid case of Wilson v. Layne is one such example.

In *Wilson*, federal and county plainclothes officers invited a reporter and a photographer for the Washington Post along on an attempt to execute an arrest warrant for felony suspect Dominic Wilson. As it happened, the police computer listed as Dominic Wilson's home a residence that was actually the home of Dominic Wilson's parents. Dominic Wilson was listed on police computers as likely to be armed, to resist arrest, and to assault police officers. The arrest warrants were addressed to "any duly authorized peace officer" and made no reference to media accompaniment to, physical presence at, or witnessing of, the arrest.

The federal and state officers, along with the two invited media representatives, entered the residence of Dominic Wilson's parents at 6:45 a.m. The arresting group was greeted angrily by Dominic Wilson's father, who was initially believed by the arresting officers to be Dominic Wilson, and who was quickly subdued on the floor. The mother of Dominic Wilson directly witnessed some of these proceedings.

The Washington Post photographer "took numerous pictures" of the proceedings. The arresting officers, along with the media representatives, left when their mistake was realized. At no time did the media representatives materially assist the officers in actually executing the arrest warrant. *The Washington Post* published no photographs of the incident.

The plaintiffs sued the arresting officers in their personal capacities for money damages, claiming that their civil rights were violated. The Supreme Court denied any financial recovery, because at the time the officers executed the search warrant, state law did not clearly prohibit them from bringing the media into the Wilson's home. Since their actions were not clearly unlawful, the officers were immune from money damages liability. (Wilson v. Layne, 1999 (citing, inter alia, Anderson v. Creighton, 1987; Harlow v. Fitzgerald, 1982)) But the Court did address the constitutional merits of the plaintiffs' claims. The plaintiffs' underlying constitutional claim was that the officers' bringing along the private newspaper reporter and photographer to document the intended arrest crucially contributed to what amounted to an unreasonable search and seizure of the plaintiffs in violation of the Fourth and Fourteenth Amendments.

The Court began its constitutional analysis by assuming that the arresting officers, based on their warrant, were entitled to enter the home in question in an attempt to arrest Dominic Wilson. But bringing along the reporter and photographer was not explicitly within the terms of the arrest warrant, and in effect expanded the scope of the warrant. The reporter and photographer did not help execute the warrant, in the literal and direct sense of somehow helping in the attempt to arrest Dominic Wilson.

The officers did argue, however, that the presence of the reporter and photographer served a number of legitimate purposes related to proper law enforcement. These included the value of publicizing government efforts to combat crime, promoting accurate reporting on law enforcement activities, minimizing police abuses, protecting suspects, and even protecting the safety of the arresting officers.

In response, the Court took no issue with the value of these specified interests in the abstract. Instead, the Court emphasized that such interests are irrelevant to the judicially authorized purpose of actually serving the particular arrest warrant in question. Further, such purposes could in some respects be served as well or better by utilizing official police photographers or videotape operators. Certainly a private photographer might in some cases protect police officers, but it seems at least as likely that private journalists could themselves pose an additional risk for the officers to manage. Parenthetically, we might suppose that the risks to the photographer discussed above in *Lashinsky* could be paralleled by risks to journalists and others in ride-along felony arrest cases.

Most deeply, though, the Court granted the possible press and public interests at stake, and recognized the value of private journalists informing the general public about the administration of the police and criminal justice system. (See Wilson v. Layne, 1999) Generally, "in a society in which each individual has but limited time and resources with which to observe at first hand the operations of his government, he relies necessarily upon the press to bring to him in convenient form the facts of those operations." (Wilson v. Layne, 1999 (quoting Cox Broad. v. Cohn, 1975)) There was thus a substantial free press interest at stake in *Wilson*.

Against this undoubted First Amendment interest, however, the Court weighed the plaintiffs' Fourth Amendment interest in the security and privacy of their home. (See Wilson v. Layne, 1999) The Court determined that under the circumstances, the presence of the private journalists could not justify the burden on Fourth Amendment rights. The Court concluded by holding that "it is a violation of the Fourth Amendment for police to bring members of the media or other third parties into a home during the execution of a warrant when the presence of the third parties in the home was not in aid of the execution of the warrant." (Wilson v. Layne, 1999)

The language and logic of *Wilson* cover search warrants as well as arrest warrants, as was explicitly confirmed by the Court in a companion case. (See Hanlon v. Berger, 1999) But in other respects, the precise scope of *Wilson* is unclear. The actual publication of photographs or of a news story, for example, could interestingly cut in opposing constitutional directions. Any resulting publicity may aggravate the invasion of the plaintiff's privacy. But such resulting publicity may, on the other hand, also enhance the extent, depth, and significance of any contribution by the media to public understanding of police practices. Thus in some cases, greater invasion of the plaintiffs' privacy may actually be linked to greater fulfillment of the main constitutional press function.

As with any search case, however, the weight of the interest tends to vary under the circumstances, including the degree of intrusiveness, the degree of the sense of personal violation, the length of the search, the extensiveness of the search, and of course the degree of publicity given to what is intimate, personal, or private. Any balancing of individual privacy interests with conflicting public interests or free press rights must be sensitive to these considerations.

The proper judicial result might vary, for example, if an arrest were carried out on a busy public sidewalk, or if the identity of the arrested parties was electronically obscured in all media images. Then there is the further, separate problem of media presence at searches of non-residential business premises.

One variation on the latter theme was developed in an Ohio appellate case, State v. Covey. *Covey* involved repeated visits by a local Humane Society cruelty investigator to business premises with a number of poorly housed and poorly cared for animals. The defendant was charged with and convicted of animal cruelty. On appeal, but not at trial, the defendant claimed a violation of her Fourth Amendment rights because members of the media, with no relevant law enforcement function, were present along with the officers executing the search warrant.

Reviewing for the presence of plain error, the appellate court recognized the force of the above case of Wilson v. Layne, but found the actual case at bar not to fall within its scope. The court read *Wilson* as involving a police invitation to media members to accompany the officers on the arrest, and distinguished the case at bar on its facts. The court concluded in particular that "since there is no indication in the record that the Toledo Humane Society invited the media to accompany it on the raid, we cannot say that the media's presence at the scene violated appellant's constitutional rights."

The court in *Covey* thus distinguished *Wilson* not on any difference in the character of the premises or the nature of the warrant, but on the basis of a lack of invitation to or actual accompaniment by the media in *Covey*. The latter considerations may prove of special legal interest. What constitutes an "invitation" to the press may not always be clear. The idea of an 'invitation' may be taken in either a narrow, formal sense, or a broad, informal sense. If the police merely inform selected media in advance of the time and place of a search or arrest, and then leave the door open or do nothing to discourage media presence, have the media been "invited" on or to the raid?

It is difficult to believe that the fact of quite literally riding along with, or actually physically accompanying, the police some distance to the site in question will typically be constitutionally crucial. The degree of the privacy invasion, though perhaps not the fullness of the reported story, will typically not vary depending upon whether the media accompany the police or arrive independently, shortly before or after the police. The focus should thus be on the degree to which the police facilitate or somehow specially permit the presence and activity of the media.

If members of the private media are permitted at the execution of any search or arrest warrant, questions of selectivity, favoritism, and bias on the part of the police, and on the part of the favored journalists, will inevitably arise. It seems imaginable that the police might tend to offer special access, promoting immediate first-hand news coverage, to those inclined to report relatively favorably on police activities. There might eventually arise an understanding that unfavorable coverage of the police may result in the withdrawal of valuable special access. It is, after all, one thing for a newspaper merely to interview witnesses and participants after the fact, and another to have spectacular photographs and eyewitness reports from the event in progress.

It is possible that the public might come to discount favorable police coverage by those media outlets granted any sort of informal advance notice of special events. And it is also possible that the major problem may eventually come to be not conscious bias on the part of the favored media, but the natural inclination to sympathize with those persons and institutions to whom we have been granted specially privileged access.

It is also certainly imaginable that the uninvited, disfavored media may, by way of contrast, take up some of the slack in criticizing police activities. But they would then be doing so partly on the basis of questionable motives of their own, and they would still lack direct access to the events in question. They would continue to suffer whatever disadvantages in circulation or viewership their absence from the actual arrests or seizures might bring.

Overall, it is fair to say that the police hindrance cases and the police cooperation cases are really not entirely removed from one another, as though they were at the far ends of a spectrum. This is because the interests of the police and press, realistically, cannot be either entirely adversarial or entirely shared. Even where the police, for legitimate or illegitimate reasons, would prefer that the press not be present, the press can serve the public interest, and even the ultimate interests of the police, by accurately reporting on police conduct. But on the other hand, too much cooperation between the police and police-preferred media may increase the physical and legal risks faced by the police, and may tend to distort press coverage and public understanding of police activities.

NOTES

1. The Court made no specific reference at this point to any general requirement of content-neutrality, or to any difference in the level of judicial scrutiny applied to content-based restrictions on press activity.

2. The Court understandably did not attempt to address the "Who counts?" issue of the definitional scope of the press, or any issues of official recognition or accreditation of members of the press.

3. The dissent by Justices Clifford and Mountain would have required a showing of either actual physical interference or specific intent to interfere on the part of the defendant photographer.

4. For discussion, see, e.g., Rodney A. Smolla, "Privacy and the First Amendment Right to Gather Information," 67 *Geo. Wash. L. Rev.* (1999) 1097; Erwin Chemerinsky, "Balancing the Rights of Privacy and the Press: A Reply to Professor Smolla," 67 *Geo. Wash. L. Rev.* (1999) 1152.

5. See, e.g., the cases and analysis in Tom A. Collins, "The Press Clause Construed in Context: The Journalist's Right of Access to Places," 52 *Mo. L. Rev.* (1987) 751, 795; Timothy B. Dyk, "Newsgathering, Press Access, and the First Amendment," 44 *Stan. L. Rev.* (1992) 927, 948–49; Note, "And Forgive Them Their Trespasses: Applying the Defense of Necessity to the Criminal Conduct of the Newsgatherer," 103 *Harv. L. Rev.* (1990) 890; Hannah Shay Chanoine, Note, "Clarifying the Joint Action Test for Media Actors When Law Enforcement Violates the Fourth Amendment," 104 *Colum. L. Rev.* (2004) 1356.

6. See O. Marie Anderson, "Mine Accident Investigations: Does the Press Have a Right to Be Present?," 98 *W. Va. L. Rev.* (1996) 1121.

7. See Karen S. Precella, "Freedom of the Press: Does the Media Have a Special Right of Access to Air Crash Sites?," 56 *J. Air L. & Com.* (1990) 641.

8. See, e.g., David F. Freedman, Note, "Press Passes and Trespasses: Newsgathering on Private Property," 84 *Colum. L. Rev.* (1984) 1298.

11

Press Access to Persons, Sites, Proceedings, and Documents

The press has a legitimate interest in a wide variety of what might be called access rights. The law of press access cannot be quickly summarized with useful precision, because the interests at stake vary in different contexts. Any attempt to catalog press access law exhaustively will prove merely exhausting. This chapter, however, illustrates some general press access themes and formulas in some important contexts.

THE PRISONER INTERVIEW CASES

The scope of press rights in prisoner interview cases was established in two cases decided by the Supreme Court on the same day, Pell v. Procunier and Saxbe v. Washington Post.[1] *Pell* involved a First Amendment challenge by inmates and by professional journalists to a recently revised section of the California Department of Corrections Manual. The section at issue provided that "[p]ress and other media interviews with specific individual inmates will not be permitted." The Supreme Court recognized that the rights of prisoners and of journalists may be intertwined in this context. The Court's analysis began with the distinctive status and purposes of the prison system. The First Amendment rights of inmates, and any derivative rights of journalists, must therefore be consistent with the status of prison inmates, and with "the legitimate penological objectives of the corrections system."

With this general limitation on First Amendment rights in mind, the Court then determined that the prison regulation at issue should be considered in light of any available alternative channels of communication remaining available to the prison inmates. The Court recognized that the available alternative speech channels might not be a perfect substitute for journalist-controlled individual interviews. But the possible availability of such alternative speech channels was at least a constitutionally "relevant factor in the analysis." (Pell v. Procunier, 1974 (citing

Kleindienst v. Mandel, 1972)) In particular, the Court found it "clear that the medium of written correspondence affords inmates an open and substantially unimpeded channel for communication with . . . the news media." (Pell v. Procunier, 1974) With regard to illiterate or simply less than fluent writers, the Court pointed to the presumed availability of writing assistance from other inmates, family, or friends.

There is actually little to complain of if alternative speech channels really are as good from a free speech standpoint as the channels currently available, bearing in mind especially the speaker's own judgments as to message, timing, medium, and so forth. But often the only alternative speech channels will serve the speaker substantially less well from the standpoint of the speaker's own message priorities.

Some speakers, for example, will care greatly about the size, or the demographic makeup, of their audience. Other speakers will care strongly about cost considerations. Some will care most about avoiding any distortion in their message. Others will care more about a sense of immediacy and conveying emotional fervor. Some will care most about the sheer volume of information conveyed. Respecting the First Amendment rights of each of these speakers means respecting their own choices as to message, timing, and medium, and not assuming that one size of an alternative speech channel fits all.

Recourse to written correspondence may be fine in some First Amendment context and for some First Amendment purposes. Doubtless Dr. King's *Letter From Birmingham Jail*, in its printed form, has had a greater impact than any number of standard filmed prison interviews would have had. Sometimes a thousand words will be worth any number of pictures. But this will hardly be the case with many prisoners. Prisoners will often legitimately have quite divergent First Amendment priorities.

Nor should we forget the broad changes in our communicative culture since Dr. King's 1963 *Letter*. By and large, mass reform movements today are not galvanized by epistolary eloquence. A televised interview may convey a sense of visual immediacy and dynamism far beyond the capacity of typical letter writing and letter reading.

One's sympathies in this sort of case may depend upon one's vision of the media's role in such cases. The perspective of the prison authorities on the interaction between individual, media-selected inmates, and the interviewing media figure may well differ from that of the media. Prison authorities may have legitimate or illegitimate motives for limiting media access. Until required by the Supreme Court to revise its regulations, the prison in *Pell* had censored statements in letters that 'unduly complain' or that 'magnify grievances.' (Pell v. Procunier, 1974) This administrative perspective emphasizes the potential for deception and exaggeration in prisoner speech and emphasizes the disciplinary problems that prison interviews may create.

In contrast, the press might be concerned with persons allegedly wrongly convicted or excessively sentenced, or with prisoners who articulate a particular political cause or a broad grievance with special eloquence and authority. In the extreme case, such a figure could be classified as a political prisoner. Here again, we might think of the arrests of Dr. King in the United States, Mahatma Gandhi in India, and Natan Scharansky in the Soviet Union.

There is a conflict between the perspectives of prison administrators and at least some journalists as to the overall social value of individual interviews of media-selected inmates. The Supreme Court in *Pell* was forced to somehow resolve this conflict. The Court took the matter of security concerns in these sorts of cases to be within the special province of prison administrative expertise, and thus upheld the restrictive press interview regulations.

What the majority opinion in *Pell* undervalues, however, is that both the prison administration and the press bring their own distinct, relevant expertise to bear on the problem of prisoner interviews. Doubtless prison officials bring special insight into questions of security. But it is equally clear that the press brings special insight into how, in a prison setting, to best serve the public informational interest in whatever prison inmates may wish to convey.

In the prison interview context, the Court's deference should thus have been two-sided, rather than one-sided. The press is in a position to shed light on the informational value of an exchange of letters, or of videotaped personal interviews with prisoners selected neither at random nor by a prison administration recently intent upon avoiding the undue magnification of grievances. Neither the prison administration nor the press need be thought of as really neutral and dispassionate. But this may be all the more reason for courts to not defer to the judgments of either institution at the expense of the other.

The *Pell* court went on to observe, however, that inmates who wished to communicate with the outside world were not confined to letter writing. Inmates could also communicate through limited personal visits with family, clergy, attorneys, and "friends of prior acquaintance," all of whom could in turn communicate with the press. (Pell v. Procunier, 1974) Indirect contact with the press was thus possible. The Court again deferred to administrative security concerns and observed in particular that the prison visitation rules seemed not to be content-based.

It should be noted, though, that the distinction between content-based and content-neutral restrictions on prisoner communications is realistically of only limited value. Typically, newsworthy prisoners tend toward unfavorable views of the criminal justice and prison administration system. Of course, there are also human interest stories of genuinely repentant prisoners. But it is fair to say that many prison administrations would be pleased to hear only limited public praise from prisoners, in exchange for also hearing only limited public criticism. There is thus a crucial sense in which limiting the flow of both praise and criticism from prisoners is not neutral in its effects.

The Court's legal analysis acknowledged the value of a free press in maintaining an informed, open society, the constitutional disfavoring of any prior restraint on free expression, and the constitutional status of seeking out and gathering news itself prior to publication. (See Pell v. Procunier, 1974 (quoting Branzburg v. Hayes, 1972)) The Court observed that "'without some protection for seeking out the news, freedom of the press could be eviscerated.'" (See Pell v. Procunier, 1974 (quoting Branzburg v. Hayes, 1972))

On the other hand, "some" protection for newsgathering hardly approaches absolute protection. Press access to what is newsworthy is often limited. The press is typically excluded, for example, from grand jury sessions, Supreme Court conferences, public bodies justifiedly meeting in closed executive session, and meetings of private organizations. The press can also be barred from accident or disaster scenes where the general public is excluded as well. (See Pell v. Procunier, 1974)

In *Pell*, the court observed that press access to specified prisoners was no less than that of the general public. This relative press equality was deemed crucial. The press has "no constitutional right of access to prisons or their inmates beyond that afforded the general public." Broadly, "[t]he Constitution does . . . not require government to accord the press special access to information not shared by members of the public generally." After all, virtually any denial of press access to any source or site could be argued to involve a constriction of the flow of information. (See Pell v. Procunier, 1974)

By implication, the *Pell* court also believed that there is no general constitutional right of public access to specified prisoners under the First Amendment. No doubt there could be no public access right involving, say, a dozen conversations per day with any given prisoner. But in the prisoner interview context, and in other contexts as well, it is difficult to know precisely how to assess the Court's comparison of the respective rights of the press and of the general public.

Let us assume that the press seeks access to specified prisoners for the purpose of interviewing them, and perhaps then publishing a story. How, precisely, are we to envision comparable activity by the general public, as opposed to friends, relatives, clergy, and attorneys? For what comparable purpose, then, would a member of the general public seek access to a particular prisoner? Should we imagine an amateur, non-press interview? If we cannot specify the relevant purpose in such a case, we can hardly determine the constitutional strength of the general public access claim. Or we might assume that such a vague sort of activity on the part of the general public, as opposed to the press, cannot be of much constitutional weight.

In either case, it would be disturbing to then, and on that basis, quickly conclude that the rights of the press to interview specific prisoners must rise no higher than the right of the general public to act for no particularly comparable reason. But if we assume, instead, that the general public would be seeking prisoner access in order to conduct an amateur, non-press interview and then possibly somewhere publish a story, the constitutional picture is still a bit murky.

It would at best be merely unhelpful for the Court to say that the rights of the press and of the general public are the same, if the general public is doing essentially the same thing that the press is doing. But we should still wonder whether the First Amendment right of the press should rise no higher than the right of the general public to prisoner interviews, where the general public makes no pretense to journalistic competence. If the press has any special competence or any special informative role, why wouldn't non-journalist members of the general public often be an inadequate substitute for the press, and therefore of lesser practical constitutional value?

Consider, by way of analogy, the respective rights of the press and of the general public at an accident scene. Can we uncontroversially say that the rights of the press to cover the story should rise no higher than the rights of the public merely to gawk, mill about, chatter, and then tell their friends? This is not to assume that journalists are invariably serious and more adept at observing or interviewing than the general public, but instead that a journalist's efforts are more likely to result in a more informed general public. By virtue of what we might call the social division of labor, there is thus obvious reason not to confine the relevant press rights to those appropriate to the non-press general citizenry.

Any holding in *Pell* that the rights of the press rise no higher than those of the general public, even if somehow defensible on their merits, may nevertheless be unnecessarily broad. After all, the prison's motive in barring interviews of prisoners selected by the press was based on particularized institutional discipline and security concerns. It is not clear that visits by the general public to an uncooperative prisoner invariably tend to elevate that prisoner to prison celebrity status, or to embolden further intransigence, as readily as visits by the press, particularly if any sort of further publicity arises from the press interview. If, under the specific prison circumstances, the press inadvertently posed a significantly greater risk to prison discipline and security than did the general public, a holding on those grounds alone would have been narrower[2] and less controversial than generally limiting press rights to those of the general public.

In the simultaneously decided case of Saxbe v. Washington Post, the Supreme Court majority took essentially the same tack as in *Pell*, over the dissents of Justices Powell, Douglas, Marshall, and Brennan. *Saxbe* involved a federal prison limitation, at least in non-minimum security federal prisons, on press-selected prisoner interviews similar to that upheld in *Pell*. The Federal Bureau of Prisons cited similar discipline and security concerns to those in *Pell* in justifying the interview restrictions. The Court majority in *Saxbe* found the case "constitutionally indistinguishable" from, and thus controlled by, *Pell*.

The dissent in *Saxbe*, on the other hand, emphasized the journalistic and public informational value of genuine, face-to-face interviews of the crucial figures in a news story, as opposed to brief conversations with randomly selected inmates. The dissent then took issue with the majority's suggestion in both *Saxbe* and *Pell* that the key First Amendment consideration should be non-discrimination against the press relative to the general public. The dissent urged that

[a]t some point official restraints on access to news sources, even though not directed solely at the press, may so undermine the function of the First Amendment that it is both appropriate and necessary to require the government to justify such regulations in terms more compelling than discretionary authority and administrative convenience.

Further, the dissent would have required the prisoner interview regulations to be more narrowly tailored, in the sense of not being so broadly restrictive as to unnecessarily limit the rights of a free press.

The dissent in *Saxbe* recognized legitimate concerns that press interviews can contribute to prison discipline and security problems, and increase costs by requiring individual decisions in every case of a prospective interview. Ultimately, the dissent suggested the possibility of limiting "the number of interviews of any given inmate within a specified time period."[3] Such a limitation might conceivably reduce interview-dependent prison discipline problems to acceptable limits.

MILITARY BASES AND VIEWPOINT-NEUTRAL RESTRICTIONS

Some additional grasp of the issues in *Pell* and *Saxbe* can be drawn from the factually quite different District of Columbia Circuit case of JB Pictures, Inc. v. Department of Defense. *JB Pictures* involved a media request for access to photograph or film the casketed remains at Dover Air Force Base of American war casualties. For some time, American troops killed abroad were returned to the United States and to their final resting place through Dover Air Force Base, with ceremonies at the Dover base honoring the war dead. Under a revised policy, ceremonies honoring the war dead were instead to be held closer to the homes of the deceased's family, with the families holding the option of excluding the press from the local ceremonies. The plaintiffs challenged their exclusion from seeing or photographing the caskets at the Dover facility. Their argument raised the issue of viewpoint bias in the federal regulation of media access. Access to war dead was generally denied, while access to other, presumably more favorable or more positive events was generally available.

As an initial matter, the court recognized that there was no universal right of press access to publicly-owned facilities merely because of the possibility of better news coverage or enhanced public insight. (See JB Pictures, Inc. v. Dep't of Defense, 1996 (quoting Zemel v. Rusk, 1965)) The court distinguished between facilities or events that are traditionally open to, and likely to benefit from, public access, and those that are not. Criminal trials, for example, typically fall into the former category, and the working areas of the White House, the Supreme Court, and the FBI into the latter. (See JB Pictures, Inc. v. Dep't of Defense, 1996) A long tradition of open access in a given context argues in favor of a right of press access in that context. But some courts maintain the possibility of a right of press access to some kinds of facilities or events even without an open access tradition in that particular context, based on a balancing of the government's institutional concerns against the severity of the burden on press rights.

The Court in *JB Pictures* applied a balancing test, but was unwilling to review the press access regulations with any further stringency. The military base access regulations at issue did not overtly discriminate on the basis of favorable or unfavorable press views. More interestingly, the Court concluded that the actual effects on public sentiment of viewing the war dead need not be invariably negative.

The plaintiffs had argued, in effect, that some military-related images, including the somber spectacle of the return of flag-draped coffins to grieving, perhaps distraught family members, are less likely to convey a pro-government message than, say, the stirring ceremonial send-off to foreign military action of resolute, determined troops. There seems to be something to this argument, at least as a matter of popular belief. It is often argued that the American public cannot remain supportive of military action in the face of constant, graphic images of American casualties, or of grief and mourning. It is certainly arguable that the differences in television coverage of the Vietnam and Persian Gulf Wars—often, of American casualties in the first case, and of precise long-distance air strikes in the second— may have affected the degrees of public support for American policy.

But the Court in *JB Pictures* rightly pointed out that historically, for many cultures, images of returning war casualties have evoked contrasting moods and responses. While such images may provoke reassessment or demoralization, we can also imagine cultures in which similar images galvanize righteous indignation and fortify a will to prevail. By way of loose analogy, a military force can never be sure whether bombing or blockading enemy civilians will tend to break their will, or instead steel their resolve.

It is thus possible that even in our culture, which sets a high value on each individual casualty, any government attempt to manipulate press coverage and public reaction via press access regulation may backfire. At least this prospect of "backfiring" seems a more realistic possibility in this context than in the prison interview cases. The realistic content-bias in the prison interview regulation cases will normally be more predictable than the content-bias of the regulation in *JB Pictures*. If the Supreme Court majority is untroubled by such bias in the prison cases, it is unlikely to be disturbed by the less predictable bias of the press access regulation in *JB Pictures*.[4]

JOURNALISTIC HYPERLINKS FROM OFFICIAL CITY WEB SITES: THE PUBLIC FORUM CATEGORIES AND A "REVERSE ACCESS" PROBLEM

The Sixth Circuit case of Putnam Pit v. City of Cookeville raised interesting free press issues in a new technological context. The Putnam Pit was "a small, free tabloid and Web page," whose publisher sought extensive Cookeville records and the opportunity to establish a hyperlink from the Cookeville official Web site to that of the Putnam Pit. The City provided the requested records in hard copy, as opposed to electronic form, and denied the opportunity to establish a hyperlink from the City's Web page.

Ultimately, the Sixth Circuit upheld the granting of the defendant City's summary judgment motion on the question of the form in which the records were delivered. But the Sixth Circuit also addressed the plaintiff's request for a hyperlink to the Putnam Pit Web site.

Doubtless there are occasions when delivery of time-sensitive records or other materials to the press—unindexed random boxes of documents when either an indexed set or an easily explored electronic version is also cheaply available—is more of a burden upon than assistance to the press. But the court concluded that whether the Putnam Pit counted as a genuine press outlet or not, its rights were not violated by the City's failure to provide electronic versions of the materials sought.[5]

On this point, the Sixth Circuit cited cases involving the deposition of President Clinton (United States v. McDougal, 1996) and the audio tapes of President Nixon. (Nixon v. Warner Communications, 1978) In the case involving President Clinton, the press and public were denied access to the videotaped deposition, where the "information" contained in the videotapes was readily available in other formats. (Putnam Pit v. City of Cookeville, 2000) In the Nixon case, the press was held to have no constitutional right of access to copies of White House tapes where the public at large had no such rights, and where the press did have access to the contents of the tapes. (See Putnam Pit v. City of Cookeville, 2000)

It would create too much of an adminstrative burden on government if a government agency had to provide information in whatever form the recipient wanted. Sometimes, however, the format in which information is provided can affect its practical informational value. The courts in these cases may actually be making the essentially journalistic judgment of whether the meaning, impact, content, and informational value of one medium is, in context, the same as that of another. It is odd to assume that a videotape does not relevantly differ from a printed transcript. It is hard to square such a belief with court rulings in other contexts. Appellate courts, for example, generally recognize that there may be useful information in the observed bearing and demeanor of a trial witness that is not conveyed by a bare printed transcript. (See, e.g., United States v. Wolf, 1987; In re Clay, 1994; Hartselle v. Dr. Pepper Bottling Co., 2000)

For a court to say that a transcript is as good as a videotape is for the court to substitute its judgment for that of the press. The court, lacking any claim to journalistic expertise in such a case, in effect decides that whatever loss of information as may result from denial of press access to information in a particular format is trumped by other sorts of values, including administrative costs and the protection of privacy or fair trial rights.

The second issue in *Putnam Pit* involved the City of Cookeville's denial of a hyperlink from its official Web site to the Putnam Pit. The City's purpose in allowing a limited, non-distracting number of hyperlinks from its Web site was to promote the City and its services, amenities, construction and tax policies, and its governmental activities and job openings. (See Putnam Pit v. City of Cookeville, 2000) The City denied the Putnam Pit's request for a hyperlink to the City Web site because the hyperlink would not be consistent with these particular purposes.

The Sixth Circuit held that the Putnam Pit had raised a triable issue of fact as to whether the City of Cookeville had denied the hyperlink request based on impermissible viewpoint discrimination. There was some evidence to suggest that the City refused the hyperlink because the Putnam Pit had criticized city officials. This would provide an issue for trial even if the City's Web site were considered a non-public forum.

The basic problem, however, lies in the ability to characterize the disagreement between the City and the Putnam Pit in two distinct ways, pointing in opposing legal directions. Certainly, one can easily see the Putnam Pit's critical, muckraking journalism as presenting an alternative point of view to that of the City. This approach would help the Putnam Pit's First Amendment case. The City's denial of a hyperlink would on this approach be seen as viewpoint discrimination, and as a violation of the Putnam Pit's First Amendment rights.

On the other hand, though, the intended purpose of the official City Web site was presumably to promote, rather than critique, the City and its general policies. The official City Web site is on this approach therefore an instance of government speech, loosely akin to an official government position paper, a government report, or a "fireside chat."[6] Presumably, government speech itself is generally intended to present the government's position in a favorable as opposed to even a neutral or bipartisan fashion. Government officials presumably defend their policies and their regimes. The purpose of the forum itself would therefore be inherently incompatible with some sorts of criticism of the City, and thus with some points of view. This alternative approach would thus undermine the Putnam Pit's First Amendment case.

Perhaps the best defense of the Sixth Circuit's result in this case would draw a distinction between an official city Web site and instances of government speech that allow for criticism and response only in other places. There may thus be important differences between a general city Web site and a city policy position paper. And more specifically, there may be important differences between providing a hyperlink away from a city Web site and an extensive critique of a city on the city's own Web page. It might well undermine a city's promotional purposes for that city's own Web site to feature criticisms of the city, even if the city disclaimed and attempted to rebut the criticisms. But it is more difficult to claim that the mere presence of one or a few innocuously named hyperlinks on a city's Web site would significantly impair the city's promotional, image-enhancement purposes. A city could disclaim agreement with the content of any or all hyper-linked Web sites if it feared that allowing a mere hyperlink amounts to an endorsement of whatever content that hyperlink may lead to.

PRESS ACCESS TO DOCUMENTS HELD BY STATE AND FEDERAL EXECUTIVE BRANCH AGENCIES

In Capital Cities Media, Inc. v. Chester, newspaper plaintiffs sought access to documents concerning water contamination that were held by a state environmental agency. The Third Circuit Court of Appeals held that press access to the documents was not guaranteed by the First Amendment. The underlying news story in *Chester* involved contaminated drinking water that made over four hundred water company customers ill. The *Times-Leader* published numerous articles on the subject, including articles on the enforcement strategy and priorities of the Pennsylvania Department of Environmental Resources. The plaintiffs sought a large number of potentially relevant documents, many of which were then made available, at least for review, at the agency's regional offices or at the state capital.

Access to a number of the documents, however, was withheld. Such documents included citizen complaints, attorney-client communications, internally generated technical memoranda on enforcement strategy and alternatives, and the results of the Department's own investigation into contamination problems. Departmental guidelines also exempted disclosures barred by law, or which would impair personal reputation or personal security, or which would result in the loss of federal funds. (See Capital Cities Media, Inc. v. Chester, 1986)

The newspaper plaintiffs urged that the exemptions from disclosure be judicially tested by strict scrutiny under the First Amendment, requiring the government to show that barring press access to specified documents was necessary in order to promote a compelling governmental interest. The Third Circuit Court of Appeals, sitting en banc, declined to impose such a test.

The court began its analysis by conceding that a major purpose of the First Amendment is to promote the circulation of information necessary for responsible democratic government. Legitimate newsgathering by the press is generally a protected activity. (See Capital Cities Media, Inc. v. Chester, 1986 (quoting Houchins v. KQED, Inc., 1978 (in turn quoting Branzburg v. Hayes, 1972))) The federal government and most state governments have codified some right of access to government documents by the press and other persons, along with limitations on such access, in federal and state Freedom of Information Acts, Privacy Acts, and Government in the Sunshine Acts.[7] (See Capital Cities Media, Inc. v. Chester, 1986)

The court in *Chester* observed, however, that the very prevalence of such statutory grants of access throws the distinctive language of the First Amendment into relief. The Freedom of Information Acts and related statutes do not merely specify what is already implicit in the First Amendment. Instead, such statutes supplement the scope of the first amendment. The Third Circuit distinguished between a "negative" right to freedom *from* governmental interference with speech and the press, and a "positive" right, not protected by the First Amendment, amounting to "a right to know and a concomitant governmental duty to disclose." No constitutional source demands disclosure of particular governmental documents.

The court in *Chester* cited a number of Supreme Court cases denying a general First Amendment right of access to government information, beyond a right of equal access once access has been granted to another class of persons. The court recognized, as well, Supreme Court authority upholding a First Amendment right to attend various sorts of trials and trial-related court proceedings. But these cases, according to the Third Circuit, generally require access only to those court and other governmental proceedings that historically have generally been open to the public.

The most that could be drawn from the Supreme Court case law, the court concluded, would be a two-part test for a constitutional right of document access. First, is there an historical tradition of access to the sorts of documents in question? And second, would public access play "a significant positive role in the functioning of the particular process in question?" (Capital Cities Media, Inc. v. Chester, 1986 (quoting Press-Enterprise v. Superior Court, 1986)) The Third Circuit held that the party claiming access must prove that both prongs of the test are met, rather than treating the two prongs as merely relevant considerations, more of one of which might compensate for less of the other.[8] The Third Circuit was willing, for summary judgment purposes, to assume the presence of the second prong, but not the first.

The court's crucial focus was thus on the historical access issue. The Third Circuit in *Chester* focused not on the history of access to the specific records held by the particular state agency, but on the history of access, more generally, to the kinds of records more broadly described. The latter, broader sort of historical access inquiry would be less subject to manipulation by individual agencies. And here, the court concluded, there was no allegation by the plaintiffs that executive agencies had generally granted access to the type of agency records involved here. (See Capital Cities Media, Inc. v. Chester, 1986; Calder v. IRS, 1989; Foto USA, Inc. v. Board of Regents, 1998) Thus, no First Amendment right of access to the records attached. (See Capital Cities Media, Inc. v. Chester, 1986)

Applying such a two-part test, whether as merely two relevant considerations or as two necessary elements, will often prove difficult. Historical practice, after all, may well be clearer and more unequivocal at a specific level than at a broader level. Particularly if we describe the relevant records broadly, it will often be possible to find some exceptions to whatever the more prevailing pattern of access may have been historically. Are such exceptions merely exceptions, or can they operate like a waiver? What if the "exceptions" appear to be relatively recent? Could they constitute a developing trend?

More importantly, though, we must ask why we should give historical traditions of access a possible veto over public access in the era of computer files,
micro-miniaturization, and the Internet. Surely there may be differences in the
practicality of hand copying documents in the late eighteenth century and merely
sending an electronically locatable file as an e-mail attachment. Agency documents that were once impossible or inconvenient to provide plainly may no
longer be so.

Nor should we assume that historical practice and the effects of public access
on agency functioning are both entirely neutral criteria. In a narrow sense, an
agency's having to devote time and expense to providing access to agency records
will of course typically impair, rather than promote, agency functioning. But in a
broader sense, it could also be said as a matter of law that an agency's being
responsive to reasonable public access requests, with appropriate exceptions, is
important to the functioning of a responsive administrative branch. In a broad
sense, then, the second consideration in the Third Circuit's two part test is always
met by any reasonable and appropriate access request.

As well, it is hardly clear that historical tradition and governmental functioning, in a narrow sense, should exhaust the relevant constitutional considerations.
There is surely more to the First Amendment than merely the smooth operation of
the relevant government agency.[9] (But *cf.* Calder v. IRS, 1989) The public interest
in document disclosure may go beyond proper agency functioning. In some cases,
we should weigh the interests of press freedom and of an informed public against
the interest in efficient agency functioning.

On any analysis, all relevant First Amendment values should be taken into
proper account. The First Amendment, admittedly, is not itself[10] a specific, constitutionally binding Freedom of Information Act.[11] (See also ACLU v. Mississippi,
1990) But on the other hand, focusing too narrowly on historical traditions of
access and on narrow issues of specific agency functioning underserves basic
First Amendment values and purposes.

PRESS ACCESS TO CONFIDENTIAL DISCIPLINARY
PROCEEDINGS

Media access to professional disciplinary hearings has been litigated in a number
of contexts. The informative North Carolina Supreme Court case of Virmani v.
Presbyterian Health Services Corp. involved a civil suit filed against a hospital
arising from a confidential medical peer review committee proceeding and decision. The occasion for the published opinion in *Virmani* was the trial court's decision to seal the peer review committee records and to close the judicial
proceedings discussing those records.

The North Carolina Supreme Court in *Virmani* applied essentially the two-part
test discussed above in connection with the *Chester* case. Thus, the court consid-

ered the historically open or closed status of the general kind of trial and administrative committee determinations at issue, as well as whether public access would promote or impair the functioning of the type of proceeding at issue.

Ultimately, the court determined that the portions of the civil proceeding at issue in *Virmani* could be closed. Both prongs of the test pointed away from a constitutional right of access. First, the court observed that "[f]or many years now, the workings of medical review committees and the materials that they consider have been closed to the public and have been deemed confidential." (Virmani v. Presbyterian Health Services Corp., 1999; See also, e.g., Johnson Newspaper Corp. v. Melino, 1989)

As to the agency functioning element, the court recognized prior case authority that "external access to peer investigations conducted by staff committees stifles candor and inhibits objectivity." The state legislature's view was, to similar effect, that "public access plays a negative role in the functioning of the medical peer review process." Thus, both historical tradition and agency functioning argued against accessibility of the hearings in question. Whatever public health interest there may be in fuller access to such hearings was thought to not rise to controlling significance.

Interestingly, despite the fact that the court found that there was no historical tradition of access to such documents and that access would not contribute to agency functioning, the court did not end the analysis there. Instead, it assumed the existence of some sort of First Amendment right of access to civil proceedings in general. The court therefore went on, remarkably, to apply strict scrutiny to the closure in the *Virmani* case. Applying this standard, the court found a compelling public interest in maintaining peer review board confidentiality, and narrow tailoring in that no means less restrictive than closure would secure that confidentiality in the civil trial setting.

There is a critical difference between the two constitutional standards that were applied in *Virmani*. Requiring the press to prove both a history of open access and a positive effect on agency function is clearly more demanding on the press than requiring the agency to show that its denial of press access can pass strict scrutiny. Consider, for example, a case in which press access has historically been denied, but in which the only current public interest in denying press access can somehow be outweighed. Such a denial of press access will be upheld under the two-part history and function test. But the denial of press access would fail a strict scrutiny test, for lack of a compelling public interest in barring press access.[12]

Of course, even where the media are constitutionally denied access to confidential disciplinary proceedings, they may still hold some related First Amendment rights. The absence of a constitutional right to attend a proceeding does not by itself tell us whether, or in what circumstances, the publication of information stemming from such a proceeding can be criminally punished. This is a separate constitutional issue.

One set of such circumstances was involved in the Supreme Court case of Landmark Communications, Inc. v. Virginia. A newspaper, the *Virginian Pilot*, published an article accurately discussing a judicial commission's pending investigation of the conduct of a state judge. The newspaper was then indicted for violating a statute prohibiting public disclosure of such information.

The United States Supreme Court emphasized the context and narrowness of the issue presented. The newspaper did not claim a First Amendment right to attend the meetings of the Commission. No question of prior restraint, or of publishing illegally obtained information, was involved. Nor was there any issue of the power to punish actual participants in the judicial investigation for publishing confidential information. Instead, the case focused on the constitutionality of punishing media defendants, or other persons, for publishing lawfully obtained accurate information bearing upon the confidential commission inquiry.

The United States Supreme Court concluded, based on an ad hoc balancing of interests, that the threatened punishment violated the newspaper's First Amendment rights. The publication itself was said to lie "near the core of the First Amendment." (Landmark Communications, Inc. v. Virginia, 1978). The state's interests in criminalizing the publication were, vaguely, "insufficient to justify the actual and potential encroachments on freedom of speech and of the press which follow therefrom." The Court then affirmed the value of a free press in promoting an independent and responsible judiciary. While the usefulness of the press in this context doubtless does support the result in *Landmark Communications*, there is a strong argument to be made that it also equally supports a constitutional right of press access to judicial disciplinary commission proceedings. However, the Supreme Court has always distinguished between imposing an affirmative obligation on the government to provide access to information versus punishing the publication of lawfully acquired information.

PRESS ACCESS TO CIVIL TRIAL PROCEEDINGS

The status and scope of press access rights to various sorts of civil trial proceedings have not yet been decisively determined by the Supreme Court. Courts confronting such cases are often guided, to one degree or another, by broad language from the Supreme Court's decisions in the context of access to criminal trials, which we address in this section.

A useful case to consider in the civil trial context is the California Supreme Court case of NBC Subsidiary v. Superior Court. This case involved a trial judge's order preventing the public, including the press, from being present for any courtroom activity in the particular case conducted outside the presence of the jury. The transcripts of such proceedings were to be sealed until the conclusion of the trial. The trial court's main consideration was the effects of extensive media coverage of the case, which involved a well-known Hollywood celebrity marriage.

The California Supreme Court vacated the trial court's restrictive order as insufficiently justified under a California "open courts" statute, as construed in light of the First Amendment. The court adopted what it took to be the appropriate standard in criminal trial cases:

The First Amendment of the federal Constitution generally precludes closure of substantive courtroom proceedings in criminal cases unless a trial court finds that (i) there exists an overriding interest supporting closure; (ii) there is a substantial probability that the interest will be prejudiced absent closure; (iii) the proposed closure is narrowly tailored to serve that overriding interest; and (iv) there is no less restrictive means of achieving that overriding interest.

The court then argued for the relevant similarity of criminal and civil cases. In particular, the court quoted Justice Holmes, before his elevation to the Supreme Court, to the following effect:

It is desirable that the trial of [civil] causes should take place under the public eye, not because the controversies of one citizen with another are of public concern, but because it is of the highest moment that those who administer justice should always act under the sense of public responsibility, and that every citizen should be able to satisfy himself with his own eyes as to the mode in which a public duty is performed.

The court concluded that a First Amendment right of access to civil trials and associated documents obtained. (See NBC Subsidiary v. Superior Court, 1999)

Such access rights do not extend, the court assumed, to the products of the discovery process or other litigation documents not involved in the trial itself. (See NBC Subsidiary v. Superior Court, 1999) Nor does the First Amendment provide the public or the press access to appellate court conferences and deliberations, or to the trial notes of a trial court judge. (See NBC Subsidiary v. Superior Court, 1999) But as to ordinary civil trial cases, the California Supreme Court applied criminal trial closure standards and concluded that with which it began:

[P]ublic access to civil proceedings serves to (i) demonstrate that justice is meted out fairly, thereby promoting public confidence in such governmental proceedings; (ii) provide a means by which citizens scrutinize and check the use and possible abuse of judicial power, and (iii) enhance the truth-finding function of the proceeding.

In addition, the availability of a mere paper transcript, post-trial, was not a constitutionally adequate substitute for live press and public access to the proceedings in question. (See NBC Subsidiary v. Superior Court, 1999; See also Whiteland Woods, L.P. v. Township of West Whiteland, 1999)

One problem requiring much further general attention is that of the constitutional adequacy or inadequacy of any one form of access as opposed to another, whether in an administrative, civil, or criminal trial context. This general problem of "substitutability" is a broad one, but a single example will suffice. Why, precisely, is it that a transcript is not a constitutionally adequate substitute for attendance at a court hearing where no jury is present, but mere physical presence at a civil trial is a constitutionally adequate substitute for videotaping the proceedings for broadcast to a large audience? What are the relevant tests for the constitutional substitutability of one means of access for another? What considerations are relevant? Much judicial work remains to be done in this area. As yet, there is little guidance.

PRESS ACCESS TO CRIMINAL TRIAL PROCEEDINGS

The Supreme Court has provided extensive guidance, however, on the constitutional right of access to criminal trials. Among the most authoritative and useful Supreme Court decisions with regard to press access to criminal trials is that of Globe Newspaper Co. v. Superior Court. The underlying case involved a rape trial where the three testifying victims were, in two instances, 16 years old, and the other 17 years old, at the time of trial. The trial court, on its own motion, ordered that the courtroom be closed to the press and public during the course of the trial. The *Globe Newspaper* intervened to bar the closure.

On the First Amendment merits, the Supreme Court pointed first to its recent plurality decision in Richmond Newspapers, Inc. v. Virginia. Richmond Newspapers, in which seven Justices recognized a constitutional right of public and press access to attend criminal trials. The *Globe Newspaper* majority cited the First Amendment's value in protecting "the free discussion of governmental affairs," and in ensuring that "the individual citizen can effectively participate in and contribute to our republican system of self-government" as underlying the logic of public access to criminal trials. The *Globe Newspaper* majority then emphasized that historically, criminal trials have generally been open, and that access tends to enhance the quality, integrity, and the perceived fairness of such trials, as well as contributing more broadly to overall governmental legitimacy. The Court concluded with the observation that "the institutional value of the open criminal trial is recognized in both logic and experience." In other words, the Court concluded that there was an historical tradition of access to criminal trials, and that access contributed to the positive functioning of the trial process. (See Globe Newspaper Co. v. Superior Court, 1982)

Even so, the Court recognized the non-absolute character of the criminal trial access right. Denials of access to criminal trials must be limited: "the State's justification in denying access must be a weighty one." The Court, however, then rather oddly characterized the specific interest in closing the trial case to public access as that of seeking to "inhibit the disclosure of sensitive information," even though it then recognized clearly separate interests, such as the psychological well-being of a minor.

In any event, the Court then held that strict scrutiny should apply to the denial of public access to a criminal trial. The Court recognized that content-neutral time, place, and manner restrictions on trial access, as in the case of physically limited seating space for a popular trial, should not draw strict scrutiny. But the Court clearly treated the concern for minimizing trauma for rape victims as somehow more akin to a content-based restriction on the press, in the sense of requiring strict scrutiny.

In any event, the Court held that protecting the minors' psychological well-being and encouraging accurate testimony were compelling governmental interests. But the Court was unwilling to find a broad closure rule in such cases to be narrowly tailored.[13] (See also Bell v. Jarvis, 2000) A case-by-case approach to closure issues, instead, would be sensitive to the realistic differences among the young victims, their maturity levels, and their psychological states. Of course, the press and public must in such instances be given an opportunity for a meaningful hearing on their possible exclusion. (See Globe Newspaper Co. v. Superior Court, 1982)

Not all criminal trials, however, are like the rape prosecution in *Globe Newspaper*, and not all criminal case access issues involve the actual trial stage itself. Different state interests, and different alternatives bearing upon narrow tailoring may be involved. In Gannett Co. v. De Pasquale, for example, the Supreme Court applied a Sixth Amendment public trial analysis, and found such a right to be personal to the accused. *De Pasquale* involved not press access to the trial itself, but to a pretrial suppression hearing.

The Supreme Court in *De Pasquale* assumed that a constitutional right of access exists in such circumstances. The Court then found that the trial court had permissibly balanced First Amendment access rights against the criminal defendant's fair trial rights, including the potential prejudice stemming from an open pretrial suppression hearing. The Court emphasized that the complete lack of public access was only temporary, in that (at least) a transcript of the suppression hearing was made available once the danger of unfair pretrial prejudice had passed.

The courts have attempted to follow the general guidance of the Supreme Court in a variety of criminal case-related, non-trial contexts. Such cases have, for example, involved hearings in chambers in mid-trial regarding alleged juror misconduct, plea hearings, and bail hearings (United States v. Edwards, 1987; See In re Washington Post, 1986; United States v. Chagra, 1983) Recurringly, courts must consider the real differences between live press access to a proceeding of whatever sort, and the eventual availability of a verbatim paper transcript of that proceeding. These cases again raise what we have called the general "substitutability" problem.

The Supreme Court itself has distinguished between grand jury proceedings, where the necessary secrecy would be impossible with general press access, (See Press Enterprise Co. v. Superior Court, 1986) and other sorts of preliminary criminal case hearings. In the preliminary hearing at issue in Press Enterprise Co. v. Superior Court, for example, the Supreme Court found both a general tradition of accessibility and a possible role for public access in the "functioning of the process." The Court then imposed the following stringent standard:

If the interest asserted is the right of the accused to a fair trial, the preliminary hearing shall be closed only if specific findings are made demonstrating that first, there is a substantial probability that the defendant's right to a fair trial will be prejudiced by publicity that closure would prevent and, second, reasonable alternatives to closure cannot adequately protect the defendant's fair trial.

Note, in particular, that prejudice to the fair trial right must be not merely a reasonable probability—a slightly lower legal standard—but a substantial probability. (See Press Enterprise Co. v. Superior Court, 1986; El Vocero de Puerto Rico v. Puerto Rico, 1993)

Finally, at the borders of criminal trial litigation, the courts have addressed several constitutional and often non-constitutional access claims to materials at least loosely relevant to criminal adjudication. Such cases have included, for example, disputes over access to FBI rap sheets, (See Dep't of Justice v. Reporters Committee For Freedom of the Press, 1989) mug shots of federal grand jury indictees, (See Detroit Free Press v. Dep't of Justice, 1996) post guilty-plea mug shots, (Times-Picayune Publ'g Corp. v. Dep't of Justice, 1999) and to automatically sealed records of acquittal or of no probable cause (Globe Newspaper Co. v. Poraski, 1989). These cases generally reflect the rules discussed above, often supplemented by some sort of balancing of the competing interests at stake in the given case.

NOTES

1. *Pell,* but not *Saxbe,* involved claims made by prison inmates as well as by journalists. While there is no reason to assume that the rights of prisoners and of the press will even in this narrow context be identical, some similar issues arise, whether the plaintiff is a prisoner or a journalist, due to some overlap in interests.

2. For the classic discussion of the virtue of avoiding unnecessarily broad constitutional holdings, see Justice Brandeis' concurring opinion in Ashwander v. TVA, 297 U.S. 288, 341, 346–48 (1936).

3. For a summary and critique, see Daniel Bernstein, "Comment, Slamming the Prison Doors On Media Interviews: California's New Regulations Demonstrate the Need For a First Amendment Right of Access to Inmates," *30 McGeorge L. Rev.* (1998) 125. For brief discussion of *Pell, Saxbe,* and *Houchins,* see "The Supreme Court, 1977 Term: Media Right of Access," 92 *Harv. L. Rev.* (1978) 174. For discussion of *Pell* and *Saxbe,* see "The Supreme Court, 1973 Term: Bans on Press Interviews of Prisoners," 88 *Harv. L. Rev.* (1974) 165.

4. For general free speech expressive purposes, neither prisons nor military bases, as public property, have traditionally functioned like public streets and parks as largely unregulated public space for the expression of one's sentiments on any subject of public interest. See, e.g., United States v. Albertini, 472 U.S. 675, 684–86 (1985). For a sense of the fragile logic, and occasionally rather arbitrary dynamics, of categorizations under the public forum doctrine, see, e.g., Arkansas Educ. Tele. Com'n v. Forbes, 523 U.S. 666 (1998) (non-public forum as opposed to limited purpose or designated public forum).

5. Apparently, the parking ticket and other information sought was not ordinarily kept in electronic form in the ordinary course of the City's business.

6. For general discussion of the exceptionally difficult problems posed by constitutional challenges to speech by the government itself, see, e.g., Mark G. Yudof, "When Government Speaks: Politics, Law, and Government Expression in America" (Berkeley: U. of C. Press 1983); Randall P. Bezanson, "The Government Speech Forum: Forbes and Finley and Government Speech Selection Judgments," 83 *Iowa L. Rev.* (1988) 953; Richard Delgado, "The Language of the Arms Race: Should the People Limit Government Speech?" 64 *B.U. L. Rev.* (1984) 961; John E. Nowak, "Using the Press Clause to Limit Government Speech," 30 *Ariz. L. Rev.* (1988) 1 (arguing for a limited "right of reply" to some government speech).

7. The amended federal Freedom of Information Act, including the specified exemptions from disclosure, is codified at 5 U.S.C. § 552.

8. The Supreme Court itself referred to the two inquiries as "complementary considerations."

9. For discussion of the First Amendment checking value, and its broader applicability, see Vincent Blasi, "The Checking Value in First Amendment Theory," 1977 *Am. B. Found. Res. J.* 523.

10. See Potter Stewart, "Or of the Press," 26 *Hastings L.J.* (1975) 631, 636 ("[t]he Constitution itself is neither a Freedom of Information Act nor an Official Secrets Act").

11. There is a large body of case law involving journalists and other plaintiffs seeking access to government documents withheld under one or more exceptions to the Freedom of Information Act. As examples, see, e.g., Nation Magazine v. United States Customs Service, 1995 (challenging the denial of access to agency files involving Ross Perot's attempts to aid agency drug interdiction efforts pursuant to law enforcement records); Copley Press v. City of Springfield, 1986 (city liquor license as an occupational license for Freedom of Information Act exemption purposes); Dep't of Justice v. Landano, 1993 (rejecting the agency argument that all informational sources for FBI investigations should be presumed confidential for Freedom of Information Act purposes); Accuracy in Media, Inc. v. National Park Service, 1999 (photographs of deceased were compiled for law enforcement purposes and disclosure would amount to an unwarranted invasion of personal privacy); Cf. Favish v. Office of Indep. Counsel, 2000 (despite Freedom of Information Act's personal privacy exemption, the district court was required to view photographs of deceased in camera in order to balance personal privacy interests of the deceased's family against relevant public benefits); But see National Archives v. Favish, (2004); New York Times Co. v. NASA, 1990 (discussing the possible release of the last conversation of the Challenger shuttle astronauts in light of family privacy concerns); Dep't of Justice v. Reporters Comm. For Freedom of the Press, 1989 (balancing privacy exemption interests against the possible public interest in disclosure).

12. Curiously, the court in *Virmani* had earlier concluded, apparently, that even if a history of open access and a positive effect on agency function were shown by the press, the agency could still negate the resulting qualified right of access by passing a strict scrutiny test.

13. The court carefully noted that the real focus should be not on the effects of testifying, but on the incremental differences between testifying in closed or in open court.

Table of Cases

Index

ABOUT THE AUTHORS

LYRISSA BARNETT LIDSKY is the University of Florida Research Foundation Professor at the Levin College of Law in Gainesville, Florida.

R. GEORGE WRIGHT is the Michael D. McCormick Professor at the Indiana University School of Law, Indianapolis.